HOMEGROWN RADICALS

HOMEGROWN RADICALS

A STORY OF STATE VIOLENCE, ISLAMOPHOBIA, AND JIHAD IN THE POST–9/11 WORLD

YOUCEF SOUFI

NEW YORK UNIVERSITY PRESS
New York

NEW YORK UNIVERSITY PRESS
New York
www.nyupress.org

Library of Congress Cataloging-in-Publication Data
Names: Soufi, Youcef L., author.
Title: Homegrown radicals : a story of state violence, islamophobia, and jihad in the post–9/11 world / Youcef Soufi.
Description: New York : New York University Press, 2025. | Includes bibliographical references and index.
Identifiers: LCCN 2024007842 (print) | LCCN 2024007843 (ebook) | ISBN 9781479832262 (hardback) | ISBN 9781479832293 (ebook) | ISBN 9781479832309 (ebook other)
Subjects: LCSH: Muslims—Canada—Social conditions—21st century. | Terrorism—Religious aspects—Islam. | Jihad. | Canada—Ethnic relations—21st century.
Classification: LCC F1035.M87 S68 2025 (print) | LCC F1035.M87 (ebook) | DDC 305.6/97097107—dc23/eng/20240410
LC record available at https://lccn.loc.gov/2024007842
LC ebook record available at https://lccn.loc.gov/2024007843

This book is printed on acid-free paper, and its binding materials are chosen for strength and durability. We strive to use environmentally responsible suppliers and materials to the greatest extent possible in publishing our books.

Manufactured in the United States of America

10 9 8 7 6 5 4 3 2 1

Also available as an ebook

In Memory of Hélène Clément, "Ma Tante" (1952–2024)

CONTENTS

Introduction: "They Found Him" 1

1 Can the Muslim Speak? Grief, Suspicion, and Social Responsibility 33

2 Lives That Mattered and Lives That Didn't: Muslim Canadians and the War on Terror 69

3 The Emergence of the Homegrown Jihadist 97

4 Under Suspicion: Targeting, Harassment, and Abuse of Power 137

5 "I Want Out": Disillusionment with Utopian Jihad 161

6 Prosecuting Terrorism: National Security, Treason, and the Impossibility of Justice 189

Epilogue 223

Acknowledgments 230

Notes 231

Index 257

About the Author 263

INTRODUCTION

"THEY FOUND HIM"

July 2016. I am walking through Ottawa's Parliament security. My phone rings: "Private number." It's the third time that someone blocking their number has tried to reach me. I wonder who it could be, what they want. I answer hastily and slightly nervously: "Hello."

"Hi, is this Youcef Soufi?"

"Yes."

"This is Detective Paul from the RCMP in Winnipeg, I've been trying to reach you. I've left voicemails but you haven't gotten back to me."

The Royal Canadian Mounted Police? I start to think about all the possible reasons why Canada's national police force might want to talk to me. I haven't murdered anyone, and last time I checked, I don't sell or do drugs. Did I accidentally do something? A tax problem? A traffic violation? Library fines are the most probable crime I can come up with. But most of all, I can't shake the impression that this has some connection to my Muslim identity—in one way or another.

Voicemail? I don't have voicemail on my phone. No bother: "What can I do for you?" I ask Detective Paul.

"Well, is this a good time to talk to you?"

"It's not, actually, is there a way for us to speak in a couple of hours—say, noon Winnipeg time?" That would mean 1 pm Ottawa time.

"Sure, I'll call you then."

Before he ends the call, I quickly ask whether everything is alright.

"Oh yeah," Detective Paul replies; then, tentatively, trying to avoid telling me too much, he adds: "it's just in relation to what we talked to you about a few years ago." I complete the security screening and enter the building's gathering area for tourists.

My thoughts are racing as I wait for my tour to begin. I stand looking at the posters and video displays in the waiting area, but I am not all there. I have an idea of what the RCMP wants, but Detective Paul has still given me very few details to go on. I see my sister. She is the tour guide, and she is ushering in visitors from security, directing them to the waiting area. A second-year student at the University of British Columbia, where I am starting as an assistant professor in the fall, she is thirteen years my junior and working at Canada's federal legislative assembly to save money for school. I had taken the bus the night before from Toronto to Ottawa to visit her, and she had reserved tickets for me to take her tour. I wonder if she knows I am unsettled. I try to mask it. I know how much she is looking forward to showing me her presentation.

The tour begins in the visitors' chamber, where golden plaques listing the elected members of each parliamentary session are on display. I locate the 23rd Parliament (1957–1958). There, I see my grandfather's name: "LOUIS DENISET," written in engraved black letters, alongside other members of Parliament. As my sister speaks, I wonder how the other visitors read her. She is wearing a headscarf. Are they reading her as foreign to Canada? As a new and welcome addition to Canada? Born of immigrants from overseas? How many of them would be perplexed to know her grandfather represented the parliamentary constituency of St. Boniface, Manitoba, long before most of them were born? How many of them would suspect her French Canadian origins? I think about how being Muslim involves continual reassertions of one's Canadianness—continual claims of entitlement to the nation.

The tour begins. I know the building well—exceedingly well. I had been a parliamentary tour guide myself in the summers of 2004 and 2005. My sister leads us from the House of Commons to the Library of Parliament. We walk through the Hall of Honour. Here, my mind wanders back to my phone call with Detective Paul. My gaze lingers on a small alcove. The other visitors don't know the significance of this place. A year earlier, the alcove's Tyndall limestone had been riddled with bullets. Michael Zihaf-Bibeau, a self-declared ISIS supporter, had run into Parliament armed with a Winchester rifle. Before entering, Zihaf-Bibeau had gone to the Tomb of the Unknown Soldier across from Parliament and shot and killed Corporal Nathan Cirillo, an unarmed soldier and young father symbolically guarding the tomb. The attacks rattled Canada. Zihaf-Bibeau hid in the alcove before being killed. Decidedly, I tell myself, these are troubling times.

The tour ends. "Good job, kiddo. That was amazing," I tell my sister.

"Thanks, bro—I'll see you later, alright, once my shift is done."

"Sure thing, see you soon." I make my way to the lawn in front of Parliament. Seven minutes to 1 pm. I lie down and wait. The sun is bright and the air humid. I am exhausted from the long bus ride the night before and I need to rest. A few minutes pass and my phone rings; I sit up. "Hi Youcef."

"Hi," I say, pausing. "So what can I do for you?"

Detective Paul answers plainly. "The Americans would like to interview you. It's about Muhanad Al Farekh."

Surprised, I respond in a slow, inquisitive tone: "That's fine with me. But why Muhanad? What do they want to know about him specifically? Why not the other two guys?"

Detective Paul answers: "Well, because the trial is coming up."

The trial? I ask myself, puzzled.

"You do know they found him, don't you?"

What? The statement doesn't fully sink in. I shake my head in consternation and move the phone away slightly. What did he mean they found him? How could that be? Muhanad had disappeared; all three of them had, without a trace. It had been nine years.

Detective Paul continues, "Yeah, the Americans picked him up in Pakistan last year."

"No, I didn't know. I had assumed he was dead a long time ago."

"Well, the Americans have him in custody and they've decided to put him on trial."

I come back to my senses. "Yeah, I get it," I say. "Muhanad was an American citizen."

"Yes, that's right. The Americans want to gather evidence for the trial. That's why they want to interview you."

"That's not a problem, I'm coming to Winnipeg in a few days to visit family. I'll be there until the end of July and then I'll be back in Toronto in August."

"Great, I'll inform the Americans and get back to you. I'll send you my email address so you can reach me." We end the call.

I look around me. Swarms of tourists everywhere are enjoying the beautiful day. My mood could not contrast more sharply with theirs: With furrowed eyebrows, I am pensive, absorbed in my thoughts. The events surrounding Muhanad's disappearance had greatly impacted my life. All our lives. Now, just like that, he was back. I look behind me to the imposing neo-gothic clock tower of Parliament. Detective Paul had said Muhanad was on the news. How did I miss that?! I pull out my smartphone. I can't remember exactly how to spell his name. I enter "Muhannad El-Ferekh." Google corrects his name for me. I see a series of news sources that have covered the story in recent months, and select an article from the CBC (the Canadian Broadcasting Corporation). It features a sketch from a New York City courtroom. Plain as day, it is Muhanad. He has gained weight, his beard is long and scruffy, and he has a receding hairline. But it is him. Same short height, oval face, blond hair, and round nose. The sketch even shows the distinct crease marks on his forehead. His eyes are different though. They have lost their life. Muhanad's eyes used to twinkle, but here he looks pitiable, forlorn, and broken. As I read the article, I quickly learn why. He had been in solitary confinement for the last year: in a room little larger than a closet, for twenty-three hours a day.

So he wasn't dead, I thought. It had been nine years. Nine years I had waited for answers. And not just about Muhanad, but also Ferid and Miawand. All three had disappeared in March 2007. I remember my friend Dawud's words: "When they left, they left a mess." We resented them for that. They left a mess that the Winnipeg Muslim community would have to deal with. A mess and a mystery. What had happened to these three men? Where were they, what were they doing, and why had they left? There had been whispers. Whispers of Pakistan, radicalization, terrorism. But whispers were all we heard. Now, with Muhanad in custody, perhaps, finally, we would have some answers.

I lie back down on the grass. I think of our increasingly precarious and polarized world. The emergence of ISIS has led to a proliferation of acts of terrorism worldwide—Paris, Brussels, San Bernardino, Istanbul. In the days prior to my trip to Ottawa, Omar Mateen carried out the largest mass shooting in American history at the Pulse Nightclub in Orlando, Florida. Muslims are increasingly under the microscope. Donald Trump's proclamation to ban all Muslims from America is gaining a degree of support that would have been hard to imagine a short while earlier. The road ahead seems arduous, to say the least.

THE PROBLEM(ATIZATION) OF RADICALIZATION: QUESTIONING THE MODERATE/RADICAL DIVIDE

Radicalization is the greatest threat we face, or so we were told.[1] And while national security experts have also recently labeled white supremacist groups as radical, Muslims are the original and paradigmatic bearers of this term.[2] The post–9/11 era gave rise to the emerging discipline of radicalization studies. Experts—typically white, non-Muslim social scientists—now dedicated themselves to studying how and why Muslims became radical. Lorenzo Vidino, director of the Program on Extremism at George Washington University, explains that "radicalization is the term of art used by academics and policy makers to describe the process that an individual undergoes when [he] embraces an extremist ideology, and then, in some cases . . . undertakes acts of violence in furtherance of that ideology."[3] Radicalization studies emphasizes a whole host of social and individual factors that might serve as causal variables in a Muslim's trajectory toward embracing a jihadist ideology in which violent political action is legitimated in the name of the Islamic faith. The emergence of ISIS's self-proclaimed caliphate in 2014 gave renewed impetus to attempts to understand radicalization. Thousands of Western fighters flocked to ISIS's lands, and several others heeded its calls to wage a war against the West. Muhanad Al Farekh, Miawand Yar, and Ferid Imam were three University of Manitoba students who allegedly underwent radicalization years before the exodus of ISIS fighters from the West. This book historicizes their ideological journey from "normal" young men to dangerous jihadists and accused terrorists. But it is only partly *their* story.

The problem with radicalization discourse is that it hides the historical complexity of political and religious life. Radicalization is a discourse in the service of the state's management of suspect populations. A century ago, the disciplines of anthropology and Oriental studies served a similar purpose, allowing experts on colonized peoples to provide advice to Whitehall in the UK or the Quai D'Orsay in France on how to govern potentially unruly populations.[4] While anthropologists and Islamic studies scholars continue to advise governments today, they have generally adopted a more critical stance toward violence against the non-"Western" world. In contrast, radicalization studies emerged as a response to September 11, amid concerns about understanding the jihadist enemy. Moreover, radicalization experts have often served within national security agencies like the CIA. But how would we see radicalization differently if we examined it not as an object located in suspect individuals, but as a strategy of the state? What new histories would emerge about our post–9/11 world? What new understandings not only of Islam and jihad but also of national suspicion, policing, and violence in the United States and Canada might this methodological shift produce? And, most important, what new political solidarities might become possible at both the domestic and international levels? In "bringing the state back in,"[5] this book attempts to answer these questions. It is not the story of Muhanad, Miawand, and Ferid so much as it is the story of a small Muslim community on the outskirts of the American empire, just an hour's drive from the US border in the Canadian prairies. The book seeks to understand this community's experience of the War on Terror after September 11 by focusing on the traumatic event of the radicalization of three of its members. What emerges is a very different narrative from the common story of a community whose faith renders it susceptible to violent politics. Instead, we find a community tragically caught in the crossfire of an unprecedented and aberrant type of global war—one without borders and without clearly defined enemies.

In hindsight, the War on Terror could have unfolded differently. The Bush administration could have declared war against al-Qaeda. Perhaps no war at all would have materialized, considering the Taliban's willingness to negotiate Osama bin Laden's extradition. But America was wounded and demanded its pound of flesh. The result was an act of Congress establishing the globe in its entirety as a potential battleground. Obama inherited this borderless war and, despite his criticisms of the Bush administration, normalized it. The day after bin Laden's death in 2011, his Secretary of State Hillary Clinton declared, "The fight goes on."[6] The spectacular failures of the War on Terror are difficult to deny—the Iraqi insurgency from 2003 to 2011, the many terrorist attacks on civilians throughout the world, the emergence of ISIS, and two decades of Taliban resistance in what became America's longest war. In contrast to Obama's claims during his vaunted Cairo speech in 2009, the United States did have a choice in the weeks after September 11.[7] The choices it made then and afterward have continued to reverberate throughout the world up until today, particularly within a handful of Muslim-majority countries that have suffered from extensive military campaigns. But while exempt from direct military violence, Muslims in Winnipeg were placed in the distinctly uncomfortable position of proving their innocence and loyalty to an imagined entity called the West. This central condition of my interlocutors pervades the series of events I document throughout this book. This condition also makes this history larger than the community I focus on.

If the book is about a small Canadian prairie community, it nonetheless sheds light on a wider history of North American Muslims. The history of Canadian Muslims is intimately shared with that of their American counterparts. Both countries drew from analogous immigrant Muslim populations after the 1960s, namely large, educated South Asian and Arab populations who would quickly integrate into the middle class.[8] The shared medium of English within most of Canada (North African and West African Francophones in Montreal are the major exception) means that culture and ideas easily cross the border. The border is porous in another sense too. Canadian Muslims live close enough to maintain intimate connections with American Muslim communities. As a US Muslim academic once told me, "I'm from Michigan: I grew up knowing Canadian Muslims."[9] Sometimes these ties were forged because families or friends from back home ended up in different North American cities, and sometimes diasporic ties were forged after settling in North America.[10] Several Winnipeg Muslims found their spouses in cities like Dearborn, Chicago, and Houston, where large communities of Muslims settled. Moreover, Muslim organizations in the United States were often connected to Canada. During the 1990s, a group of Winnipeg Muslims drove down to Chicago every year to partake in the annual conference of the Islamic Society of North America (ISNA)—the largest and most influential Muslim organization in the United States at the time.[11] One Winnipeg Muslim called it the equivalent of the hajj pilgrimage for North American Muslims: "Mecca's far, Chicago's right there."[12] In the late 1990s, a prominent member of the Winnipeg community moved to Washington, DC, to join the team of the Council of American Islamic Relations, which fought for Muslim civil rights. And it was Ingrid Mattson, a Canadian Muslim convert from Ontario, who served as the first woman president of the ISNA from 2006 to 2010. The central difference between the Canadian and US Muslim communities is the presence in the United States of a prominent African American Muslim demographic shaped by the experience of slavery and an ongoing struggle against anti-Black racism.[13] Even in Canada, though, Canadian Muslims have increasingly found inspiration from Black Muslim activism in combating anti-Muslim racism.[14] The legacy of Malcolm X, while complicated and subject to change from one era to the next, was already deeply entrenched before 9/11.[15]

At the level of the state, the Canadian Muslim experience has also been shaped by American foreign policy. Canada's membership within the North Atlantic Treaty Organization (NATO) and the North American Aerospace Defense Command (NORAD) has made Canada a junior—and occasionally reluctant—partner in the United States' military adventures in the Muslim world. The two nations' Smart Border Declaration solidified their intelligence sharing in the years after 9/11.[16] Information on Muslim populations has crossed the border with devastating consequences for individuals like Ottawa resident Maher Arar, who found himself the object of extraordinary rendition by the United States to Bashar al-Assad's Syrian prisons, where he was tortured for a year from 2002 to 2003.[17] As a consequence, Canadian Muslims have experienced their state's security agencies as an extension of the American state's security imperatives.

But why make a case of radicalization the focus of this book? Is it not curious to try to uncover a history of state suspicion against a vulnerable population by focusing on an example that appears to justify the state's worries? It might seem better to do as many others have and to show that Muslims are regular citizens trying to live peacefully, provide for their families, and give back to society.[18] Such studies have been immensely important in showing that the War on

Terror has had an unmerited impact on innocent people with no connection to terrorism. But these works are not able to transcend the state's own terms, which posit a clearly delimited moderate Muslim majority against a small set of radical Muslims who threaten the nation. In the end, they evoke sympathy for a beleaguered Muslim majority who should not have to pay for the crimes of a few of its members. If, however, we study the moderate Muslim in relation to the radical, then we will come to see the history that produced both. At its foundation, the history of the moderate Muslim and the radical Muslim in North America began with little to differentiate one from the other. Both experienced deep discomfort at the War on Terror's legitimation of violence abroad and suspicion at home. Both relied on the same Sunni Islamic tradition, including its central beliefs and practices.[19] Their divergence related to the small but consequential question of proper political action in response to the War on Terror. But for this divergence to come about, something had to happen first to convince the radical that his path was the right one. The radical and the moderate North American Muslim were therefore the products of contingent circumstances in the years after 9/11, circumstances that can and should be the object of study. Rather than absolve the moderate Muslim from the guilt of the radical, this book holds the moderate and the radical Muslim in proximity to each other to show the different paths each took.

In historicizing the formation of the moderate/radical divide, both empirically and discursively, I seek to shed new light on the operation of anti-Muslim racism, i.e., Islamophobia. Islamophobia has often been associated with a history of Western colonial tropes about the Orient. Thus, legal scholar Khaled Beydoun writes that Islamophobia is "the presumption that Islam is inherently violent, alien, and unassimilable, a presumption driven by the belief that expressions of Muslim identity correlate with a propensity for terrorism. Islamophobia is the modern progeny of Orientalism . . . a worldview that casts Islam as the civilizational antithesis of the West that is built upon core stereotypes and baseline distortions of Islam and Muslims embedded in American institutions and the popular imagination by Orientalist theory, narratives, and law."[20] Specialists on anti-Muslim racism widely acknowledge that these Orientalist stereotypes have been fueled by

Western states' foreign policy. This foreign policy can be attributed to a history of colonial rule and to the United States' strategic interest in the Middle East for its oil and geopolitical value during the Cold War. But a central argument of this book is that anti-Muslim racism has operated since 9/11 through the blurring of the porous lines between the moderate and radical Muslim.[21] Anti-Muslim racism functions through the state's and the pseudo-expert's drawing and redrawing of the line separating the moderate from the radical Muslim. As a result, actions that were once deemed part of "moderate" Islam are subsumed under the label of radicalization. Forms of suspicion and state violence are legitimized through these kinds of discursive interventions concerning who or what constitutes radical Islam. This book is therefore an attempt to explain how the moderate/radical divide emerged and to trace its subsequent impact on Canadian Muslim communities.

THE NATION AND ITS ENEMIES

If we want to understand the condition of Winnipeg Muslims in the post–9/11 era, we might begin a few hundred miles westward where the Canadian prairies turn into the imposing Rocky Mountain range. There, in Banff National Park, a stone's throw away from the hot springs that attracted scores of people in the nineteenth century seeking their purported medical benefits, sits a small wooden hut. On a typically busy summer day when Canadian and American tourists fill the park to view its breathtaking snow-capped peaks, large evergreens, and emerald-colored lakes, this wooden hut is remarkably empty. But, were one inclined to forsake the great outdoors for a history lesson, the hut is unlocked, unattended, and open to anyone to walk in without payment. The hut is something between a museum and a shrine, serving as a site of national contrition and atonement. It informs its visitors that Banff National Park has not only been a location for amusement and vacationing. A century ago, Canada's national parks were used as internment camps during the First World War.[22] The entry of the United Kingdom—and by extension its Canadian colony—into the war created great suspicion of Canadian citizens with origins in what were now enemy states. Canadian politicians and men of influence inflamed sentiments of fear against Germans, Turks, and peoples of the Austro-Hungarian Empire. Ukrainians who had recently settled on the Canadian prairies were a particular object of suspicion.[23] The fear of these populations was compounded by earlier stereotypes that presented them, not unlike Muslims today, as possessing a culture opposed to the Western European and particularly British values of the Canadian nation. The Banff exhibit quotes a politician who stated that Eastern Europeans would corrupt the Canadian nation if allowed to migrate. In 1914, the War Measures Act paved the way for the imprisonment of approximately 8,579 "enemy aliens." Many had little relationship to their original homelands and still less to the politics of the day. The North Western Canadian Police counseled the government that there existed little reason to worry about the loyalties of these new immigrants to Canada. But this was a time of war, and the least threat was still deemed too much. More sober voices were drowned out, with serious consequences. The Banff exhibit features a desperate letter from a nine-year-old daughter to her imprisoned Ukrainian farmer: "My dear father: We haven't nothing to eat and they do not want to give us no wood. . . . It is better with you because we have something to eat. . . . It is cold in that shack. Goodby my dear father. Come home right away." The internment of new immigrants in the First World War notably also paved the way for the internment of suspect Canadian citizens, particularly Japanese Canadians, in the Second.[24] In documenting this past injustice, the government recognized that its suspicion of Eastern European immigrants to Canada was misguided and unjust. Jason Kenney, the Minister of Multiculturalism at the time, attended the opening of the exhibit in 2013 and declared that, after decades of denying the history of the camps, "it was time to put things right."[25] By remembering, the nation demonstrated that it had learned from its mistakes and progressed toward a multicultural and pluralistic society in which all were afforded equal individual rights.

At first glance, the Canadian government had learned from its mistakes even earlier, in 2001. In the weeks after the Twin Towers in New York City fell, the Canadian government made clear that Muslim citizens were not to be blamed for the carnage meted out on Canada's southern neighbors. In this regard, it followed the Bush administration, who called Islam a religion of sound teachings. The government's actions were meant to allay national anxieties about the enemy within. In the days after 9/11, suspicion of the Muslim had intensified. Fears of divided loyalties and fifth columns emerged, compounded by a legacy of Orientalist stereotypes and images of brown-skinned terrorists that became fodder for countless 1980s and 1990s action movies.[26] But upon closer examination, it would be more accurate to say that the state sought a monopoly over the representation of the nation and the right to defend it. The government resorted to a dual strategy of publicly positioning Muslims as allies to Western civilization while privately sanctioning the pervasive state surveillance of Muslim communities.[27] The strategy reflected the government's aim of keeping the peace at home while avoiding overt violations of the democratic and liberal values upon which Canada's national identity and civilizational superiority had been constructed during the Cold War. The policy protected Muslim communities from vigilante violence, which, also in the name of the nation, had begun to target mosques and Muslim individuals across North America. At the same time, it made Muslims particularly vulnerable to state forms of violence.[28] In effect, the state arrogated to itself the right to distinguish "rational" national suspicions from excessive populist ones.

My Muslim interlocutors in Winnipeg were subject to this determination on the part of the state to neutralize a suspect population with little regard to either the reality of the threat they posed or the consequences on their lives. The state's system of surveillance functioned according to a scale of suspicion. Muslims' shared faith with al-Qaeda and the Taliban rendered them suspect by default. This suspicion was not entirely new: Muslims had already been on the radar of the Canadian Secret Intelligence Services (CSIS) and the Royal Canadian Mounted Police (RCMP). Arabs were particularly subject to monitoring during the First Gulf War.[29] After 9/11, CSIS increasingly sought to infiltrate Muslim communities by pressuring their members to become informants. But it was typically young, male Muslims, whom the state worried *might* hold radical beliefs, who attracted especially heightened state suspicion. Most of my interlocutors in this book fit within this category. The principal reason to suspect radical belief in the years after 9/11 up until at least 2007 was knowing a radical. The paradigm of "guilt by association," to which I give great attention in this book, led to sustained and intrusive investigations into men who had never articulated radical positions (however loosely defined), let alone partaken in terrorism. My interlocutors' interactions with security agencies left them with long-term mental health issues, significant losses to their livelihood, and a deep distrust of the state. A common descriptor for the experience was "trauma." Of course, these interlocutors fared much better than radicals themselves did. When Canadian and American security agencies felt that a Muslim had become radicalized (even when that judgment was based on shoddy intelligence), they shifted to threat elimination mode, often collaborating with foreign governments to imprison or assassinate the threat. In effect, the strong presumption of radicalization turned the radical from an "enemy within" to a full-fledged foreign enemy, with little regard for the alleged rights afforded by citizenship. What becomes clear is that (1) the state's suspicions of Muslims after 9/11 were no more "rational" than those of the vigilantes—only more predictable and controllable, and (2) though its tactics may have changed since the First World War, its objectives have not.

By outsourcing the more unsavory treatment of Muslims to security agencies, the state's violence largely remained in the shadows. The paradigm of guilt by association has had a mystifying effect on the public's awareness of the War on Terror. To the general public, state security services appear to have done their job well by targeting the minority of Muslims who are radicals if not terrorists and leaving the moderate majority alone. Human rights violations are viewed as the unfortunate by-product of keeping us safe. They are lamentable but they neither reflect who we are as a nation nor provide grounds for a wholesale indictment of our security agencies. This impression is compounded by the silence—or, rather, cautiousness—of the vast majority of Muslims in North America who want to live in peace without rocking the boat. Most Muslims have had sufficient interactions with the state's security apparatus to know the power the state can exercise over them. Typically, it is through travel—particularly border crossings—that they get a brief glimpse of this state power.[30] They have come to accept this minimal intrusion upon their lives and have had little reason to protest en masse, especially because the paradigm of guilt by association would mean the risk of appearing to stand with those accused of terrorism. Many Winnipeg Muslims privately sympathized with those caught within the crosshairs of the state's suspicion and recognized the discriminatory foundation of these practices, but others, in a bid to protect a majority of Muslims, sided with the state in its search for radicals. Of course, it is uncertain whether state security agencies have made us at all safer. It is telling that an intrusive FBI surveillance operation led a US Imam to formulate the jihadist theory that would appeal to Ferid, Miawand, Muhanad, and scores of other Anglophone Muslims.

The suspicion and violence against Muslims during the War on Terror reveal something about our deep-seated national fears. The "enemy within" raises the specter that perhaps nothing is really holding the nation together. In times of war and peace, the state's function is to define the nation by mobilizing symbols and instituting practices that can sufficiently justify the notion of a united people.[31] Managing the affective bonds between citizens and the nation is as important as managing the economy.[32] In effect, the state needs to continually *reimagine* the national community.[33] The assumption is that liberal democratic states have met this challenge by building multiethnic nations premised primarily upon political rights rather than language, race, or religious background. Quebec's language and history might make it a separate nation, but its democratic values make it an easy partner within a larger multicultural Canada. Many have contended that liberal democratic nations are exempt from the violent ethno-nationalism of the postcolonial world.[34] But the War on Terror suggests that the language of political values is still deeply wedded to a racial and territorial origin story. The liberal and democratic rights that are meant to bind us together are tied to a civilizational project with deep colonial roots that saw white Europe as the natural teacher to the colonized "savages" of the non-European world. It was this impulse that had previously led Canada's First Prime Minister, John A. MacDonald, to seek the elimination of Indigenous Peoples' cultures through the Indian Act.[35] Canadian and American leaders explicitly used this colonial imagery in the War on Terror. In so doing, they helped define not only the foreign enemy but also the Canadian and American nations themselves. This defining of the nation has consequences at home and abroad, where it makes certain types of violence palatable and even righteous.

The question before us is whether it is genuinely possible to surmount the parochial nature of the imagined national community or whether we are bound to continue to reproduce the same forms of violence in the future. Revisiting the history of the War on Terror in this book has not made me very optimistic. It is easy to repent for sins committed a century ago when those populations are no longer suspect. It is telling that Jason Kenney saw no contradiction in atoning for internment camps for Eastern Europeans even as he instrumentalized anti-Muslim racism in his party's reelection campaign two years later by calling for a "barbaric cultural practice hotline" to alert the government about the intrusion of "foreign" practices into the Canadian nation.[36] This fact was not lost on those who sent a letter to an Edmonton Mosque in 2019 after Kenney was elected to lead the Provincial government: "We are white. We are Christians. We are proud. . . . you will not force your savage laws on us. . . . Our Premier to be Jason Kenney will take Alberta back for us."[37] It is striking that Eastern Europeans in the First World War and Muslims after 9/11 were subject to similar racial exclusions: Both the Eastern European "slav" and the Muslim were deemed "backward," even though anti-Ukrainian sentiments were also shaped by derisive accusations of uncleanliness and poverty.[38] The construction of racial difference with the nation appears to precede the identification of a national security threat and intensifies as the state moves toward the neutralization of that threat. Even as North American society moves toward a greater critical race consciousness, the end of righteous violence abroad and suspicion at home will depend upon the construction of new affective bonds that transcend the nation-state. In this regard, I believe my Muslim interlocutors have something to teach us.

The view of the state (Canadian and US) that emerges in this book is a segmented one, made up of a loose assemblage of ministries, departments, and agencies, whose respective heads, institutional norms, and objectives are often at odds with each other. This view of the state departs from a recent influential monograph in Islamic studies that sees civil society as an extension of the state. Noah Salomon's study of Sudan as an *Islamic* state has alerted us to how individuals can be simultaneously said to embody and contest the state.[39] Yet the description of the state I adopt here stems less from my commitment to a particular theory than to an attempt at empirical clarity when documenting my interlocutors' experiences with different state representatives after 9/11. I therefore keep the state distinct from the public sphere, even though I show how the two constantly influence each other.[40] Prime ministers and presidents seek to impart coherence to the state machinery by providing a vision that gives direction to its different bodies. However, these government leaders inherit bureaucracies whose mandates have essentially been set and whose operations have already been routinized. The men and women who work in these bureaucracies, particularly their frontline workers, have already acquired work skills that define how they interact with their target public. It often takes an ambitious alternative and sufficient public support to drastically restructure these bureaucracies. Two important consequences follow from this institutional inertia. First, the tactics of security agencies have endured with only minor modifications despite changes to government leadership. An Obama or a Trudeau may be more receptive to acknowledging and fighting anti-Muslim racism than a Bush or a Stephen Harper. But continuities with the past system of suspicion are also readily discernible. Second, the state has not been univocally anti-Muslim or pro-Muslim since the War on Terror began. Paradoxically, one ministry can push for the same rights for Muslims that another ministry undercuts. My Muslim interlocutors have often encountered what can only be described as a schizophrenic state, which treats them in wildly divergent ways. Even their experiences with different security agencies diverge in important respects.

Last, this book cautions against excessive attention to states of exception in telling the history of the War on Terror. The War on Terror brought with it a renewed academic interest in the thought of Nazi political theorist Carl Schmitt and German-Jewish cultural critic Walter Benjamin, especially as read through Italian philosopher Giorgio Agamben, on the topic of sovereign exceptions to the normal rights afforded by law.[41] Bush's Patriot Act and his imprisonment camps in places like Guantánamo Bay cemented the view that the state of exception was becoming ever more widespread and liberal laws would not be enough to protect citizens from gross human rights violations. Sherene Razack's pathbreaking 2008 book *Casting Out* used the notion of *homo sacer*—Agamben's term for the figure expelled from the law—to great effect.[42] Razack contended that Canadian Muslims were being expelled from the law and left at the mercy of a state that saw them as either brown terrorist men or abused brown women. Since then, the notion that Muslims experience a state of legal exception has often been repeated in monographs and articles. But my research has led me to a different conclusion. Paying attention to "exceptional laws" or executive orders has sometimes led academics and activists to focus on the wrong sites of state power in the War on Terror. For instance, Canada's Anti-Terrorism Act has been the object of protracted study and debate.[43] It first came into effect in 2001 under a Liberal government and has been subject to several amendments since.[44] The law allowed the state to imprison citizens without charge (for up to three days) and to compel answers in interrogation through investigative hearings. Yet for all the fanfare around its potential violation of citizens' rights, these measures have only once been invoked in the decade after 9/11.[45] In contrast, CSIS's operations intensified after 9/11 without need for either legislative changes or executive decisions overriding the customary working of the law. CSIS felt the law as it stood offered them sufficient leeway to achieve its goals, and in many cases it applied tactics that predated 9/11. Of course, CSIS repeatedly acted in ways that flirted with and sometimes actually were legal violations, but it was always careful to present itself as following unexceptional state laws. In particular, we will see that CSIS made great use of state borders in order to violate the expected rights of Muslim citizens while simultaneously absolving itself of legal wrongdoing. Likewise, on the surface, the United States took great care to ensure that Muhanad would receive a proper trial, as any other American citizen would. But on closer examination, Muhanad's ambiguous position between national security threat and indicted criminal made a fair trial an impossibility. My point is that we should look for abuses of power and violations of customary legal rights in the everyday workings of the law of liberal democratic states and not only in measures whose flagrance grabs our national attention.

THE EMERGENCE OF THE HOMEGROWN JIHADIST AND THE MUSLIM UTOPIAN IMAGINARY

In the days after 9/11, the United States and Canada feared that another attack on the West was imminent; the Bush and Chrétien administrations envisaged the possibility of al-Qaeda cells operating all across North America. There was, of course, no data on whether this was the case. But what is certain is that few threats materialized for several years.[46] In Canada, the first credible threat occurred a full five years after 9/11, with the Toronto 18 plot of 2006, which saw a group of Muslims contemplate attacks on the Toronto Stock Exchange. In 2007, the US Department of Homeland Security still boasted that the country's system of liberal rights and integration should be credited with preventing radicalization among US Muslims.[47] But a steady stream of terrorist plots in the following years would belie this statement. By 2010, US Homeland Security Director Janet Napolitano affirmed that threats to national security had shifted from the foreign terrorist to homegrown radicals: "those who have lived for years in the West and who move seamlessly—often with the advantage of citizenship—in and out of target populations."[48] Ferid, Miawand, and Muhanad were part of this new wave of radicals—pioneers in fact. They left Canada in 2007, only a year after the Toronto 18 plot unraveled. But they were not the last. By the time ISIS's Caliphate took its last breath, hundreds of Canadians and Americans had joined the jihadist organization.[49] How do we account for this shift? What happened within Muslim communities that created the homegrown jihadist?

Answering this question must begin by considering the relationship North American Muslims had to political violence before the emergence of the homegrown terrorist. On the eve of 9/11, the Muslims of Winnipeg constituted a highly politically engaged community. It was a community comprised of various diasporic groups with different concerns about politics back home. What happened in Pakistan, India, Bangladesh, Lebanon, Libya, Bosnia, or Ethiopia often mattered deeply to the people who emigrated from these lands. New media like the internet and satellite news from the Middle East or South Asia made it possible to follow political analysis more quickly than ever before. But beyond typical diasporic immigrant concerns, many mosque-going Muslims were also preoccupied more broadly with events affecting their Muslim sisters and brothers the world over. For instance, during the Second Intifada starting in 2000, Winnipeg Muslims often spoke about Palestine from the mosque pulpit or during Friday night learning circles (*halaqas*).[50] The mosque basement became a classroom for lessons on the Balfour Declaration and the Sykes-Picot Accord, which sealed the fate of the Middle East after the First World War. The community organized marches and protests to pressure the Canadian government to take a critical stance toward the Israeli occupation of the West Bank and Gaza,[51] and to express their anger at continued US support for an Israeli state that disregarded Palestinians' internationally recognized rights. This concern with the Muslim world stemmed from the modern history of pan-Islamic movements, which fostered affective bonds among co-religionists during the nineteenth and twentieth centuries.[52] The mixing of diverse peoples at the mosque—a veritable multicultural space—made the notion of an international Muslim community all the more tangible. This concern often translated into sympathy with the cause of armed groups abroad. Many viewed Kashmir, Chechnya, Palestine, and Kosovo as sites of legitimate political resistance to foreign invasion, occupation, and ethnic cleansing. Before 9/11 placed Muslim fighters under suspicion, it was not unusual for Winnipeg Muslim camp leaders to sing a popular 1980s ode about the Afghan mujahideen resistance to the Soviet Union. The song would make most Canadian Muslims blush today because of its references to God's army banishing the disbelieving Soviets to hell.[53]

Darryl Li has aptly contended that modern international jihadism is driven by a sense of solidarity rooted in the concept of the *umma* (the global Muslim community).[54] Li grounds his analysis on the empirical data about international volunteers who fought in Bosnia in the 1990s. He focuses on how solidarity among jihadist fighters enacts a form of universalism insofar as it seeks to encompass all humankind and rival the international legal system forged after the Second World War. Li succeeds in moving away from the reductive analysis of the jihadist as either pathological or immoral. However, my interest in this book is in asking how Muslim solidarity is cultivated through mundane reminders, religious exhortations, and acts of international and local care—from Friday sermons to organizing charity efforts in lands devastated by natural disasters. These practices shape sensibilities and mutual affections that give life to the concept of the umma and become the basis of various social and political mobilizations, whether nonviolent or violent.

Curiously, despite many Muslims' sympathies with armed rebel groups the world over, the concept or doctrine of armed jihad was largely absent from Winnipeg mosque discussions. This might seem paradoxical: How do you sing about mujahideen and not think about jihad? But it should be easy enough to recognize the difference between supporting an armed faction—e.g., the US troops engaged in various combat missions—and theorizing why that faction warrants support. As Khalid Blankinship notes, jihad (a term that literally means "to struggle" and also includes struggling on a spiritual path) is the equivalent of the Christian or Modern European philosophical theory of a "just war."[55] Throughout history, Muslim jurists have debated what makes a war just. When should war be undertaken? What rules of engagement must be observed? And under what conditions should peace be sought? If my Winnipeg Muslim interlocutors had little awareness of this doctrine of jihad, it is because it was irrelevant to their lives. They lived in a country whose soil had not witnessed battle since 1885. More importantly, knowing debates about jihad was immaterial to being a good Muslim.[56] For the vast majority of my Winnipeg Muslim interlocutors, in 2001 as today, Islam is centered on cultivating a relationship with God. This work requires self-discipline through various spiritual practices—like prayer, fasting, and charity—that continually remind oneself of the ultimate return to God. War was never a central feature of the faith for my interlocutors—nor was it for most Muslims throughout history.[57] For the homegrown radical to emerge, then, concern with the theory of jihad first needed to be revived. Doing so would necessitate great creativity.

One of my key arguments is that the jihadist ideology that gave birth to the homegrown terrorist was, and could only have been, the product of a post–9/11 world. This is because it was a direct response to the War on Terror: Jihadist ideology provided a diagnosis of and a solution to the violence that the War on Terror had inflicted upon

Muslim-majority countries like Iraq, Afghanistan, Pakistan, and Somalia. Ferid, Muhanad, and Miawand discovered this jihadist ideology in 2006 and, as we shall see, it spoke to them. The doctrine made sense of the anti-Muslim racism they witnessed in the West and the seeming apathy among Muslims toward the continuous bombings and killings of Muslim peoples. The author of this jihadist ideology was a US Imam named Anwar Al-Awlaki who himself gradually became disillusioned with the US security state after 9/11.

Al-Awlaki's thought is best understood through the concept of the "utopian." In Western political thought, the utopian has figured prominently within the Marxist tradition. Marx famously and derisively spoke of "utopian socialisms" to refer to various forms of nineteenth-century socialist visions that competed with his own for intellectual and political popularity in Western Europe.[58] Marx dismissed thinkers like Fourier and Saint-Simon for peddling visions of a society that could not exist—much the same way Thomas Moore used the term utopia in his novel to designate an implausible place. In contrast, Marx claimed his socialism was the product of scientific laws rooted in a rigorous understanding of the workings of a capitalist economy. By deploying the concept of utopia, Marx captured the imagination of future theorists inspired by his thought, but not always in deferential ways. In 1954, Ernst Bloch published *The Principle of Hope*, providing a positive revaluation of the utopian and applying its relevance to the development of human culture. Rather than seeing the utopian as the unscientific and irremediably impossible, Bloch spoke of "utopian yearning" as the means to bring about a more just world—what he called the "Not-Yet Being."[59] Here, the utopian imagination is not an escapist fantasy but the mechanism through which a new reality is created.

Bloch ushered in an enduring shift within Marxist thought in understanding utopian thinking as birthing new worlds. Herbert Marcuse, Bloch's colleague within the Frankfurt School, would reaffirm the transformative potential of the utopian, particularly in art. Still, later Marxists emphasized the limitations of utopian thought. Marcuse distinguished between utopian thought that upheld the existing capitalist system and the one that transformed it.[60] Even more insightful was Fredric Jameson's intervention in his *Archaeologies of the Future*.[61] Jameson pointed out the fact that utopian thought is mediated by one's social and cultural conditions. The utopian is not an unmoored imagining of a new and more just reality so much as it is tied to one's material conditions. Jameson reminds us that all ideas are situated, even the most fantastic and imaginative ones.

In many ways, Muslims' past and present cannot be understood without considering the ways in which the utopian, understood as the longing for a seemingly distant but immeasurably better world, periodically shaped their social and political movements. How could it not when Islam began as a utopian movement? The Prophet Muhammad and his companions were few in number when they fled their hometown of Mecca with limited possessions and took refuge in the city of Medina. They had been persecuted relentlessly by their own kin, the tribe of Quraysh, some tortured and even killed. And yet they were guided by the Qur'anic vision of spiritual, social, and political reform. The Qur'an preached care for the poor, the enslaved, the social outcast, and the vulnerable. Most of all, it preached an Abrahamic vision of transforming the polytheistic Arab society into one dedicated to a single omnipotent and merciful God. This vision carried the Muslim refugees in Medina and within ten years, against all odds, they would control the entire Arabian Peninsula. Along the way, they would continue to face the military ire of the Quraysh. At a place called Badr, they would meet an army three times their size, but the Qur'an would tell them that God sent them angels to strengthen their ranks: "It was not you [Muhammad] that threw [sand blinding your enemies], but rather it was God that threw" (Qur'an 8:17). By the time of the Prophet's death in 622 CE, the spiritual, social, and political utopian vision of the Qur'an had become reality. A prophet, guided by God, had established peace and justice through military might but also through the forgiveness of his most bitter enemies.

Early Muslims would look back at the time of the Prophet as a source of inspiration. God's just rule is not only "to come,"[62] but also near if only Muslims strive to bring it about. The utopian impulse gave way to different sociopolitical movements throughout history seeking to correct the ills of the world. The 'Abbasids who took over the Muslim Empire in 750 CE were driven by the desire to place a righteous member of the Prophet's family on the throne.[63] The eleventh-century Almoravid dynasty in North Africa began as an attempt to strengthen and revitalize religious practice. When their dynasty became too religiously lax in the next century, the Almohads again preached religious adherence and an end to political corruption. Closer to home, we can think about the religious fervor that propelled the Saudi family to power in 1927, facilitated by the vision of the Ikhwan troops seeking to purge the Arabian Peninsula from what it considered to be idol worship.[64]

The problem with utopian thinking in Muslim history is that it never really lived up to the justice of the Prophet. Sunni Muslim legal scholars realized early on that utopian political movements could often lead to civil strife and internecine Muslim fighting. Utopian thinking was at the root of what was to be called the *Fitna* or Civil Wars that pitted different companions of the Prophet against each other after his death.[65] It even led to the slaughter of the Prophet's beloved grandson, Husayn, when he sought to take the reins of the Muslim Empire from a corrupt and licentious ruler. As Near East historian Patricia Crone points out, the tempering of the utopian impulse among the masses began in the ninth century with the *ahl al-hadith*—a pietistic movement known for its political quietism.[66] By the time Sunnis wrote mature texts of legal thought, they paid homage to the ideal of justice while accepting the limits imposed by reality. A telling example is how the eleventh-century Iraqi scholar, Abu al-Hasan al-Mawardi, simultaneously claimed that the leader of the Muslims ideally should be the most virtuous and knowledgeable among them, while accepting a less qualified Muslim leader that can preserve political stability.[67] They had harsh words for those who rebelled against the ruling authority, calling them *ahl al-baghy* (the people of corruption). Sunni jurists applied the same consideration to war, a point that will be pursued in later chapters. Although a just empire under Muslim rule spanning the entirety of the earth would in theory be desirable, they saw that endless imperial expansion was impractical. The Kharajites, a group of Muslims who rebelled against the fourth Caliph ʻAli, would become the paradigmatic example in their collective memory of how the search for justice could go terribly wrong, leading to bloodshed in the quest for eradicating human political fallibility. By the tenth century, Twelver Shiʻa scholars had also embraced a political discourse that recognized the disconnect between the ideal and the possible.

But the impulse toward the utopian never fully disappeared from Muslim life. So long as justice was an aspiration demanded of God, some would find it necessary to change the status quo—often militarily. Sometimes the utopian overlapped with the messianic, as in the case of the Safavid empire whose leader, Shah Isma'il I, claimed to be appointed by God to spread Twelver Shi'ism, or the Mahdi movement in nineteenth-century Sudan, whose leader Muhammad Ahmad bin 'Abd Allah proclaimed himself the righteous one who is promised to bring justice according to Islamic eschatology. But most utopian movements were not millenarian, seeking to enact the end of times. Rather, they dreamed of correcting wrong and emulating the Prophet's justice. As the Prophet was reported to have said: "If any of you see an injustice, let him change it with his hand. If this is too difficult, then with his tongue. And if this is still too difficult, then let him hate it in his heart, but this is the weakest of faith."[68] The utopian impulse within Islamic history attempts to implement a vision of a just state of affairs, one that harkens back to the Prophet.

Al-Awlaki's thought should be interpreted as a modern iteration of a utopian theory of jihad. He was part of a coterie of thinkers who departed from a Sunni tradition that was committed to a pragmatic understanding of politics, war, and peace. Al-Awlaki's role in radicalizing North American Muslims is well known. Journalist Scott Shane has tied countless plots under the Obama administration back to Al-Awlaki's influence, and radicalization studies scholar Alexander Meleagrou-Hitchens notes that "Awlaki's works are, and have been for some time, on the essential reading (or viewing and listening) list for Western Salafi-jihadists." But what our historical record lacks is sufficient attention to North American Muslim communities' engagement with Al-Awlaki's theory of jihad and, especially, to his creative rupture with the Islamic tradition.

My claims about the utopian strain within Islamic history should not be confused with past anthropological attempts to reduce Islam to historical constants. I do not seek to replicate the likes of Ernest Gellner's typology of an urban and rural Islam forever in tension.[69] Such approaches have lost favor in the last three decades to what we may call the Asadian turn.[70] Talal Asad's contention that Islam be treated as a discursive tradition makes us attuned to the various ways in which Muslims draw eclectically upon the scriptures and intellectual resources of the past to shape their religion in the present. This book is fully indebted to the Asadian turn. It contends that Al-Awlaki's theory of jihad was a product of selectively drawing on past sources to make claims about the present. But it also recognizes the power of specific stories and teachings in shaping Muslim practice across time and space. Not all scripture is equal, in other words. While there are thousands of hadith, a relatively smaller number have figured disproportionately in the shaping of popular Muslim practice. To speak of a utopian impulse, then, is to recognize the power of Islam's early political and religious triumph in shaping Muslim imaginaries in the present.

The claim that Muslims are shaped by a utopian impulse does not suggest that Muslim politics is in any way determined by scripture or religion—at least not univocally. The Islamic tradition in this book functions neither as a site of ideology that produces predictable political action nor as a mask for other "real" causes of violence. Instead, Islam functions as a rich repository of material from which Muslims can draw (should they choose to do so) in orienting themselves in a political arena. Islamophobia studies scholar Arun Kundnani appropriately speaks of this Islam as a "lens" in making sense of the world.[71] The vastness of this Islamic tradition—made up of thousands of Qur'anic verses, tens of thousands of reports about the Prophet (the *hadith*), as well as historical accounts of the early Muslim community, books of Islamic law, Qur'anic exegesis, hadith commentary, theology, and spirituality (Sufism)—makes the possibilities of political engagement virtually limitless. To give but one example: Premodern Muslim jurists have paradoxically seen in the Prophet Muhammad's Hudaybiyya Peace Treaty with the rival tribe of Mecca both a justification for war and a justification for peace. The eleventh-century jurist Abu al-Hasan al-Mawardi claimed that since the treaty was for ten years, Muslims should sign peace treaties only for ten years or less.[72] In contrast, the fifteenth-century jurist, Ibn Humam's *Sharh Fath al-Qadir*, took the peace treaty to be an example of how peaceful relations enabled non-Muslims to see the virtues of the Islamic faith.[73] Of course, the variability of the Islamic tradition can be found throughout Muslim belief and practice. Muslims will often pray slightly differently or abide by different rules in the hajj pilgrimage to Mecca. But, today at least, the sphere of politics is amenable to greater variation precisely because for most Muslims it is not a site around which questions of Islamic orthodoxy or Muslim belonging turn. It is telling that past ethnographies of Muslims have often sought to examine how pious self-fashioning *indirectly* shapes Muslim politics. This is to say that Islamic practice and thought leaves immense space for Muslims' discretion in how they relate religion to politics. Our customary division between the radical and moderate Muslim is lazy and misses the multiplicity of different political visions among Muslims. And it is worth mentioning that none of these visions are truly innocent—as politics rarely is. In this sense, Muslims are not very different from other religious communities in the West whose members possess different and competing political ideas. It is high time we introduce specificity over generality in our historical analysis of the War on Terror.

Instead, the emphasis on the utopian impulse within Islamic history is meant to add precision in understanding the Islamic lens with which a jihadist thinker like Al-Awlaki approached the political realities of his time. Al-Awlaki, and many men who heeded his call to violence, were less convinced of the inherent need to wage war against non-Muslims, as they were unwilling to accept the status quo. Without attending to the Islamic impulse to utopian justice, we inevitably distort the past in two ways. First, we strip agency from the jihadist by failing to understand what made Al-Awlaki's solution to the War on Terror convincing. Here we fall into a secular bias, dismissing religious claims about righteous violence as so obviously wrong that they need not be engaged with.[74] Alternatively, we construe such claims as covers for other problems (political, psychological, etc.). We therefore miss why jihadists like Ferid, Miawand, and Muhanad agreed with Al-Awlaki after carefully listening to him.[75] Although we might critique the three men's acts or beliefs—and indeed many of my interlocutors called them "naïve" and "foolish"—there was nothing irrational about them.[76] They had reasons for believing that picking up a gun was a proper solution to the problems they faced. Only a careful account of Al-Awlaki's ideas and of the men's own reception of those ideas can shed light on what made them compelling.

Second, by missing how the War on Terror produced a novel ideology of jihad, specifically addressed to Anglophone Muslims, we absolve ourselves of our own role (as citizens of North American states) in producing the ideology we seek to eradicate. We fall back on the erroneous view of a stable radical Islamist ideology (often called Salafi-jihad) that allegedly won over a minority of North American Muslims because we lost the "battle for hearts and minds."[77] This misses the dynamism of human thought—even jihadist thought—in the face of shifting politics. A proper historical analysis demands that, instead of sweeping our insecurities under the rug, we ask in what ways the War on Terror could be so problematic that some of our own citizens came to formulate and embrace a theory of just war against it. Note that acknowledging our complicity in producing violence does not excuse the jihadist. Historians who argue that the Treaty of Versailles in 1919 produced the conditions for the Second World War do not thereby justify Nazi ideology or actions. But they do add complexity to historical analysis—which is difficult when we are still party to the violence.

METHODS AND POSITIONALITY

This was not an easy book to write. And not only because of the emotional toll of revisiting and discovering systematic state abuses and miscarriages of justice. Would it were only this. Unfortunately, I discovered a community with great reluctance to contribute to my research project. One of my key interlocutors initially refused an interview by tersely writing that he "respectfully declined" to speak to me or anyone else he knew from the Winnipeg Muslim community. I thought perhaps he had experienced the men's radicalization as a type of traumatic event that he wanted to forget. But I eventually discovered that his reluctance resulted from his deep fear of security agencies. He wrote, "I'm still quite shaken by the entire experience and the tactics that ensued, as you can imagine I'm very apprehensive . . . my first question to you is, and forgive me for being so frank, are you involved with any intelligence agencies yourself?" I came to see during my ongoing research that there was a pervasive fear among Muslims who had been approached by CSIS. Some politely but flatly refused to contribute to the research. I understood why. As a member of their community, I too would have distrusted someone asking questions about the three men. The problem is not only the fear of reprisals from the state. It is also the fear of social ostracization and stigmatization. My participants were men with careers and families to protect. They could not afford to be linked to radicals, even in a study that promised to reveal the injustices they suffered. Another interlocutor agreed to speak on condition that I strip him of even the most obscure identity marker. In an attempt to protect my interlocutors, I have used pseudonyms throughout—a convention that is odd in history but common in anthropology. My interlocutors showed great courage in participating in my research. Until the narrative shifts away from seeing Muslim men during the War on Terror as suspect and toward seeing them as equal citizens, with the same right to the presumption of innocence as anyone else, they remain a vulnerable community.

I have little doubt that someday there will be deep national contrition for the treatment of Canadian and American Muslim citizens during the War on Terror. But my interlocutors' responses suggest we are not there yet. There are, however, signs of change on the horizon. When Detective Paul called me in 2016, I would not have had the courage to write this book. Two developments have changed matters significantly for me. First, during his time as president, Donald Trump's overt anti-Muslim racism forced liberal America and Canada to reckon with the grossly harmful perceptions and treatment of Muslims.[78] Just as it was under Trump that Black Lives Matter broke through to the mass US consciousness, Trump's repugnant attitudes toward Muslims forced many to embody his antithesis. The Muslim Ban prompted historic solidarity, with crowds gathering at airports—the paradigmatic site of Muslim exceptionality. Under Obama, the assumption was that if you were a Muslim in trouble, you must have done something wrong. Under Trump, there was an acceptance that perhaps the security state had gone overboard. Second, the end of ISIS has coincided with a reduction in terrorist attacks and anxieties about the proliferation of terrorists. The new fault lines of Middle East politics no longer appear to be between religious and secularist ideologies, but rather among competing authoritarian alliances, occasionally reinforced by sectarian identity (Saudi Arabia, the United Arab Emirates, and Egypt versus Qatar and Turkey on the one hand, and versus Iran, Iraq, the Yemeni

Houthis, and Hezbollah on the other). And in addition to these two shifts, I have the privilege of writing to fellow academic audiences who, for all of their biases, are trained to examine scholarly analyses and to engage questions of power and ideology critically. In this regard, I am more fearful of a bad review than accusations of jihadist sympathies.

This book is the product of four different methodologies. First, I employ the historian's craft of finding the past by scouring archives. These archives come predominantly from the Canadian and US governments, court transcripts, private emails, and various Winnipeg Muslim community organizations. Second, I use my training in classical Islamic law to analyze the historical ties and ruptures between jihadist ideology and past Muslim thought; I draw on premodern treatises that define and detail the norms of war and peace in Islam. Third, I conducted more than twenty interviews. My interlocutors are typically members of the Winnipeg Muslim community. All are Sunni Muslims (though the community itself contained Shiʿa Muslims as well). Most were in their early twenties when Ferid, Miawand, and Muhanad disappeared and are now in their late thirties. They have helped me better understand who the three men were, why they left, and especially how Muslims have been treated by state security agencies. They have also helped me understand the role that politics and religion played within the Winnipeg Muslim community in the years before and after September 11.

Last, I rely heavily on the methods of auto-ethnography by drawing on my own observations and experiences in the Winnipeg Muslim community from 1999 to 2007. That I was not an academic during this time raises many methodological questions. For one, can my memory be relied upon? Have my later life experiences prejudiced these data? My approach here is to follow other ethnographies that acknowledge memories of the past as something that changes with life circumstances.[79] Documentary evidence is therefore used in two different ways. First, I turn to such evidence to ascertain where my memories and those of my interlocutors depart from the facts of the past, and to attempt the most faithful reconstruction of events. Second, in order to question why our perceptions have changed over the course of the thirteen years that elapsed between 2007 and the starting point in the writing process of this book, I ask what wider politics, interests, and fears have shifted our perceptions of Islam, jihad, the Winnipeg Muslim community, and the three men. Another worthwhile question is whether my work is truly ethnographic or more of a memoir. The problem here is that I did not go to the "field" armed with the questions or the theoretical tools that ethnographers typically possess. Rather, I entered the field as an insider, undifferentiated from those I now call my interlocutors. I have therefore had to ask my questions retrospectively. But this may be a necessary constraint of my subject matter. How does anyone write an ethnographic account of radicalization otherwise? Radicalization is a process of becoming, and the researcher has no way of knowing who will become a radical. What I can do is apply the various insights of anthropological studies on Islam to a community that I did observe and try to understand over eight years—and beyond.

What, then, was my relationship to my interlocutors during these years? I joined the Winnipeg Muslim community in 2000 after converting to Islam. My conversion was a slow process. I had been raised by a white Christian single mother who baptized me in the Catholic Church. Hers was the only family I knew up until the age of about thirteen. They were part of a French Canadian community that had settled on the Eastern banks of the Red River in the nineteenth century (in the former town turned neighborhood of St. Boniface). Franco-Manitobans have successfully struggled to retain their language against a historically assimilationist Anglophone provincial government. I therefore attended Franco-Manitoban schools of the newly forged Franco-Manitoban School Division (DSFM), where whiteness overwhelmingly predominated. I had a typical Franco-Manitoban name at the time and I was sufficiently white-passing to fit in. I felt I was part of a minority—but a linguistic, not a racial or religious, one. Only on rare occasions was I made conscious of the physical traits I inherited from my North African father. A strange mix of events brought my father more prominently into my life at the beginning of my teen years. He introduced me to the Islamic faith and to the Muslim community. My first experience in a mosque was a cultural shock. I had never seen so many non-Europeans in one room and I felt out of place and uncomfortably worried they might identify me as an intruder. But by the age of sixteen, I had attended enough Muslim community events to feel comfortable with Muslims and their faith. I wrestled with the faith part for some time, as anyone exposed to new beliefs should.

When I did embrace Islam in early 2000, I went all in. I told my teachers at school I wanted to be called "Youcef," which had been one of my middle names at birth. I joined various Muslim youth organizations and attended Saturday Islamic school, Friday prayers, and Friday night learning circles at the mosque. In the process, I developed a circle of Muslim friends. I tried to understand the Muslim vision of the world—religious, social, and political—and contrasted it to my upbringing. The philosopher of ethics, Alasdair MacIntyre, speaks of the novice's need to defer to authority when learning a tradition, and I was an eager pupil. In a characteristically white convert manner, I saw myself as a spokesperson for an unjustly maligned religion and felt my Western culture had much to learn from Islam. Of course, before preaching its virtues, I would have to learn more about the faith. After high school, I studied Arabic and Islamic studies in Damascus, Syria. Upon my return, I began an undergraduate degree at the University of Manitoba in 2003. There, I met Ferid, Miawand, and Muhanad, alongside most of the interlocutors of this book. We were all part of a sizable Muslim student body that constituted a fraternity of young men. I speak of these men throughout the book as "the brothers"—a shorthand within Muslim communities that gestures toward an aspiration of intimacy among fellow believers. I consciously use gender-binary language in accordance with my interlocutors' understanding of gender. I left Winnipeg in 2007 to pursue graduate school. This led to forging ties with Muslim communities in Victoria, Montreal, and Toronto. Though these communities do not figure within this book, they contribute to my practical knowledge about a wider Canadian Muslim community.

With the passage of time, my religious beliefs and practice have become much more private. Today, there is no single mosque, association, or school of thought to which I belong or subscribe. This privacy is the product of a multiplicity of factors. One is simply growing up and busying oneself with a career, livelihood, and raising a family. This busyness often results in spiritual laziness. Perhaps someday, when things settle down, I will follow in the footsteps of the eleventh-century mystic al-Ghazali and give myself wholeheartedly to the Sufi path.[80] But there is a second and more conscious reason for my distance from any particular Muslim group. The more I delved into the Islamic tradition, the more I found it richly laden with a variety of competing and meritorious views and practices. I have come to appreciate and dwell in Islam's multiplicity of perspectives on God and ethics. This journey makes me reluctant to speak with certainty about any single way of being in the world (Muslim or otherwise). In many respects, I now seek to emulate the premodern jurists I have studied so closely who, while possessing personal convictions about what God wants of them, recognized that they could very well be wrong and others right. I am more useful to my students and to society when presenting the complexity and diversity of thought and practice within Islam than I would be pontificating on "correct" doctrines. During the 2010 and 2020s, I continued to be invited to speak at Muslim community events, but when doing so, I have taken on the posture of a historian of ideas who can shed light on the past or the present without ultimately voicing an opinion on the truth of the matter or prescribing a way of acting. Despite my uncertainties about life, I do know that I love my Muslim communities very much. I love them from their most conservative to their most progressive members. I love them for their commitment to bettering themselves, for their recognition of our human frailty, and for their aspiration to find truth. What pains them pains me. The Winnipeg Muslim community continues to hold a special place in my heart. I found a home among them in the formative years of my life. I learned from them a new way of seeing the world and forged friendships that remain to this day. This book is for them.

* * *

A note on terminology: I have chosen to use the term "jihadists" to refer to individuals belonging to militant groups that justify their activities by reference to the Islamic tradition. I have avoided using the Arabic term *mujahid*, which literally means a fighter engaged in jihad, because the identity of a true mujahid today is a matter of disagreement among Muslims. The one exception is the Afghan fighters of the 1980s anti-Soviet jihad, since the media often used the term "mujahideen" to speak of them. The reader should nonetheless remember that the term jihadist is a loaded one because of its frequently contemptuous deployment within North American policy circles and media. Likewise, I speak of Ferid, Muhanad, and Miawand as radicals not because the term gives us a great understanding of the men's beliefs but because it allows us to interrogate our assumptions about those we call "radical."[81]

1

CAN THE MUSLIM SPEAK?

GRIEF, SUSPICION, AND SOCIAL RESPONSIBILITY

The Meccan air is warm and dry. Sunset is approaching, offering the coolness of the desert winter night. I am walking from ʿArafa to Muzdalifa. I have spent the day in worship; Ferid, Muhanad, Miawand, and Sabir are with me. The heart of the hajj pilgrimage is the day spent on Mount ʿArafa. There, the pilgrims had asked God for forgiveness, for goodness, for mercy. We asked him to make our circumstances easy; to cure our ills, to provide for orphans, to grant us success in our studies, to bless our parents, to bring peace and security to the oppressed, the poor, and the destitute worldwide. Up until then, the journey had been smooth and easy. We had stayed in comfortable tents in Mina before going to ʿArafa, and the morning walk to ʿArafa had been pleasant. In the late afternoon, pilgrims were preparing to make their way to Muzdalifa to spend the night there. Many boarded buses, but we decided to walk. The buses were slow, stuck in the traffic of the one-million-plus pilgrims there that year. Walking might be quicker, we thought. It wasn't too far; we anticipated a couple of hours at most. Besides, we are able-bodied and recognize that the pilgrimage is about effort and sacrifice for God's sake. The road is paved. Pilgrims are all around us. Our spirits are high.

I see the sign for Muzdalifa. We have arrived. I wonder where exactly we will camp for the night. As we cross the threshold of Muzdalifa, suddenly and without warning, the crowd starts becoming ominously larger. The space between us and the other pilgrims is shrinking at an alarming speed. I feel shoving and pushing from all sides. I look to my travel companions. They mirror my expression of concern. We all know the stories. Pilgrims, sometimes hundreds of them, trampled to death by crowds too large to be gathered in a single space. We are stuck and jostled one way and the other. If we fall, we are finished. There would be no way we could get back up. The crowd has a mind of its own and the pilgrims, despite their best intentions, cannot control where they step. I start to drift from my companions, lost in the crowd. I see Muhanad; we link hands. "Let's stay close," Muhanad tells the group. We all take each other's hands. We are in this together. The minutes are passing and the crowd is not getting any smaller. Suddenly, I feel a strong push from my left side. Oh my God, I'm losing my balance. My hand slips from Muhanad's. I'm about to trip, to fall. Ferid sees me losing my balance. He sees the expression of fear on my face. As I fall, he takes my hand. "I got you, brother," he says. I give him a look of gratitude.

* * *

This is how I remember them. The hajj trip was where I got to know them best. We spent two weeks together, and shared special experiences: we prayed at the Ka'ba (the temple in Mecca believed to be built by Abraham and Ishmael) and at the Prophet's mosque in Medina. Many Muslims consider the hajj a once-in-a-lifetime duty for those able to undertake it. It is a time when pilgrims leave the mundane preoccupations of their lives—studies, money, family and social duties; in short, what Muslims call *al-dunya* (this worldly life)—and focus on spirituality, or what Muslims call *al-akhira* (otherworldly matters). We returned from Saudi Arabia on January 4, 2007. Just over three months later, Ferid, Muhanad, and Miawand disappeared. We will get to the specific circumstances surrounding their disappearance in due time. For now, I want to focus on who these men were, or at the very least, how I and fellow Muslim community members knew them. Through memories—not just of hajj, but also of the four years prior during which we attended the same university—we will understand each person's complex life histories, aspirations, and understandings of self, community, and God.

The biographical stories I tell here resemble those that social scientists present when seeking the causes of radicalization.[1] These radicalization experts scour the lives of individual jihadists and seek patterns to understand why someone would turn to violence. In the case of Ferid, Miawand, and Muhanad, these experts would find variables—age, criminal history, religious orientation—that confirm the conclusions of previous studies of jihadists. But they would also concede that these variables are not uncommon among other Muslims.[2] This commonality, coupled with the fact that the radicals were seemingly "ordinary" young men with little in common except for religious conviction, would then feed the harmful narrative that any Muslim could potentially become radicalized[3]—a point often repeated in the investigation into the disappearance of our three men.[4] Moreover, the search for variables misses the historical specificity that made violence a seemingly viable political option for them. Thus, while my biographical sketches overlap with the methods of radicalization experts, I depart from their studies in two ways. First, rather than search for variables, I examine the men's lives as part of an attempt to shed light on what is to come. I take to heart Alasdair MacIntyre's contention that we cannot understand individuals' motives without a sense of the historical narratives within which they situate their lives. The continuities and ruptures the three men would later undergo can only be fully understood once we know the ethical assumptions, commitments, and motives guiding their engagement with their social world. Second, I tell their story as a means to examine the often-neglected tragedy that befalls a Muslim community when it loses one or more of its members to militancy. I therefore present the lives of these three men as part of an attempt to document how their life histories intertwined with and changed those of their fellow community members.

The communal memories of the three men that I present here have been shaped by the state's suspicion of the Winnipeg Muslim community. This suspicion, in turn, has hindered its members from properly grieving the men's radicalization as loss. For years, I myself refused to acknowledge the men's departures as a communal tragedy. I was prevented by feelings of anger and frustration toward them. We all were: Dawud, Mahdi, Nabeel, Sabir, Ryan, and the others. The three men had created such a spectacular mess for their families and Muslim community, and we resented them. It was an unlikely person who reminded me that it was alright to grieve the loss of these men. The day before Muhanad's trial, I spoke to US prosecutor Saritha Komatireddy and suggested that she must be excited about the upcoming trial. "It's a big day tomorrow," I added. "You've been working toward it for years now."

Her countenance became serious, and with a pensive expression she answered softly: "No, not really." She lingered for a moment. "What I really feel is sadness. I've seen what this case has done to so many people, to the families in particular. I think the overriding feeling is sadness." For so long, those belonging to the Winnipeg Muslim community have been unable to mourn properly and to heal. By exploring the Winnipeg Muslim community's pain at the loss of its members to radicalization, this chapter not only documents the significance of the men's radicalization for community members but also carries out an act of grieving through remembering. It is an act that pushes back against the normalized suspicion of Muslim communities that prevents grieving from taking place. It relies on seeing historiography as more than facts and their interpretations. The writing of history is also about reckoning. It is about looking into the mirror and coming to terms with pains we have been harboring for too long. The Muslims who knew the three men have a right to restore intelligibility to their individual and collective lives by constructing narratives of themselves and the men through an Islamic idiom that is true to their embodied sensibilities and self-understandings.

But sharing experiences is not only a means to better understand Muslim loss and pain during the war on terror. It is also a means to gain a different and more complex view of the figure of the radical, and of social responsibility. Moving beyond the view that reduces the radical to a national security threat, the Muslims I interviewed instead saw the three men through an Islamic tradition that acknowledges human frailty and folly. They viewed humans as continually prone to misguidance but never beyond hope: a perspective that not only de-exceptionalizes the radical but also posits a different view of mutual care. While my interlocutors acknowledged the radical's accountability for illegal actions, they also felt a communal responsibility to guide their members toward the right path. I suggest that this Muslim view of radicalization has the potential to make us think differently about our political commitments and our collective belonging.

A YOUNG AND GROWING COMMUNITY

Winnipeg is a mid-sized city in the center of Canada. It is situated in the vast Canadian prairies where fields of wheat are abundant and where the terrain is so flat that, as the joke goes, it's the only place you can lose your dog and watch it run away for days. Winnipeg is a sparsely populated city, regionally fragmented, and hard to get around without a car. Each neighborhood has its own history with distinct communities that settled there at historical junctures. For instance, my family is part of the French community, many of whom mixed with the Indigenous peoples of Manitoba and settled on the Eastern banks of the Red River where it crosses the Assiniboine River.[5] To the French, one might add Indigenous, Anglo-Saxon, Jewish, and Ukrainian as prominent communities who helped build Winnipeg in the nineteenth and early twentieth centuries.[6]

In the 1950s and 1960s, Muslims arrived in Winnipeg the way most of its past communities had: with minimal resources but a determination to carve a place for themselves in the city's landscape.[7] This itself is something to marvel at. As my friend Dawud, who studied environmental design at the University of Manitoba and left Winnipeg in his mid-twenties for Toronto, says, Winnipeg is an odd place to live: the winters are absurdly cold, easily reaching below 30 degrees Celsius for months on end, and the summers, while warm and pleasant, mark the arrival of swarms of mosquitoes on every enjoyable green patch of grass. And yet some of the founding families of Winnipeg's Muslim community have expressed how Winnipeg grew on them until it became home: Community elder Laila Chebib reminisces that after spending some time in Winnipeg for studies, "the Ford Foundation offered [my husband] Farouk to [fund] his PhD [studies] . . . and they asked us where you would like to go, anywhere in the world? And I said Winnipeg."[8] Laila and her husband, Farouk Chebib, came to Winnipeg in the 1950s around the same time as a handful of Muslim students and young families. Most of them were of West Indian, Arab, and South Asian descent. For several years, they searched for a place where they might pray together and teach their children their faith.

At first, they were resigned to makeshift spaces, sometimes provided by churches. But eventually they formed the Manitoba Islamic

Association (MIA) and gathered sufficient funds to build their own mosque—or almost. The families found a plot of land in the region of St. Vital in the south of the city—a predominantly white, middle-class area, and, incidentally, the neighborhood where I was raised. But they soon encountered a challenging problem: Their contractor had underestimated the cost of the mosque and went bankrupt, leaving the mosque only partially completed. Undeterred, the group of largely white-collar workers—university professors, doctors, and engineers—rolled up their sleeves, picked up hammers and nails, and finished the job themselves. They completed the structure in 1978, and for the next three decades this mosque—built on a residential street and no larger than a house—became the heart of the Winnipeg Muslim community.[9]

Until 2004, this was Winnipeg's only mosque.[10] The Hazelwood Street Mosque—recently baptized Pioneer Mosque in honor of those who lay the groundwork for the growth of the Winnipeg Muslim community[11]—organized community bonds among incredibly diverse groups of people distinguished along cultural, racial, linguistic, and socioeconomic lines.[12] As increasing numbers of immigrants from formerly colonized countries settled in Winnipeg, the mosque came to include Muslims from every corner of the earth. They worshipped during the five daily ritual prayers, and the mosque barely contained them during Friday service. They attended evening and weekend lectures about their faith's ethical and ritual injunctions. And they partook in communal celebrations like Ramadan meals, marriage ceremonies, and commemorations for the births of new children. The mosque helped shape a new generation of North American Muslims who, though a minority, were fluent in the majority language and culture. Ferid, Miawand, and Muhanad were part of this new generation. Despite their different backgrounds, they, like me and my interlocutors in this book, found a home in this Winnipeg Muslim community.

A LIVELY UNIVERSITY PRAYER ROOM

I met Ferid, Miawand, and Muhanad while studying at the University of Manitoba between 2003 and 2007. We were all connected through the University's Prayer Room (*musalla*). For many Muslim students living on or near campus, the Hazelwood Mosque (and, after 2004, the downtown mosque on Ellice Avenue) was too far to travel to frequently for one's daily prayer obligations: It was not a walkable distance from the University, and Winnipeg's transit system has never been very good. For many of these students, the prayer room served as the equivalent of a mosque where they could congregate to pray between a busy class and study schedule. It also permitted Muslims from all over campus to fulfill their Friday prayers—and by far, it was the Friday prayers that brought together most student congregants. This prayer space would become the heart of Muslim student life on campus; and like the mosque, it would create ties of solidarity across a diverse group of Muslims. It was here that Ferid, Muhanad, and Miawand met and developed friendships.

When I began my undergraduate studies at the University of Manitoba in the fall of 2003, the Muslim Student Association (MSA) prayer room was scarcely larger than an office space. Tucked away in a tunnel that permitted engineering students to walk to the Student Union Building without being subject to Winnipeg's cold winter weather, Muslims praying there seldom lingered. As such, friendships were rarely generated in that space. Instead, Muslim students often met and socialized in the Muslim Student Association office, which, while also small, had a microwave, a TV, and a comfortable sofa.[13] The size of the prayer room made it impossible to accommodate the Friday congregation, which numbered into the hundreds. The MSA executive committee would reserve various rooms in the Student Union Building to host the large Friday gatherings.

All of that would change the next year. The MSA president, a thirty-plus-year-old Libyan PhD student in engineering, had entered into lengthy talks with the university administration over the summer and had secured a new prayer space in the Education Building. Having visited several university prayer spaces in my life, I can attest that this one was a cut above. For one, its size matched that of the Hazelwood Mosque, ensuring that all Friday prayers could be conducted there. For another, the space was incredibly thoughtfully designed. The carpet was new and clean (an important feature since Muslims prostrate themselves in prayer), there was a large basin with running water at the back where Muslims could perform ritual ablutions before prayer, and the room had a separate, large vestibule at the entrance lined with coat hangers and shoe racks to ensure that the actual prayer space would remain neat and tidy.

From 2004 to 2007, I saw how this prayer space created social ties like those of a mosque. The space was always open and students would come to pray at all times of the day. Even when staying only briefly, they would chat in the entrance hallway about everything and anything—courses, upcoming events, travel plans, fashion, movies, and pop culture. Ferid, Miawand, and Muhanad would become regulars—among a host of others who encompassed all Muslim nationalities one could think of, from Syrians to Pakistanis, Sudanese, Afghans, Turks, and Iranians. A natural division occurred between older, often Arab, graduate students and younger students with fluency in English and Canadian culture. In Ramadan, the prayer room served as a meeting place for Muslim students to break their fast together, and students would often spend time there poring over their textbooks during exam periods. A student named Sabir even conducted a weekly martial arts class in the prayer room.

Ideals of Islamic modesty concerning interactions between genders meant that Muslim men typically fraternized with other men within the campus prayer room. I did not have much insight into the communal ties that shaped the women's prayer space, which had a separate side entrance and was partially closed off.[14] The men encouraged each other to adopt spiritual virtues applicable to both genders: steadfastness in ritual practice, patience before hardship, forbearance, kindness, and hospitality toward others, and sexual abstinence outside wedlock. But, although most of the men were bachelors, they nevertheless saw themselves as one day leading a family, just as they then led the congregation in prayer. As such, they would be the breadwinners and moral guides for their wives and children. Thus, the virtues promoted in the prayer space were always inevitably gendered and always shaped by the knowledge that the men were still in a state of becoming. In particular, the students' idea of what constituted good leadership—emphasizing such virtues as courage, wisdom, temperance, strength, and kindness—was inflected by the men's future roles as husbands and fathers.

The prayer room also became a site to promote MSA activities. Regular events included a welcome dinner at the start of the school year, the annual Ramadan "Fast-a-thon" where non-Muslim students and faculty were invited to fast with campus Muslims, and an annual conference, organized jointly with the University of Winnipeg.[15] Other events were more ad hoc, such as movie nights, religious classes, or soccer games.[16] These events further generated a sense of community among Muslim student attendees. Although the students were too numerous for everyone to know each other, faces became familiar and the friendships that did form ran deep. Even in 2005–2006, when the MSA executive committee was in disarray and did little in the way of organizing events, the prayer room continued to be a lively site where students got together, informally and formally.

Our three men found their campus home within this lively prayer space. Each came from a different ethnic group, academic discipline, and socioeconomic background. Each had lived immensely different lives and had personalities that an outsider might think were strangely incongruent. And yet the prayer space was a place where they all belonged as practicing Muslim students.

FERID: THE CONTEMPLATIVE SALAFI

October 2006. It is Ramadan. I am fasting but not too hungry. It is nearly sunset, the point at which we can eat again. I usually break my fast at home but I have an assignment due tomorrow and I am staying late on campus. I go to the prayer room, braving the cold; I know the MSA is providing food there. I walk in and see Ferid. I greet him, but I also see he is busy organizing the food on tables. "It's time," someone tells him. Ferid walks to the front of the hall and begins melodiously reciting the *adhan*—the Muslim call to prayer. Ferid's voice exudes calmness and serenity. I don't know of a more beautiful call to prayer than Ferid's.

Dates and water are passed around as Ferid continues the adhan. The water trickles down my throat, bringing life back to my sluggish body. I make my way to the table of food and serve myself. The meal is plain: rice, potatoes, and salad. I am surprised: Ramadan is a time of fasting, but also of post-fast feasting; I expected more elaborate dishes. I sit down with Ferid, nonetheless grateful to have food. "How are you doing?"

"Good," he tells me, smiling. "It's just been a very busy time." His voice is measured, as always.

"So are you in charge of the MSA now?"

"Yes, kind of," Ferid answers.[17] "I'm just covering for now. *In sha'a Allah* [God willing] a properly elected executive will take over soon."

"I see." Then, after a pause, I say, "Ferid, you didn't feel like ordering from Chicken Delight today? I know their food is crazy greasy, but when Ezzedin ordered it, it was a hit with most of the students. Are you trying to minimize costs?"

Ferid answers, "No, actually this was a lot more expensive. Unfortunately, I can't order from Chicken Delight because the University has a policy that food can't be brought in from outside. I needed to order from the University catering service, and since they don't prepare halal meat, the food needed to be more plain."

A man eating to Ferid's right chimes in, "But just bring the food in and don't tell anyone, like we used to do. Are you afraid of getting caught? Our room is secluded, no one comes here except Muslims."

"Ferid," I add, "I think the university rule is supposed to be for large gatherings. We're not that many students here, thirty at most. I don't think it's a big deal."

Ferid looks up from his plate. "I know we wouldn't get caught and I know no one would think it's a big deal," he says plainly. "But we are using this space under agreed-upon rules clearly stipulated by the University. As Muslims, we are not allowed to cheat people or violate contracts. The rules are the rules, and we should respect that."

* * *

Ferid always played by the rules. His morality was like that. He wanted to be a person of integrity who did not contort his religious commitments for personal gain. He desired to do the right thing and act in the right ways toward God and his fellow humans. This desire shaped his persona. He was a sober and pensive person. He was calm, taciturn, and displayed great maturity. Of the three men, he was the most natural leader. He was sure of himself, even as he pondered matters deeply. I am not the only one to remember Ferid this way. Dawud, who, like Ferid came from Ethiopia to Winnipeg as a child, noted Ferid's confidence and self-assuredness: "He had a clear sense of his convictions."

Ferid's maturity is attributable to numerous causes. For one, he was older than all of us, born four years before me, in 1980. By the time I started university, he had already spent years studying the natural sciences and planned to start a Pharmacy program in the near future. For another, Ferid had been raised by a devoted Muslim family who had sought to inculcate in him Prophetic manners and respectability. He embodied the Prophet's teaching that one should "speak well, or keep silent."[18] Ferid knew that speech was often vain: It could lead to backbiting, gossip, and preoccupation with frivolous topics. His older brother Tamim had been a role model for him growing up. Tamim was the *muadhdhan* (prayer caller) at the Hazelwood Mosque, and like Ferid he often attended the congregational prayer there. The family consciously chose to live near the mosque so as to worship with ease.

Ferid left Ethiopia at the age of eleven, shortly after his mother passed away. His eldest sister, who was already settled in Winnipeg, took him under her wing and raised him. She became another mother to him and preoccupied herself with his intellectual, physical, and moral well-being. Ferid came from the Amharic ethnic group and his family traces their Islamic faith to the time of the Prophet, when some of the very first Muslims sought refuge from religious persecution in Ethiopia. For many immigrant children, the disparity between their childhood culture and their new Canadian society can be difficult to reconcile.[19] For some time, Ferid struggled too. His sister remembers an episode where a classmate cruelly asked Ferid "where he was" in a picture showcasing poverty in Ethiopia. But this period of tension was short-lived, and Ferid quickly found a way to fit in with his Muslim and wider Canadian communities. He made new friends at Dakota High School and was a well-respected member of its soccer team. He came to understand Canadian culture as much as any Canadian-born Muslim like myself. He dressed in stylish, well-fitted, and ironed preppy clothing, often looking like he could be a model for The Gap. He was likable and got along with his non-Muslim colleagues and classmates. Whenever I had something to purchase at the University of Manitoba bookstore, I would see Ferid socializing with his co-workers, a warm smile on his lips. But the Muslim identity of the Ferid I knew was never in doubt. He was a constant presence at the prayer room and the Hazelwood Mosque during my university years from 2003 to 2007. And Ferid felt comfortable establishing his moral boundaries on campus, whether by exempting himself from venues serving alcohol or limiting interactions with members of the opposite gender. His sense of self as a Muslim and his religious practice were remarkably consistent throughout the years I knew him.[20]

Our Ramadan story also sheds light on Ferid's approach to Islam. The prayer room was a space that brought together diverse sets of Muslims from different sects and orientations. Ferid's insistence, despite objections, that Muslims must respect university rules, tells us much about his understanding of religion, society, and God. Ferid wanted to obey God, unconditionally. This sentiment is not foreign to other Muslims. The word *Islam* itself means "submission" or "surrender," as in to surrender oneself to God. Moreover, obeying God's rules in the Qur'an and Prophet's hadith is a persistent theme of Friday sermons. But, as Ebrahim Moosa notes, most Muslims do not approach their religion as a set of clear-cut duties to God.[21] Their ways of acting—morally and religiously—are also shaped by their cultural norms and their considerations of fairness, justice, mercy, and love.[22] For Ferid, all these values mattered, but invoking them could not trump what he considered the plain meaning of scripture. "Obey God and obey his Prophet," the Qur'an says. Taking this approach inevitably meant that there would be moments when Ferid felt he needed to go against the grain. There would be moments, like the one that Ramadan night, when he felt it necessary to firmly defend God's rules against a public morality that leaned in a different direction—Muslim and non-Muslim alike.

Ferid's approach to religion could be traced back to his increasing immersion within Salafi Islam. Salafism is a complex social movement that took root in Saudi Arabia in the 1970s.[23] It emerged from efforts by Saudi scholars to champion a plain reading of scripture that would determine the morals and ritualistic rules Muslims should follow. In championing this plain reading, Salafis largely bypassed the centuries of legal, theological, and mystical debates that comprised the vastness of the Islamic tradition. The move was meant to simplify the religion by taking recourse to unmediated texts, typically in the form of statements or actions attributed to Muhammad (hadiths). As Islamic studies scholar Caner Dagli notes, the problem with this hermeneutic approach is that it overlooks the inherent multiplicity of Muslim scriptural interpretations.[24] Salafi religious authorities have often failed to recognize that their understanding of scripture is simply one of many. Instead, they have assumed that—and acted as though—their interpretation conforms to a text's plain, common-sense, or literal meaning. Following this interpretation, for Salafi authorities, becomes a sign of obedience to God. Those who depart from this plain interpretation are guilty of religious innovations that pervert the religion. Moreover, as Islamic legal scholar Abou El Fadl notes, Salafi teachings typically have ended up promoting the religious interpretations of Saudi Arabian society, whose distinct social realities, including lack of diversity and worry about sexual morality, did not match our Canadian context at the time.[25]

Salafism was generally well-regarded among mosque-going Winnipeg Muslims in the early 2000s.[26] For instance, the MIA hired a new imam in 2000: Hosni Azzabi, who had obtained his degree from the University of Medina, the preeminent Salafi institution at the time. His credentials did not provoke open opposition or debate and many were pleased that their mosque leader had been trained in the historic City of the Prophet. But the positive attitude toward Salafism rarely resulted from a conscious decision. Most Muslims who adopted Salafi ways of thinking had never heard the term. Rather, Salafism was simply part of the environment, so to speak.[27] It was present in Friday sermons that cautioned people against innovations in religion and falling into polytheistic practices, like participating in Christmas celebrations or Halloween parties.[28] It was present in exhortations to be careful not to lose one's Muslim identity by resembling non-Muslims too much,[29] and it was present in the almost obsessive calls to avoid sexual temptation.[30]

But in contrast to most Winnipeg Muslims, Ferid quite consciously settled on Salafi thought as the correct religious path. What Salafism had to offer Ferid was a straightforward rendering of the faith. Whatever the Qur'an and the hadith exhorted Muslims to do, they should do it. Thus, Ferid often read texts from the Saudi-based Dar-us-Salam press, which quoted Salafi authorities such as al-Albani, Bin Baz, and al-ʿUthaymin. But because Ferid had very little knowledge of Arabic, he also listened to lectures and read blog posts by Salafis in the Anglophone world, such as Muhammad Alshareef.[31] In fact, when Ferid had the opportunity to organize a conference, he invited Abdurraheem Green, an eloquent Salafi British convert.[32] Ferid rejected other approaches to the religion. For instance, he critiqued the well-known US preacher Hamza Yusuf and other scholars for chanting the *Burda*, a popular poem celebrating the life of Muhammad. He saw their chanting as an innovation with no sanction in the religion.[33] Despite this one instance that stands out in my mind—an instance that, importantly, occurred right before he disappeared—it should be emphasized that Ferid was not typically judgmental or harsh with others. Salafism has a reputation for breeding condescending worshippers who look down upon others.[34] Ferid, however, was a gentle person. He collaborated with Muslims of varying stripes and showed great warmth to one and all. What mattered most for him was not telling others how to live their life but maintaining the integrity to live his own life the way God wanted—in short, having the moral courage to follow the rules, even when no one else did.

Ferid's concern for his fellow community members is exemplified in a story that Dawud relayed to me: "Youcef, do you remember that black jacket I used to have? I wore it for years. Do you know where I got it? It was Ferid that gave it to me. And do you know how he gave it to me? One day, I saw him wearing the jacket and I complimented him on it, the way anyone does. I just said, 'nice jacket,' and on the spot he took it off and said, 'take it, it's yours.'" Ferid's giving spirit was the product of an Islamic ethics that he tried to make central to his life. Through this ethics, Ferid forged ties of fraternal love with the other men of his community.

MIAWAND: LIKE A ZEALOUS CONVERT

October 2006. "What should I expect?" I ask Usman.

"The guys there just want a sense of brotherhood in Ramadan. It's not easy being in prison. Many of them are new to Islam. They don't have access to community members to ask questions and learn more about their religion."

The highway to Stony Mountain Penitentiary is a short drive north of Winnipeg. There is light traffic this evening. Dusty winds of snow are lightly brushing over the road ahead of us. I remember seeing the penitentiary from afar as a child on my way to football games in rural Manitoba. I remember the chills it gave me. Its imposing, enclosed structure and its location on an empty highway play on the imagination of passersby, almost to say, "you don't want to be here." It was both secretive and in plain sight.

"So how long have you been a prison chaplain?" I ask Usman.

"Two years now. I go every two weeks or so, and sometimes I deliver the Friday sermon. You'll meet Khalid; he's the facilitator of the group. He's the one that makes the formal request to the prison admin for the Ramadan dinners." Usman pulls into the prison parking lot. We enter; the prison guard recognizes him and smiles. We pass through security and are ushered into a large room. The room is simple but warm: It reminds me of a church or community hall more than a federal penitentiary. There are twenty or so prisoners there. I meet Khalid, who enthusiastically embraces Usman. Usman seems genuinely well-liked by the inmates, and I see that his visits are appreciated. I start making small talk with some of the other inmates. We break fast, pray, and then we eat. I enter into a long dinner conversation with an inmate named Tom. He tells me about how he will soon leave the prison and wishes to continue learning about Islam on the outside. But as Usman and I ready ourselves to leave, one prisoner comes to speak to me. He is short, with a shaved head, and sparse facial hair.

"So you go to the University of Manitoba? Do you know Miawand Yar?" he asks.

"I do," I answer, puzzled by his question.

"That's my cousin," he says. I am taken aback. I had no idea Miawand had a cousin in jail.

* * *

Why start a description of Miawand by speaking about his incarcerated cousin? Why start with a scene in which he himself is absent? First, Miawand's absence captures my relationship with him. I never knew him well, and I have no striking memories that would provide insight into his dreams, worries, or aspirations. A large part of who

Miawand was remained opaque to me until after his disappearance. He spoke little and his eyes hid a dark past and deep pain. I remember in him neither Muhanad's bubbly joviality nor Ferid's warmth. Others, however, have different memories of Miawand. Sabir, a Trinidadian student known in the prayer room equally for his kindness and physical strength, studied engineering with Miawand and fondly remembers how they would get together during lunches: "He would make a chicken curry and I would make a lamb curry. We both liked to cook and share food. That's my favorite memory of him." The two men built a strong bond as they joked, laughed, and took a break from the heavy demands of their engineering program. They would often meet with a group of fellow engineering students with whom they built a mutual camaraderie. This image of a kind person was shared among my interlocutors, including Dawud, who lived with Miawand for some time, and Nabeel, an Arab international student who calls Miawand "a real sweetheart."

But the second reason to start with this story is that Miawand could have very well ended up in his cousin's shoes, something I did not know at the time. Neither did I know it after he left in 2007. It took a later news report by the *Globe and Mail* in 2010 for me to learn about Miawand's troubled past.[35] The trouble started before Miawand was even born, when the Soviet Union invaded Afghanistan and Miawand's family was forced to flee over the border to Pakistan. Reduced to refugees, they settled in the northern city of Peshawar among other Pashto people.[36] Miawand was born three years later in 1983, the youngest of three brothers and one of a total of nine siblings. For some time, the family had some stability. Miawand's father was a doctor, and he found decent work at a German hospital operating in Peshawar. But Miawand's father soon aroused the anger of an armed group who were upset that he was working in a non-Muslim institution. His father was murdered when Miawand was still a child, leaving him without his love or guidance.[37] Miawand's eldest brother Ahmad and his mother made plans to flee Pakistan. They settled down in Winnipeg. But, unlike the middle-class South Asians I knew in my teenage years, Miawand's family lived in the "North End" of the city, a neighborhood of lower socioeconomic status. Miawand had trouble in school. He was expelled more than once for bullying. Then, while attending Sisler High

School, Miawand gravitated toward gangs. During this time, he paid little attention to religious practice. In 2003, Miawand was caught selling crack. He faced the possibility of heavy prison time. In fact, the case seemed airtight, as Miawand and his accomplice had tried to sell drugs to an undercover officer. The accomplice was eventually sentenced to ten months in jail. But in September 2006, Judge Menzies of the Manitoba Queen's Bench gave Miawand a second chance. The proceedings were stayed as Miawand cooperated in investigations of higher-ranking drug dealers.[38] During these years of legal problems, Miawand found religion. He became a presence in the prayer room in the winter of 2006. From that time until he left in March 2007, Miawand became incredibly diligent in his worship. Sabir characterized him well when he described him as avaricious in seeking *ajr*: an Arabic word for God's rewards to the faithful. Miawand did not only do the religious minimum: He also sought to perform optional prayers and fasts. He attempted to do whatever God wanted of him.

Though Miawand was born to a Muslim family, his dedication to changing his life from top to bottom resembled that of a convert.[39] He conformed to what Nada Moumtaz calls the aspiration to piety, acknowledging his past wayward ways and seeking to become practicing (*iltizam*).[40] There is beauty in the convert or the newly practicing Muslim's zeal to live a pious life, even if it is likely unsustainable.[41] The beauty stems from the level of dedication and self-sacrifice a person is capable of devoting to a higher purpose—not unlike Saint Paul's commitment to the Christian mission after his encounter on the road to Damascus. Miawand, like countless other newly practicing Muslims, went from being characterized by his family as "lazy," uninspired, and consumed with watching movies, to being self-disciplined, focused, and caring. Those who knew him before the change had trouble recognizing the man he had become. But the convert's zeal can also easily turn to intolerance, dogmatism, and rigidity. This is something that academics have pointed out and Muslim creatives have parodied.[42] I suspect that this turn, when it happens, is the product of a lack of religious experience. Being new to the faith—or, in the case of Miawand, never having really paid attention to it—a convert often has little sense of the depths of the Islamic tradition. He lacks an awareness of the variety with which Muslims have interpreted and lived their faith through the centuries.[43] Learning this takes time. It necessitates living with Muslims and seeing them debate, disagree, and quote scripture in wildly divergent ways. It also takes personal spiritual growth that permits one to move past the seeming arbitrariness of God's rules to considering how those rules aim at a conception of human flourishing.[44] As we shall see, this lack of religious experience would greatly impact Miawand's life.[45] But for now, I want to emphasize that the Winnipeg Muslim community embraced Miawand with all his flaws as a fallible human: They knew he had a past, but they also knew not to probe too deeply. What mattered was not where he had been but where he wanted to go in his life. In this, the Muslim community was there to offer him their love and support.

MUHANAD: THE BABY OF THE GROUP

Spring 2005. I am in the vestibule of the university prayer room putting on my shoes. Isa, a fellow Muslim student in the humanities, is beside me when we hear Muhanad's voice.

"Youcef! Isa!" Muhanad bellows with his characteristic joviality. "Salam 'alaykum. How are you brothers?"

"Wa-'alaykum salam, Muhanad. *Al-hamdulillah*, everything is well, how are you?" I respond.

"Good, good! I've been listening to a lecture. The speaker was explaining how Sufis have distorted Islam. You should listen to it, it's very beneficial."

Isa and I look at each other, sensing mutual discomfort. Isa says, "Muhanad, you have to think about who a lecturer is and what historical ideas and interests have shaped him before you take his ideas as authoritative." Muhanad listens, engaged. "You know," Isa continues, "Sufism has been a core part of Islam for a long time. Past scholars spoke of Sufism as the spiritual path to God. In modern times, some thinkers started to consider Sufi beliefs to be too supernatural or superstitious. Others considered their reverence of saints to violate Islamic notions of monotheism. I suspect your speaker is coming from that perspective."

"Hmm." Muhanad is processing the information. "So what do *you* think then about Sufism?"

I answer, "Personally I don't know, Muhanad, but I do think that you need to be aware of the different sources from which you take your religion. Remember that scholars aren't always disinterested. When reading something, you should consider the political context influencing the authors. That's all we're saying. For instance, if you read a Saudi book speaking about Shi'a Muslims negatively, you can bet that has to do with their fears about Iran and their own Shi'a minority population who live near their oilfields."

"Wow," Muhanad reacts. "You guys are really opening my eyes. I will have to think about this stuff a little more."

Other men walk in. I'm not sure how they'll respond to the conversation. "No worries, Muhanad, we can talk about this some other time," I say as I rush off to class.

* * *

Everyone loved Muhanad. My interlocutors all remember him as sociable and funny but also considerate and courteous. His ability to blend in with one and all is partly attributable to his complex upbringing. Muhanad's family is of Palestinian origins. They had become refugees in 1948 when the state of Israel was formed. Like many Palestinians, the Al Farekhs ended up in Jordan and were given Jordanian citizenship.[46] Muhanad's father became a doctor and settled with his wife in the United States for some time. Muhanad was born in Houston, Texas, in 1985, thus five years younger than Ferid and two years younger than Miawand. His father had the opportunity to work in the United Arab Emirates and Muhanad split his early life and schooling between there and Jordan. His English was excellent—the product of international schools—even while he retained a slight accent. As he was nearing adulthood, Muhanad's parents recognized the socioeconomic benefit of their son obtaining an education from Western institutions. They therefore sent the seventeen-year-old to Winnipeg, Manitoba, to live with his uncle and grandmother, and registered him at Nelson MacIntyre School in the area of St. Boniface. He graduated in 2004, moved out into his own apartment, and started at the University of Manitoba the next fall, eventually pursuing a degree in business. He was fluent in English and popular culture, but while he could fit in well in both a Canadian and Arab context, he was native to neither. When he started at the University of Manitoba, he became friends with Arab international students from countries like Syria, Lebanon, Jordan, and the UAE as well as with Canadian Muslim students. All would embrace him for his exuberance and his ability to bring levity to any situation.

Muhanad's Muslim identity was important to him from the first day I met him. I remember the day well. I was working at a computer station on campus when I heard the Muslim greeting from someone behind me, "al-salam ʿalaykum." I was perplexed when I turned around because I could not easily read him: He looked like a white convert, but his accent betrayed his foreignness.[47] Muhanad knew I was a member of the Muslim Student Association's Executive Committee and he wanted to know how he could help the organization. His enthusiasm eventually led to his appointment as secretary. From that time on, Muhanad always occupied an official position within the MSA. He helped organize every major event, from conferences to dinners. Despite his religiosity, Muhanad's desire to live a good Muslim life was coupled with a preoccupation with acquiring material luxuries that we associated with his life in the UAE. He loved brand-name colognes, luxury watches, and fancy cars.[48] During his university years, he grew out his hair and started to look like a European soccer player.

When I first met him, Muhanad did not give much attention to Islamic legal or theological debates. Islam was something his family had inculcated in him as part of what Marcel Mauss called a religious *habitus*—an embodied set of sensibilities and aptitudes linking the individual to the divine—and he held on to it within his new Canadian environment, but did not initially explore his faith in a more concerted way. Eventually, though, Muhanad was exposed to discussions, recorded lectures, and books about proper Islamic practice. His exposure resulted from being part of the campus prayer room community. As in his first interaction with me, Muhanad was very open-minded. He would ask others questions about the Islamic faith and listen to what they had to say. He was neither rigid nor self-righteous. He ardently wanted to live as a good Muslim but was willing to hear multiple perspectives about what that might entail. But perhaps he was too open-minded. Muhanad did not trust his ability to judge the opinions of others. He was younger than most students, struggled academically, and had little access to books to help him understand Islamic thought and history.[49] He was busy studying business rather than the humanities, and even when I helped him with a mandatory course for his Commerce Program titled "Critical Thinking," Muhanad barely scraped by. Muhanad's impressionability eventually led to tragic consequences. He was the baby of the trio and many of my interlocutors ascribed his disappearance to following the other two men.

AN UNLIKELY FRIENDSHIP

Our three men each had their own personalities and approaches to faith. Ferid was mature, warm, and contemplative, and he diligently studied the faith from a Salafi perspective. Muhanad was youthful and jovial, simultaneously naïve about his faith and open to hearing other viewpoints. Miawand was serious and guarded, constant in his worship and zealous in his efforts to gain God's favor. They also came from different cultural backgrounds—Ethiopia, Palestine, and Afghanistan. There was very little to bring the three of them together organically if not for their faith.

By the end of the 2006 winter term, the three men were often together. They were recognized in their community as three young men always willing to lend a helping hand and to volunteer their time in community events and charitable initiatives benefiting Muslims and non-Muslims alike. Their common interest in seeking Islamic knowledge cemented their friendship: They organized an introductory class on Islamic law and frequently shared online lectures, DVDs, and book recommendations. These materials provided basic teachings on moral conduct and functioned as a Muslim equivalent to self-help books and videos. A favorite of the group was Khalid Yasin's *The Purpose of Life*—a DVD lecture series delivered before an audience of Australian university students presenting arguments for Islam's monotheistic conception of God. It was all the more popular because several audience members converted to Islam at the end of the lectures.

By summer's end, they had gradually formed a more homogenous understanding of religion than they had previously possessed. Still, more importantly, they had developed a desire to learn about their religion. Islam had become for them a tangible "object" of inquiry in the sense that anthropologist Dale Eickelman has analyzed, where, more consciously than ever before, they asked themselves what their religion demanded of them.[50] And yet in actuality they had few sources and little intellectual guidance to draw upon. None of them knew classical Arabic in depth—Muhanad being limited to proficiency in colloquial Arabic—and very few translated books on Islam were available to them. Though the Winnipeg Muslim community itself contained members with an impressive background in the history, law, and philosophy of the Muslim world, the three men always deferred to the MIA Imam Hosni Azzabi in matters of religion because of his official position as religious guide to the community. Unfortunately, Azzabi's lack of proficiency in English or knowledge about North American culture made him particularly ill-suited to understanding the concerns of the three young men.[51] He had very little sense of what the men knew about their faith or, more importantly, the types of struggles they faced in the post–9/11 context. We will examine these struggles concretely in the next chapter, but for now, I want to note how deprived the three men were of resources that might have helped them study their religious tradition. On the one hand, the MSA prayer room had generated camaraderie and friendship among the three men who sought to learn about Islam; on the other, it left them destitute about how they might do so. Ultimately, the three men's gravitation toward one particular lecturer would be their undoing.

CAN THE MUSLIM SPEAK?

We see from the above that our three men were an intrinsic part of their Muslim community before they left. It would therefore be expected that those of us who knew them would lament their radicalization as a tragic loss. And many did. But that sense of loss has diverged wildly among us and has been subject to considerable change over the last several years. Here, I want to describe an episode to explain why. A week after the men left on March 7, 2007, an email arrived in Muhanad's inbox. It was the message of a mother, concerned about her son. Reem Al Farekh wrote:

"Habibi [My love] Muhanad. I hope you are feeling well. My prayers go to you every time I pray, five times a day and when I hear the athan [the call to prayer]. Sometimes in the middle of the night. Please send a message."[52]

It was a recognizable expression of love and worry. Islamic tradition teaches that God is closest to the believers when they prostrate themselves to him. And Reem needed God during those days. She was uncertain of Muhanad's exact activities, but she did know he had left his life in Manitoba to travel to a dangerous part of the world.

Islam was the idiom through which Reem made sense of and acted upon the world when confronted with the potential radicalization of her son. She saw the calamity of his disappearance as a spiritual test. One prominent Islamic teaching is the idea that life in its entirety is a test during which believers should expect hardships. The loss of a beloved or a threat to their safety is recognized as a particularly difficult test. In these moments of hardship, the proper response is to turn to God for help and spiritual growth. In a time of hardship, Reem increased her acts of piety. Muhanad's disappearance kindled in her the virtues of hope and trust in God's mercy. At every call to prayer, in the middle of the night, and away from anyone's gaze, she sought nearness to God. But Reem did not passively leave things up to God. Her email was also an attempt to reach out to her son directly. She explicitly informed Muhanad of her worship because she wanted him to know of her love and worry for him. Perhaps her words would make him come back. After all, the Prophet stated that paradise is attained through duty to one's mother. She also wanted him to take comfort in the hope that God would answer his mother's prayers. Reem knew Muhanad shared a religious vernacular with her. They drew on the same referents and the same belief in a benevolent God who cares for his creation. Their views and arguments were intelligible to one another.

But the Islamic idiom that Reem and her son shared also made her susceptible to state suspicion. Western states adopted two primary postures toward Islam during the War on Terror. In the years after 9/11, politicians and security agencies often spoke as though Islam itself promotes violence. This view was intimately linked to assumptions that Muslims were unable to read scripture in critical ways. Talal Asad pointed this out eloquently in the early days of the war on terror. In 2003, he wrote:

> The present discourse about the roots of "Islamic terrorism" in Islamic texts trails two intriguing assumptions: (a) that the Qur'anic text will force Muslims to be guided by it; and (b) that Christians and Jews are free to interpret the Bible as they please. . . . A magical quality is attributed to Islamic religious texts, for they are said to be both essentially univocal (their meaning cannot be subject to dispute, just as "fundamentalists" insist) and infectious (except in relation to the orientalist, who is, fortunately for him, immune to their dangerous power).[53]

This assumption about uncritical Muslim readings of scripture and classical texts endures today among various think tanks, political parties, and bureaucratic bodies.

But, as Arun Kundnani notes, alongside the view that Islamic scripture breeds violence, the state also promoted another view of Islam.[54] Although George W. Bush first articulated this view in the weeks after 9/11, it gained traction around the time our three men disappeared, eventually becoming dominant during the Obama years. This view of Islam sees the Muslim majority as moderate in its interpretation of scripture and sees radical interpretations as a product of a fringe and totalitarian reading of the faith, often labeled by scholars, as noted above, as Salafi-jihadism. This representation gives some shelter to Muslim communities who can say that their faith is not intrinsically violent. At the same time, it suffers from a major drawback from the perspective of those same Muslim communities: The line between radical and moderate is slippery, and depending on who draws it, North American Muslim communities often come under the microscope again as possible radical sympathizers. These two postures of the state have come to saturate the public sphere. Both lead to Muslims having to continually perform their distance from the radical—not only in terms of political ideology, but also in terms of shared religious tradition and communal bonds.

The Muslims who knew the three men are therefore confronted with a dilemma: They can remain true to their religious sensibilities but become objects of state and, by extension, social suspicions. Alternatively, they can adopt the view of the state in which the radical is reduced to being a traitor and a threat to the nation, and in doing so accept the resulting violence to their ethical commitments and sense of duty to their community members. As we will see, this dilemma animates the responses of Winnipeg Muslim community members as they make sense of the disappearance of the three men. We will trace how they experienced the loss of these three men and how the episode changed their lives. But I emphasize that state suspicion created a missed opportunity to explore alternative ways of understanding the radical's fall from grace: Reem's email to her son shows that Muslims have their own set of concepts to make sense of radicalization and the proper response to it. For Reem, this revolved around notions of divine tests and the power of a mother's prayer. The value of this alternative is its ability to de-exceptionalize the radical's mistakes and, in so doing, to transcend a state binary that assesses citizens according to whether or not they are loyal to the nation. Instead, it posits a view of mutual care and social responsibility that offers a different model for our political engagement with one another.

INITIAL SHOCK AND DISBELIEF

Muslim community members knew very little about what happened to the three men when they left—much less than Reem. Initial reports that they had joined a jihadist organization were met with disbelief. Most of those I spoke to could not fathom that the men they knew and befriended had become radicalized. Initially, Sabir, the engineering student who enjoyed chicken curry with Miawand, continued to think the men would come back and we would "hang out" again as though nothing had happened. This disbelief came out publicly less than three months after they left when I asked Sabir to speak at my wedding ceremony. During the ceremony, Sabir spoke about our hajj trip. It made sense: I had befriended Sabir during that trip and we had since grown close. However, I was surprised when Sabir brought up the three men. "During that trip," he said, "I felt so close to Youcef, and not only Youcef, but also Ferid, Miawand, and Muhanad." We knew of the RCMP investigation at the time and I remember thinking that these comments about our friendship could bring us unwanted attention. And yet I also understood that Sabir could not fathom that the three men would have left to engage in illegal activities. It was a moment of shock and deep confusion for all of us. Even today, Sabir still finds it difficult to believe: "I thought they were good people. How could they be a threat to anyone?" Sabir's attitude was revelatory of the loss that the Muslim community experienced when the men left. It was hard to think badly of them when all we had were memories of people who had diligently served their community.[55]

In time, I came to recognize that Sabir's stance of disbelief was not simply the consequence of past ties of friendship. It was also deeply shaped by his Islamic sensibilities. He had learned at the mosque to think well of people (*husn al-zann*), and, at least initially, he had no concrete proof that his friends had committed a crime. He was shaped by a Qur'anic verse that regards suspicion of others as sinful and a Prophetic teaching to "continue to make excuses for your brother, even up until seventy excuses." This teaching stood in remarkable contrast to the security agencies who presumed that the men, being Muslim, had left to do something nefarious. And Sabir was not alone. Many speculated that their motives for leaving had been innocuous. Perhaps they had gone to study the Islamic sciences abroad or to do charity work. Maybe they just wanted to live in a Muslim-majority country. Some wondered if Miawand wanted to escape from an arranged marriage. "I knew his family wanted him to marry his cousin," Sabir told me, "and he really did not want to go through with the wedding. I thought, maybe he's running away from the marriage."

SHAME, FEAR, AND BROKEN COMMUNAL TIES

It did not take long for my interlocutors' feelings about the three men to change. They and I gradually accepted the state narrative that they had left to join a jihadist organization. The guardedness that I felt during Sabir's wedding speech became more pronounced for all of us.

This was partially the result of the CSIS and RCMP investigations, which made us all too aware that proximity meant not only surveillance but punishment. But it was also the product of how the state shaped national sentiment about the new threat of the "homegrown radical." Security agencies and their radicalization experts explained that anyone could become radicalized—even seemingly "ordinary" people like Ferid, Miawand, and Muhanad.[56] The subject of the men's disappearance became taboo. We spoke about it among ourselves and shared bits of information that security agencies had divulged to us during interviews. But only between ourselves: The wider Muslim community preferred to ignore the entire affair. Although our community's Friday sermons would address relevant political topics at both the international and the local levels, the men's disappearance was entirely swept under the rug. Mosque administrators removed any pictures of the three men from their archives. The families, who could not easily forget the men or act as if all was normal, were left without emotional support in their time of grief.[57] The community's silence was an act of protection. It did not need the public's gaze and the implication that Winnipeg was a hotspot for radical Islam. For three years, it managed to avoid any media attention—despite the case's importance to the highest echelons of the US and Canadian executive branches of government.[58]

The reaction of one of my interlocutors when the story finally broke in 2010 illustrates the fear of social ostracization that many Winnipeg Muslims felt. Nabeel, the international Arab student mentioned above, was on a work break when he picked up a copy of the *Globe and Mail*. He was shocked to find the story of the three men he once knew. His expression of surprise was sufficient to draw the attention of one of his colleagues, who asked, "Do you know those guys?" Regaining his composure, Nabeel asserted, "No, of course not." In hindsight, Nabeel notes his deep discomfort. "Youcef, I can't tell you how embarrassed I was." Reflecting on the incident, Nabeel tells me he felt an intense fear of being judged as part of this terrorist trio. He sought at all costs to distance himself from the three men and to deny their ties or shared history. Performances of distance like Nabeel's became common among my discussants. When I began my interviews in 2020, I noted the curious opening ritual in which each individual would add the caveat that "I don't know if I can help you, I wasn't really close to them." Their claims were not lies per se: Closeness is a relative term, and few of my interviewees met with the men outside of the prayer room or community events. But it was the consistent need to express distance that was most remarkable. Nabeel, for instance, insisted that while he was close to some of the men, he was not around the year prior to their disappearance and radical turn. The need for distancing reflected a deep fear of what proximity would mean for my interlocutors' security and livelihood.

With the fear of state surveillance and social ostracization also came a new relationship to the Islamic tradition and the Muslim community. Nabeel tells me that he is no longer practicing as he once was. He remains Muslim but fears sharing his Muslim identity with non-Muslims. "I prefer not telling people that I am Muslim. A few years back, I had developed a good relationship with a colleague. At one point, religion came up and I told him I am a Muslim. I felt his expression change and I sensed a discomfort in him." Nabeel's fear of being identified as Muslim was more pronounced than that of the rest of my interlocutors. My sense is that his background as an immigrant who came to Canada as a young adult increased his worry about being deemed an outsider. But even those who speak English without an accent and navigate Canadian society effortlessly have expressed their own distancing from the Muslim community. Mahdi, Muhanad's erstwhile roommate, refuses to speak to anyone he knew from the MSA in 2007. And Sabir speaks of his suspicion of fellow community members. Now married and living in Calgary, he says, "The experience of those guys did change me. My wife often asks me why I don't go to the mosque anymore. I tell her that I don't like to go because I don't know who's there. I don't know what they might end up doing. It's changed my trust towards other Muslims." Sabir recognizes how this loss of trust has shaped his access to spirituality. The men's feelings were understandable. They wanted nothing to do with Ferid, Miawand, or Muhanad. Proximity was traumatic and dangerous. They just wanted to move on.

HUMAN FRAILTY AND COMMUNAL RESPONSIBILITY

In the silencing of Muslims about the three men lay a missed opportunity. Despite their anger, my interlocutors saw and still see the three men through an Islamic tradition that offers us a different view of the radical and of social responsibility than the one that permeates our public sphere. None of my interviewees coherently expressed this view to me: What follows is my attempt to make sense of bits of conversations through the years, and to grasp the range of emotions and perspectives conveyed to me when I asked my interlocutors about the role of the Muslim community in the men's disappearance and their opinion about the fate the men deserve. Without exception, Winnipeg Muslims saw the men as accountable for any criminal transgressions proven in a court of law: The men should face the consequences of their acts, I was told. But they also tended to make sense of the men's departure through a lens that acknowledges human frailty and the ever-present possibility of going astray (*al-dalal*). The notion of "going astray" appears in the most central Muslim prayer, *al-Fatiha*, where Muslims ask God to guide them along the "straight path, the path of those who have earned his favor and not that of those who have angered him or gone astray [*al-dalin*]" (Qur'an 1:7). The verse is sometimes interpreted as seeking protection against the type of theological misguidances that marked past monotheistic communities. And yet it also gestures toward the ever-present possibility of losing one's way. It is in this sense that the eleventh-century mystic al-Ghazali famously used the term in his autobiography, *The Deliverance from Misguidance*. Al-Ghazali presents his life as an ongoing search for truth in which misguidance lurks at every turn and he must continuously and perilously evaluate the claims of fellow humans (Muslim and non-Muslim) in his search for the straight path. The *Fatiha* and al-Ghazali's biography suggest that misguidance is a constant part of the human condition. Sometimes this misguidance can have serious consequences—as my interlocutors expressed in the three men's radicalization case. Indeed, none of my interlocutors minimized the harm the men could inflict abroad or at home. But importantly, regardless of the magnitude of the crime, they also considered that no human is beyond God's mercy.

This view of mercy is strengthened by the Islamic teaching that God expects humans to sin and transgress but that God also accepts their repentance until judgment day. Copious prophetic traditions and stories convey this message. One famous tradition speaks of a murderer who killed a hundred people.[59] When he asks a religious scholar if God can forgive him, he is told that forgiveness is possible if the man mends his ways and moves to a community where he can live a righteous life. The man begins his journey to the new community but dies on the way. As the man has not yet mended his ways, the angel of death comes to take his soul to hell. But another angel appears and intercedes on the man's behalf, claiming that his intent to repent to God should earn him a place in heaven. The two angels arrive at an agreement: They will measure the distance that the man had traveled and if his body is closer to his destination, they will take him to heaven; but if it is closer to his point of departure, he will be brought to hell. They measure the distance and determine that the man is closer to his departure point. As they prepare to take him to hell, where he will be tormented for his crimes, God intervenes, causing the earth to shrink until the man's body is closer to his destination, thereby decreeing that his mere intention to repent was enough for God. This story is but one of many traditions on repentance that my interlocutors were exposed to in their years as part of a Muslim community. They heard these traditions in Friday sermons, and many of my interlocutors tried to live by them. This view of repentance and of God's mercy therefore came unselfconsciously to them. Even as most of them appropriated and reproduced the state's language of "the terrorist" and the "radical" in uncritical ways, they nonetheless saw the radical as unexceptional in his propensity for folly.

Within this human drama, my interlocutors saw Muslim community members as morally bound to provide mutual assistance to each other as flawed individuals. Many expressed that the community was responsible for ensuring that its members receive the "correct" interpretation of Islam. This concern grew partly out of present circumstances. As Jibril, a community youth leader eight years my senior, expressed shortly after the men left, "The harm that something like this could do to us is immense." Years later, in discussing the case, Jibril told me of his desire not to stand out in society: "I don't want to be 'the enemy.'" But I also read my interlocutors' concerns through the Islamic teaching of "enjoining the good and forbidden the wrong" (*al-amr bi'l-ma'ruf wa'l-nahi 'an al-munkar*). This teaching comes from the Qur'anic verse, "You are the best of nations: you enjoin good, you forbid evil, and you believe in God"[60] (Qur'an 3:110). In premodern times, Muslim legal authorities and state leaders interpreted this verse as necessitating the public enforcement of moral standards (encapsulated in the term *hisba*). As Kristen Stilt shows, this enforcement could often be intrusive in the lives of the Muslim masses and frequently involved coercive measures.[61] Today, some states—like Iran and, until recently, Saudi Arabia—use "religious police" to uphold public standards of morality in the name of hisba. But in a Canadian minority context, my interlocutors understand this obligation as part of a collective responsibility that Muslims owe to each other. Nabeel, for instance, wishes he had been closer to the men during their period of radicalization because he is sure he could have prevented their turn. Importantly, none of my interlocutors see their community as having actively committed a wrong that demands punishment by the state. They maintain the line, repeated often since 9/11, that Muslim communities should not be punished for the actions of a few. They maintain that their community members did not expose or encourage the men to adopt a violent politics and that it was impossible to know what was happening inside the men's heads. Many insist that the state's gaze on their community is therefore unwarranted. And still, what persists is a sense of responsibility, of collective moral failure to offer the men the intellectual skills and moral judgment that would have deterred them from erroneous interpretations of their faith.[62]

This view of human frailty and social responsibility is not foreign to "Western" modernity. It finds its parallel in the celebrated nineteenth-century novel by Victor Hugo, *Les Misérables*. Hugo's protagonist, Jean Valjean, is a victim of society's disregard for the poor and destitute. This disregard, coupled with imprisonment for having stolen a loaf of bread, leads Jean Valjean to accept society's lowly view of him and embrace a life of petty crime. He resents society for his misfortune and for his continual ostracization. But he experiences a turning point when a bishop gives him sanctuary after his release from a lengthy prison sentence. Having found refuge in a church estate, where he stole the silverware before leaving the next day, Jean Valjean is caught by the authorities, who bring him back to the bishop. But the bishop makes a choice that derails the trajectory of Jean Valjean's life. He chooses to overlook Jean Valjean's crime and to recognize both human frailty and the social responsibility to help individuals find their way. Lying to the officers, he tells them that Jean Valjean has not stolen the silverware; rather, the cutlery are gifts that the bishop had given him. Moreover, he adds, Jean Valjean has forgotten to take the candle holders. The bishop concludes by telling a confused Jean Valjean: "Jean Valjean, mon frère, vous n'appartenez plus au mal, mais au bien. C'est votre âme que je vous achète. . . . je la donne à Dieu" (Jean Valjean, my brother, you no longer belong to evil, but to good. It is your soul that I am purchasing from you. . . . I give it to God).[63] Importantly, Hugo does not present an immediate turn in Jean Valjean: He lapses again soon after his encounter with the bishop. Like my interlocutors, Hugo understood that to err is human. In time, Jean Valjean finds his way.

But if the notion of human frailty and communal responsibility is easy enough to understand in a North American context, why then were those I spoke with reduced to fear and silence? Why, in other words, did their Islamic faith and proximity to the men make them objects of suspicion that rendered their understandings of self, community, and the radical indecipherable to a wider Canadian and American public sphere (especially after security agencies themselves concluded that the three men did not obtain their radical ideas from other Winnipeg Muslims)? We can answer this question by examining more closely the *Globe and Mail* article from 2010 that Nabeel read. The perception of the three men in the article is encapsulated in the descriptor that its six writers (Colin Freeze, Greg MacArthur, Patrick White, Joe Friesen, Christie Blatchford, and Marten Youssef) give them: "The Lost Boys of Winnipeg." The writers see the three men as literally "lost" in that no one knew where they were. But they were also lost because their trajectories as "normal" young Canadians (or Americans, in the case of Muhanad) on their way to becoming productive contributors to society had been abruptly cut off. This sudden biographical shift is troubling to the writers, and they seek "expertise" from the state to understand it: "None of them has been charged with a terrorism-related offence, but national security officials say the case may be an example of how unpredictable the radicalization process can be—it can take root in any part of the country and latch on to a variety of personalities."[64] What troubles the writers and their imagined readers is that Canadians cannot trust each other because anyone can turn on the nation. But they implicitly reassure Canadians that this threat of betrayal can be circumscribed within a particular racialized community whose alleged newness to Canada explains its betrayal. Suspicion of the Muslim community was a means to reassure Canadians of their national unity by containing the possibility of national betrayal to a distinct group among them—which, fortunately for them, the state is watching carefully. The authors' interpretation of the three men's departure as a national betrayal glosses over the fact that the Muslim community also considered the men along similar lines as "lost boys": as having lost their way and taken a wrong turn on the road of life.

In recent years, various Western states have embraced deradicalization and counterviolent extremism policies, which emphasize the neutralization of national security threats by reintegrating the radical into society. Prima facie, these policies also recognize that Muslims are individuals who can take a wrong turn in life.[65] But the privileging of a narrative that centers the nation as injured party has come at a cost that does not affect only Muslims. Foregrounding these policies has led to a missed opportunity to understand the radical as part of a different history—one that de-exceptionalizes his moral failures even as it does not minimize the possible threat he poses to our safety. The importance of this alternate history exceeds academic interest. When we think of the state excesses of the War on Terror—sending our citizens to be tortured, refusing to repatriate citizens, and abandoning Canadian children stranded in Syrian refugee camps where death from disease or violence is ever-imminent—the Islamic notion of mercy to the misguided has renewed stakes. It has the potential to curb the fears and indignance that lead to disavowing basic standards of decency and the rule of law. It will matter to the story of the three men too—but we will get to that in time.

I close this chapter by pointing out another lost opportunity in failing to attend to my interlocutors' Islamic view of mutual care amidst human frailty. North American Muslim communities have often been positioned as newcomers needing to learn the social and political virtues required for participation in a liberal democracy. But perhaps if we paid greater attention to Muslim forms of life, to borrow a term from philosopher Ludwig Wittgenstein, we would recognize that they have resources internal to their tradition that help strengthen our democratic societies.[66] In this case, we might learn from Muslims how to recognize and bolster our togetherness despite our individual failures. We might come in turn to see that our political unity is not premised on identity markers or common histories, but on accepting ourselves as eminently flawed individuals who always need help from our communities.[67]

CONCLUSION

December 2020. I am meeting with Dawud. I have not seen him in years, though we were very close at University. The prayer room had first brought us together, and Dawud's calm temperament and thoughtfulness had made him someone whose company I highly valued. But today I am not sure what to expect. I had begun my interviews on the three men in the preceding weeks. It has been hard to have frank conversations. Every person I speak to prefers silence over speech. The experience of the men's departure was too traumatic, especially because of the investigation that followed. No one wants to be associated with the three men, and burying the past is the preferred way of coping with their disappearance. Will Dawud feel the same way? I think about how angry we were years earlier: I remember chatting over pizza at a swanky restaurant on the University of Toronto campus. The topic of the three men came up, and we discussed the possibility that they had died. "I don't care about those guys," Dawud had said. "They were grown men. They knew what they were doing. They left such a mess behind them for the rest of us to deal with." I had chuckled in agreement, thinking about the stupidity of their actions. Will Dawud feel I am being intrusive for bringing the men up, for asking him how he remembers them, and what he thinks our community owed them? I am especially fearful because I know Dawud has suffered more than any of us at the hands of security agencies.

But as I meet my friend, my concerns dissipate. I sense the calmness I had known in Dawud in our university years. There is no anger today. We begin our walk in a park in a suburb of Toronto, socially distancing to conform to the requirements of COVID-19 prevention. I ask Dawud about his memories of the three men and the state investigation that followed their disappearance. He speaks about the men as being young, naïve, and misled. He speaks about his memories of Ferid's kind smile and generosity, Muhanad's goofiness, and Miawand's attempts at turning a new page in life. He speaks about his family's loss when CSIS turned its attention on him, and then on his brother. I sense that Dawud's openness in speaking to me has something to do with his suffering. I notice a pattern among my interviewees: Those who have suffered least from state scrutiny are most fearful of arousing its anger. But those who have suffered most have come to see the Kafkaesque nature of being Muslim and knowing a radical. I realize our anger at the three men was motivated by fear, and Dawud is no longer afraid. He is content with knowing who he is, regardless of what the state might believe; he will not let fear or anger dictate his life. At the end of our interview, he tells me, "It feels good. It's cathartic to get this stuff off my chest." Later, I tell him how different his attitude was from other interviewees, adding that many are afraid to be associated with Islam today. Dawud answers, "Things like this are a test and an opportunity. They can make you closer to God or they can make you lose your way." He explains to me how the experience of the three men's radicalization helped him immerse himself more deeply in the study of Islam. "Their example showed me I had to be careful about who I took as an authority in religion. I began to study the history of Islamic legal schools and spirituality more closely." I leave feeling happy for my friend. He has found peace through the turbulent experience of the last decade and a half. He has found his way.

The short sketches of Muhanad, Miawand, and Ferid, presented through the memories of members of their community, no doubt contain descriptions that fit the profiles of typical radicals: Ferid's Salafism, Miawand's newfound religiosity, Muhanad's heightened Arab Muslim identity, and all three men's development of strong social bonds. I do not deny that these variables impacted the three men. They shaped how they understood and evaluated claims about their faith. But they tell us very little about what happened to them. None of these variables, alone or together, have any predictive power: For every Salafi, newly religious Muslim, and international student who becomes a radical, countless others do not, as radicalization experts teach us. Thus, it is difficult to know why to focus on them, especially when the consequence is the heightened suspicion of our fellow Muslim citizens. So I have pursued a different and more fruitful line of inquiry. My concern in remembering the three men has been to move away from a narrative that situates them as enemies of the state and to capture their lives within a historical narrative that makes sense to their communities. I have sought to show this community's relationship to the three men, why they experienced their departure as a loss, and how the Muslim community's ability to grieve this loss through the idiom of its Islamic tradition was precluded by the state's suspicion. This suspicion was the product of seeing Muslims as being outside of the imagined Canadian nation, disregarding the reality that we all belong to diverse forms of life with distinct sensibilities, ethical commitments, and ways of describing our common world.

The consequences for my interlocutors are far from insignificant. Alasdair MacIntyre has pointed out how our self-understanding and, therefore, our ethical agency are dependent on the narrative unity of our lives: "I can only answer the question 'What am I to do?' if I can answer the prior question 'Of what story or stories do I find myself a part?' . . . Deprive children of stories and you leave them unscripted, anxious stutterers in their actions as in their words."[68] What state suspicion rendered difficult was the shaping of narratives that acknowledge that Ferid, Muhanad, and Miawand were part of our individual and communal histories. Instead of being situated within an Islamic vernacular that made sense to us, their lives became a subject of taboo and silence. I have sought to restore a modicum of intelligibility to the lives of their community members, not by celebrating or vilifying the men but by being faithful to the memories of those who see them in their fuller complexity. Of course, part of healing is also coming to understand why the trajectories of the three men were so abruptly cut short. In this regard, the following chapters continue the attempt to restore intelligibility to the history of Winnipeg Muslims, even as we focus on other historical and theoretical insights that the men's lives provide about the Canadian Muslim experience of the War on Terror.

2

LIVES THAT MATTERED AND LIVES THAT DIDN'T

MUSLIM CANADIANS AND THE WAR ON TERROR

I walk out of the prayer room into the vestibule littered with jackets, shoes, and bags. I see Dahawi putting on his gear. We exchange greetings and I ask him how he is doing. He expresses sadness. Today is the fourth anniversary of the September 11 attacks. Dahawi notes how the attacks have given Canadians a negative impression of Islam.

"My engineering colleagues were speaking about the anniversary today. They are all affected by it, and it pains me that they associate Islam with terrorism."

"I understand," I respond. I think about how Dahawi, a Sudanese international student, is not used to seeing Islam depicted in a negative light. "Did anyone insult you?"

"No, but they don't have the right image of the religion. All they know are the actions of murderers." I think about how common Dahawi's sentiments are. Many Muslims not only see 9/11 as a tragedy, they also see it as a PR disaster for their little-understood faith.[1]

At that moment, Ferid walks into the vestibule. I greet him: "al-salam ʿalaykum," I say, shaking his hand.

"Wa-ʿalaykum al-salam. How's it going?"

"Well, Dahawi and I are talking about the anniversary of September 11."

Ferid shakes his head in exasperation. He pauses. "I'm sick and tired of these commemorations; I simply don't care about it."

Ferid's statement startles me. This sentiment is not common among Muslims. "Ferid, you don't actually mean this."

"No, I do, I don't feel any sympathy for victims of terrorist attacks. They don't care about us, so why should I care about them?"

"Ferid . . . these are innocent people. They could be you and me—and Muslims were also among the victims of 9/11."

Ferid looks down. He wants to end the conversation. He softly and with composure says, "I'm not saying terrorist attacks are right. They might very well be *haram* [prohibited in Islamic law].[2] I don't know. I'm just saying that I can't bring myself to care." I can tell Ferid is done talking, and I will soon be late for class. I say my goodbyes to the brothers in the vestibule and rush off.

In August 2016, I first met the prosecutors for Muhanad's trial. We gathered in a room at the American consulate in downtown Toronto. The prosecution team took great interest when I told them this story about Ferid. Until then, they had pressed me to remember any information supporting their narrative arc. They wanted to show that the three men had become radicalized before they left in March 2007. But there were so few clear indications of this. Only one episode involving Miawand was seared in my mind—an episode whose analysis I leave for the next chapter—and this episode was not enough for them. They wanted more indications that all three men, especially Muhanad, subscribed to terrorist ideology.

"I know it's been a long time," stated John, the FBI investigator assisting the prosecution, "but you were all young university guys. I'm sure you would have talked about politics, the War on Terror, something."

"I'm sure we did, I know they were opposed to the War on Terror, we all were in the Muslim Student Association, but there was nothing that would distinguish their opposition from that of many non-Muslim Canadians."

John looked discouraged; I would later find out I was not alone in my assessment of the three men: No other potential witnesses suspected anything nefarious either. And then I remembered this interaction with Ferid. It had been tucked away in my mind because I had not made much of it. I described it to them, knowing that Ferid's lack of sympathy for terrorist victims could signify sympathy for terrorist action.

But I was later surprised when the prosecution used the story as standalone evidence at trial.[3] In their estimation, Ferid's reaction was unambiguously a sign of his radicalism. Who but a terrorist sympathizer could be so callous about their victims? I then realized that the prosecution did not know the proper context in which Ferid's statements were made. If they did, they would have seen that there was an alternative interpretation to Ferid's comments. Moreover, this alternative interpretation is easily comprehended by my Winnipeg Muslim interlocutors. For, although Ferid's position was jarring in its indifference to the suffering of others, it emerged from other feelings that were widespread within the Muslim community: Even as we disagreed with Ferid, we all understood where he was coming from.

This chapter fleshes out this alternative interpretation. To do so, we will first have to try to see the War on Terror through the eyes of most mosque-going young Canadian Muslims. We will proceed in three steps. First, we will examine the dominant state ideology of the War on Terror by analyzing statements made by Canadian parliamentary leaders in the aftermath of the September 11 attacks. Second, we will highlight how this ideology devalued Muslim victims of US and NATO military actions. And third, we will examine how this devaluation of Muslim life clashed with Muslim sensibilities around loving and caring for one's brothers and sisters.

What will become evident in analyzing Ferid's statements is the general sense of injury that mosque-going Muslim Canadians felt at the violence their state perpetrated abroad. The War on Terror placed them in a situation in which they were impelled to respond to violence in one way or another. Ferid, Miawand, and Muhanad eventually adopted one response, and most Canadian Muslims adopted another. But their shared injury sheds light on what it meant for young Muslims to live through the War on Terror. The chapter concludes with an unexpected suggestion: Perhaps Ferid's apathy has something to teach us, citizens of North American states, about our own histories of violence. Perhaps we might take it as the starting point of an effort to shape global relations in ways that move away from militarism.

BETWEEN THE CIVILIZED AND THE SAVAGES

"Where were you?" It is such a common thing to ask. Where were you when the two towers collapsed? The question infers the significance of the event in world history.[4] We all knew it was a cataclysmic moment that would change things forever. But for myself, as part of a Muslim minority in North America, the more salient question is: Where were you when you first wondered, "How will they treat me now?" The aftermath of 9/11 placed into relief the Muslim citizen's uncertain place within North American society. Within hours following the collapse of the Twin Towers, Osama bin Laden was labeled the prime suspect, and his Muslim extremist faith was identified as the motive for his actions.[5]

I was sitting in the chair at my optometrist's office, Dr. Champagne, when I first asked myself this question. It was the afternoon of a sunny Tuesday, a few hours after watching the attacks on a TV in our school library. My mother had picked me up from school early for my annual check-up. As I sat in the optometrist's chair, waiting for the exam to start, I wondered if Dr. Champagne would see me differently. I took comfort in the fact that he had known me since I was a child and that we belonged to the same French Canadian community. But I was known as Louis as a child, and my charts said Youcef now. Would he know that was an Arab name?

When Dr. Champagne came in, he greeted me warmly. "Today is a crazy day, isn't it?"

"Yes, it sure is," I answered. He added: "The world's going to be different tomorrow. That's for sure." I scanned his tone and countenance for anything anomalous. No, I could tell he saw me as he always had—a long-time patient, a fellow community member, and most of all, a regular person. I had never been so relieved to be ordinary. Though I began to breathe more easily, as a Canadian Muslim, my position within the nation would remain in flux for several days. During those days, mosques were vandalized and hate crimes against Muslims proliferated. A mosque in Montreal was even firebombed. When the state eventually defined my place—along with my co-religionists—within the nation, it was part of a broader evolving narrative that pitted allies against enemies. The impact of this narrative would exceed my small Winnipeg Muslim community and end up shaping world politics in lasting ways. The image of a Western civilization under siege was at the heart of this narrative. Following the US lead, the Canadian state articulated this image concretely and officially on Monday, September 17, six days after 9/11.[6]

Canadian state leadership gathered in the House of Commons—the same hallowed institution to which my grandfather had been elected, and where fifteen years later I would receive a call from the RCMP telling me about Muhanad's impending trial. Jean Chrétien, the longstanding prime minister and leader of the Liberal Party, began by presenting the following motion:

> That this House express its sorrow and horror at the senseless and vicious attack on the United States of America on September 11, 2001; that it express its heartfelt condolences to the families of the victims and to the American people; and that it reaffirm its commitment to the human values of free and democratic society and its determination to bring to justice the perpetrators of this attack on these values and to defend civilization from any future terrorist attack.[7]

A central theme of the prime minister's motion was that the 9/11 attacks threatened not only the United States but all "civilized nations." Chrétien reiterated this sentiment in his speech following the motion: "In the sad and trying days since the awful news came from New York and Washington, it has been clear that the civilized nations of the world have a solemn duty to speak as one against the scourge of terrorism." Other party leaders followed suit. The leader of the Official Opposition, Stockwell Day, affirmed, "Last week's horrific attacks in New York, Washington and Pennsylvania have shocked everyone in the civilized world,"[8] and the Progressive Conservative leader and former prime minister Joe Clark stated, "We must organize ourselves to protect and assert the civilized values that were so deliberately attacked. No nation has a greater stake in that response than Canada, and we must play our full part."[9] But this begs the question: If September 11 was an attack against civilized nations, then who exactly were these nations and, equally important, who were the uncivilized or the savages?

Historicizing the term *civilization* is useful here. To invoke civilization as these political leaders did is to tap into a broader colonial history demarcating the West from the rest. Since the Enlightenment, *civilization* has been used to speak of Europe's place at the top of a ladder of human progress. The term was employed to justify military violence and domination in places where people's skin was darker, their noses flatter, or their hair curlier.[10] In the nineteenth century, the

"Mission Civilizatrice" became a common way to describe Western Europe's duty to bring their culture to the rest of the world. Indeed, it is difficult to historicize "the West" as a geographically bounded entity without focusing on its nearly obsessive use of the concept of civilization.[11] This is because it was not only colonial officials who used the term; rather, Europe's top intellectuals theorized the term itself. The British philosopher J. S. Mill's classic essay, aptly titled "Civilization," defined the concept generally to designate any human "improvement," but also, more narrowly, to speak of the improvement that makes civilized nations superior to savages.[12] Mill identified the superiority of civilized nations by their power, wealth, arts, and sciences.[13] He located the root of this superiority in the social cooperation that characterizes civilized nations. Among savages, it is every man for himself, relying on his own physical strength and cunning, supplemented, at most, by his family or tribal affiliations. In contrast, individuals of civilized nations cooperate for the general benefit of the collective. The result is material and intellectual progress. Thus, in speaking of civilized nations, Canadian leaders were inevitably re-appropriating old violent and boundary-defining racial imaginaries between the West and the rest.

Shortly after the Canadian state was founded in 1867, Canadian leaders devised plans to "civilize" Indigenous peoples of their language, culture, and religion. Their tactic was to take children from their families and send them to what would be known as Residential Schools. In 1883, the state partnered with Anglican and Roman Catholic churches to begin opening Residential Schools (known at the time as Industrial Schools) and to enable the churches' missionizing and civilizing impulses. Alexander Morris, a Canadian minister who negotiated several treaties with Indigenous peoples of the Canadian Prairies, explained in 1880 his hopes for how the new schools would shape Indigenous children: "The new generation can be trained in the habits and ways of civilized life."[14] But beyond assimilation, the schools were rife with disease, and corporal and sexual abuse.

Within post–9/11 parliamentary imagination, Osama bin Laden figured as the paradigmatic figure of the savage, threatening civilized nations. Stuck in his cave in Afghanistan, he exemplified the medieval religious mentality of primitive peoples, incapable of grasping the higher truths of the modern sciences or appreciating the benefits of refined living. The Taliban, garbed in what appeared to be equally premodern attire, partook in savagery by offering bin Laden shelter in their lands. Stockwell Day gave voice to this sentiment more explicitly than any other leader:

> Osama bin Laden has been publicly identified as the prime suspect behind these murderous acts. He has been sheltered, if not aided and abetted, and time will tell on that question, by the Taliban regime of Afghanistan. The free world must tell all states that no matter what their ideology, supporting or condoning terror against civilians will never, ever be tolerated. . . . It is not a matter of shades of grey when it comes to these barbarous acts of evil. It is set in black and white. This is not a time for moral ambiguity. It is a moment of moral clarity.[15]

Moreover, the prime minister made clear that other nations could be included within the category of the savage enemy if they too harbored terrorists: "Terrorists are not attached to any one country," he stressed. "We must prepare ourselves, and Canadians, for the fact that this will be a long struggle with no easy solutions, one in which patience and wisdom are essential."[16]

However, if the civilized referred to the West and the savage referred to terrorist groups and their national patrons, then where did that leave the clear majority of Muslims? What was the most appropriate designation for them? Answering these questions is not straightforward, but we can begin to do so by tackling another related question: Why did Canadian leaders use the term *civilization* in the first place if it linked them to an outdated nineteenth-century colonial mentality? Part of the answer pertains to their rejection of another prevalent usage of the term at the time. In 1993, Samuel Huntington had written an article for *Foreign Affairs* arguing that the post-Soviet world order would be marked by inter-civilizational rivalry. Huntington called this a "clash of civilizations."[17] He later expanded the article into a full-length book, published in 1996, in which he argued that Islamic civilization was likely to butt heads with Western civilization.[18] In the moments after 9/11, the book seemed prophetic to many. However, the Bush administration chose to shape its civilization talk differently. Despite the explanatory appeal of Huntington's book, its thesis would have been a policy disaster if ever implemented in the United States or Canada. The theory of a clash of civilizations made it impossible to build needed allies across the Muslim world—allies that included NATO member Turkey, hosts of US military bases like Qatar, and proxy fighters like the Afghan Northern Alliance. None of these international players would take kindly to the view that the United States was at war with Islamic civilization. Moreover, the theory inevitably positioned Muslim minorities within Western democracies as part of an enemy civilization. Such a move would make Muslim citizens vulnerable to physical attack and would shatter the image of the United States and Canada as places of law and order.

In contrast, by referencing civilization in the singular, North American leaders could speak of an alliance made on behalf of civilization that could include all, regardless of religion or nationality.[19] This made foreign allyship possible. The same discursive strategy led Bush to speak of the United States as leading "the world" in its fight against terror: "The hour is coming when America will act, and you will make us proud. This is not, however, just America's fight. And what is at stake is not just America's freedom. This is the world's fight. This is civilization's fight."[20] Canadian leaders also spoke about "the world's" need to respond. Thus, while states like Saudi Arabia or Turkey might not be fully civilized, they could at least be allies to civilized nations. They could be part of the Western-led world community.

Domestically, the discourse of an alliance for civilization protected Muslim communities. North American Muslim populations had grown in number in the last decades through a combination of changed immigration policies and neoliberal globalization. They had experienced anti-Muslim racism shaped by historical prejudices about the Middle East as a land of despotism, sexual deviance, and violence and by key political events like the 1979 Iranian Revolution, the Rushdie Affair, and the 1990–1991 First Gulf War, which flattened the great diversity of Muslims and positioned them as brown-skinned terrorists even before 9/11. The Islamophobia studies scholar Deepa Kumar notes that anti-Muslim racism was shaped by particular imperatives of post-World War II American politics when the oil-rich Middle East became strategically important.[21] Now, North American Muslims were being cast by some media pundits as the enemy within. The diasporic Muslim body became what scholar of diaspora and race Junaid Rana characterizes as a figure of fear and apprehension for the West.[22] This figure was highly gendered, with the Muslim woman becoming an object needing to be saved from the violent, patriarchal, and oppressive Muslim man, as critical race scholar Sherene Razack and anthropologist Lila Abu Lughod have argued.[23] In time, fears about domestic Muslim populations would animate US and Canadian surveillance and detention policies.

But in the days after 9/11, George W. Bush attempted to prevent the emergence of populist mob violence. He clarified that Muslims were part of the American nation when he asked Muzammil Siddiqi, then president of the Islamic Society of North America, to speak at the National Prayer Service for 9/11 victims on September 14.[24] Bush reiterated his commitment to Muslim national inclusion when he visited a mosque as part of an effort to stem hate crimes less than a week later.[25] In his September 20 State of the Union Address, he emphasized that a minority of Muslims shared the terrorists' faith: "The terrorists practice a fringe form of Islamic extremism that has been rejected by Muslim scholars and the vast majority of Muslim clerics; a fringe movement that perverts the peaceful teachings of Islam."[26] Bush added that Islam is "practiced freely by many millions of Americans and by millions more in countries that America counts as friends. Its teachings are good and peaceful." Canadian leaders, likewise, emphasized that Muslim Canadians deserved support against possible bigotry and backlash. Chrétien affirmed that "the evil perpetrators of this horror represent no community or religion." He expressed sadness that there had been "demonstrations against Muslim Canadians," adding that "this is completely unacceptable" and, later, that "we are all Canadians."[27] Other party leaders expressed similar sentiments. In short, the appeal to civilization in the singular had great discursive utility in the upcoming war with the Taliban—and with any future foe: It permitted the crafting of a coalition abroad and civility at home.

Most important, the United States' and NATO's discourse of civilization served to prepare the ground for the long battle ahead. The battle would not be easy and military and civilian casualties would have to be endured. The discursive analysis of the concept of civilization in the weeks after 9/11 reminds us that the role of the state in the modern era is to reimagine the boundaries of the nation to render different political projects possible and forms of violence palatable. But while the deployment of the discourse of civilization during the War on Terror is known to many academics, as will become clear, what is less well-understood is its impact on Canadian Muslims—the radicals like Ferid, Muhanad, and Miawand, as well as the moderate majority.

Before proceeding, I want to point out that one Canadian leader stood out among the rest on September 17, 2001. Alexa McDonough, head of the leftist New Democratic Party (NDP), framed the conflict differently from the way other leaders did. McDonough put aside civilizational binaries and postures of moral superiority. Instead, she sought to frame the situation in Afghanistan and much of the Muslim world through a more complex historical analysis. She saw September 11 as a tragedy that required a response but was unwilling to condone or minimize historic violence from the world's most powerful nations. In doing so, she cautioned that a future military response could easily end up making the world a worse place:

> In the wake of these terrifying events, we need to reflect on the kind of international community we have created, where the images of mass destruction in the United States last week saw some Palestinian children actually dancing in the streets, where an international community can allow 5,000 children a month to die of malnutrition in Iraq, or hunger and preventable disease can claim the lives of thousands and thousands of children in the too many impoverished nations of the world. . . . We need to tell the world that in the eyes of Canada the wanton destruction of life and property is absolutely unacceptable. Whether it is in the United States or in Rwanda, whether it is in Washington or Beirut, Baghdad or Bosnia, we need the world to know that we practice what we preach in Canada.[28]

McDonough's comments are noteworthy for two reasons: One, she shows how civilization talk obfuscated pressing questions that could have led to a different, more thoughtful, and more internationally cooperative response to the tragedy of 9/11. Second, McDonough represents a stream of Canadian leftist thought that intimately linked self-scrutiny to the shaping of a better world. Canadian citizens of all religious affiliations would embrace this discourse at key times during the War on Terror and often petition, and sometimes force, their government to reject Islamophobic policies at home and militarism abroad.[29] Unfortunately, McDonough's voice was lost that day, with great consequence for the state's lasting framing of the War on Terror.

THE (UN)GRIEVABILITY OF MUSLIM LIFE

The discourse dividing the world between civilized and savage had immense consequences on the value of lost life in the ensuing War on Terror. The critical studies and gender theorist, Judith Butler, has invoked the term "grievability" to speak of the differing worth we accord to life lost in war. I use the term here because it is useful in capturing our striking range of emotions, from empathy to apathy, for victims of military violence.[30] Part of Butler's argument is that the state mediates and regulates our responses to justify its participation in war. In the War on Terror, the state's discourse on civilization was central to assessing the value of lives lost. To position the West as civilized was already to assert its status as the "good guys," standing above the moral censure that casualties of war and material destruction might otherwise provoke.

In this way, the War on Terror had much in common with old colonial discourses invoking civilization. As we saw above, the concept of civilization justified violence against the colonized. And this violence was considerable. Though hard to quantify, the atrocities of both direct military campaigns—like scorching Algerian peasants' crops so they would die of starvation—and indirect colonial policies—like directing Indian agriculture production to benefit English industries and thereby starving millions in the Indian subcontinent[31]—must be reckoned among the darkest chapters of human history. European powers saw the introduction of civilization to others as an unmitigated good that warranted some sacrifices from the colonized.[32] Of course, civilization talk during the War on Terror would change in its emphasis. Unlike nineteenth- and twentieth-century colonialism, the primary justification of lost human life was not the spread of civilization but its protection. The United States—and, by extension, the civilized (Western) world—had been attacked, and any response was merely a proper form of self-defense. However, the premise that civilized violence was ultimately good for those who bore it was also a common line of reasoning: one recalls how Canadian leaders portrayed the Afghan people as victims of a tyrannical regime who in the end would benefit from the coming of civilized forces. The consequence of this logic was plain and simple: Loss of life in the prosecution of the War on Terror was lamentable but acceptable to the state. No matter how many bodies piled up—civilian or military—the ends justified the means.

We can consider how the US and Canadian states' war discourse shaped the Canadian public sphere to which young Muslim men like Ferid were continuously subjected by examining two instances in which US troops killed "the wrong people." In the first, apologies were made, accountability was ensured, and the people killed were honored and mourned. In the second instance, there was no accountability, and an apology came only after political pressure made it expedient. Rather than honoring the people killed in this incident, the state and the US media left them unceremoniously nameless. For North American Muslims, and particularly Muslims in Canada whose primary source of information was often US media, such examples made clear that, depending on nationality and geographical location, some lives mattered while others did not. And in the War on Terror, Muslim lives abroad were certainly expendable.

The first case involves the loss of Canadian military lives. On April 17, 2002, US Major Harry Schmidt dropped a 225-kilogram bomb on Canadian troops of the Princess Patricia's Canadian Light Infantry, fighting as part of a NATO coalition in the Tarnak Farms area of Kandahar province.[33] The Canadian troops were participating in a training exercise when Schmidt mistook them for their enemies. It was the first time since the Korean War that Canadian troops had perished in combat. The country was devastated. The next day, Chrétien addressed the House of Commons to express his sorrow to the nation.[34] He shared that Bush had called to offer his apologies and condolences. Throughout the country, flags were flown at half-mast and schools, like my own, observed a minute of silence for the fallen soldiers. US and Canadian media named the soldiers: Sgt Marc Leger, Cpl Ainsworth Dyer, Pte Richard Green, and Pte Nathan Smith. Their biographies were shared and their images were broadcasted on Canadian national TV. Within a few days, the United States and Canada agreed on a joint military board inquiry into the incident.[35] In time, there would be two separate and detailed reports of what had happened. The United States eventually charged Major Schmidt with negligent manslaughter, before reducing the charge to dereliction of duty. Schmidt was found guilty. A US judge noted the need to show the public that the United States held its military accountable.

In contrast, most civilian casualties of the NATO occupation of Afghanistan went under- or unreported. Defense Secretary Donald Rumsfeld called reports of civilian deaths terrorist propaganda, even when the United States' newly installed Afghan president, Hamid Karzai, insisted to the contrary.[36] It took until July 2002 for the US media to focus on an incident in which the United States caused large-scale civilian deaths. On July 1, a US gunship bombarded four Afghan villages in Oruzgan province. The worst hit was a village named Kahrak, where a wedding party was gathered at the time. Official numbers varied, but at least forty villagers died while another one hundred were wounded. The story, though, took time to gain traction. The Pentagon initially denied civilian casualties. It was only when Karzai expressed displeasure at reports of the bombing that the US media began to focus on the story and the US government felt the need to take it seriously. Eventually, the United States did apologize, and George Bush even called his ally Karzai to offer an apology. But this change of heart was begrudging, to say the least. After initial denials of the deaths, the Pentagon produced a repertoire of excuses: It accused the villagers of targeting the gunship; it blamed the Taliban for using the villagers as human shields;[37] and it claimed that reports of casualties had been greatly exaggerated—in their estimation, perhaps only five people had died. When the *New York Times* dug deeper into the story, it was not to identify and mourn the lost lives, but to ascertain the facts of the case. Thus, Afghan villagers who witnessed the bloodshed are named as sources, while the deceased remain nameless. Instead, the deceased are spoken of in gruesome terms as "torsos" in a courtyard and detached flesh hanging from pomegranate trees. The description is meant to provoke disgust but not sympathy. The dead are an assemblage of body parts, not persons with histories, families, or homes. And, unlike the Canadian friendly-fire bombing, no charges were ever brought. As a contrite US army official told one of the village members: "We're sorry, but what's done cannot be undone."[38] It was time for these villagers to accept their loss and move on.

Clearly, the US government's concern for the lives of its Western allies exceeded that shown for its civilian casualties—whether in Afghanistan or other parts of the Muslim world. Part of the reason for this might be a widespread military ethos that honors fallen comrades, but I doubt this explanation goes to the heart of the matter. It is difficult to believe that the United States would have refused to apologize for a mistaken bombing of Canadian civilians in Afghanistan; and, at the very least, it is inconceivable to imagine that they would have accused them of firing at military planes or denied their deaths. The most straightforward explanation for this differential treatment is to say that Canadian lives mattered more in the War on Terror. As Butler notes, grievability is often linked to being able to see oneself as the victim of war. Canadians were part of the world's civilized nations and therefore merited US grief and recognition. And this was true regardless of racial and religious hierarchies internal to the nation.

The US response to loss of life is crucial to understanding the Canadian Muslim experience of the War on Terror. American television stations like CNN, Fox News, and CBS were widely broadcast in Canada. Moreover, American newspapers like the *New York Times* were becoming more readily available online. These media outlets made clear which lives the US state considered worthy. Because the media focused on the state's narratives of events, they also created a public sphere in which some lost lives prompted expressions of grief and others did not.

Canadian media reported the Oruzgan tragedy with more care. Some drew a parallel between the United States' carelessness in the bombing of Oruzgan and the "friendly-fire" that took the lives of Canadian soldiers.[39] And Charles Abrogast of the *Toronto Star* sought to mourn and name the victims of the tragedy: "One of the injured, a 6-year-old girl named Paliko, was brought to the hospital still wearing her party dress. Villagers said all members of her family were killed."[40] But for the most part, Afghan casualties of the War on Terror remained obscured in the Canadian press as well. Afghan lives were framed only in terms of their political worth. Indeed, Karzai was clear that it would be difficult to govern if the body count of Afghans kept rising. But their passing itself was rarely marked. After all, Afghans would benefit from our military. They would be liberated from their plight at the hands of the Taliban, as an article from the *Toronto Star* made clear the same week as the Oruzgan bombing. They, alongside other Muslim peoples, were victims of their dictatorial regimes and were waiting to be freed by our military and its allies. Devoid of civilizational purpose, Afghans' and other Muslim peoples' lives were devalued. This devaluation of Muslim life would, in turn, have enormous consequences for Winnipeg and Canadian Muslims more generally.

CANADIAN MUSLIMS' AFFECTIVE BONDS TO THE *UMMA*

In the aftermath of September 11, North American Muslim leaders often praised Canada and the United States for the freedoms these states granted their citizens.[41] They recognized that many of their home countries did not give them these freedoms. But Muslim histories and self-conceptions were more complicated than those that posited divides between us and them, between civilized and savage, and between the free and the tyrannized.[42] If the "Muslim world" lacked in wealth, opportunity, and political justice, it was nonetheless the land where many Muslims located their brethren in faith. To North American Muslims, the casualties of the War on Terror were not faceless and nameless masses with whom they had little affinity; rather, they had deep affective bonds to these people. For many, those lives should not have been sacrificed in the name of protecting or spreading civilization. In the end, the value of brotherhood and sisterhood (in Arabic, *ukhuwwa*) would alienate many mosque-going Muslims from the War on Terror. Once we understand this, we will have the necessary context to make sense of Ferid's statements about his inability to mourn the loss of life in terrorist attacks.

One episode, the year before Ferid, Miawand, and Muhanad left, shows our three men's affective relationship to Muslims abroad. The context was a conference that Ferid had organized. At the time, it was customary for the Muslim Student Association to host an annual conference at which they invited out-of-town speakers to come for two days and deliver religiously based lectures for the city's wider Muslim community. These conferences drew large intergenerational crowds; I remember attending them as early as my last high school years in 2001 and 2002.[43] Many Muslims were excited to hear new and well-known speakers. Examples included Jamal Badawi, a board member of the Council of American Islamic Relations-Canada and professor of economics, and the Islamic Studies professor Timothy Gianotti. In April 2005, though, the MSA executive committee was not functioning effectively enough to organize a conference, so Ferid stepped up and took the lead. He invited Abdurraheem Green, a white convert from the UK, to headline a conference at the University of Manitoba. To some, Green was a controversial choice. He had been barred from travel to Australia earlier that year. The reasons were unclear, but many suspected that the decision had to do with Green's brief visit to 1980s Afghanistan to meet the Afghan Mujahideen fighting the Soviet Union;[44] others speculated it related to pre–9/11 comments in which he spoke of Muslim martyrs in meritorious terms. Even though Green had consistently condemned terrorism since 9/11, one prominent Winnipeg leader wondered why local Muslims would want to attract negative attention upon themselves.

For Ferid, however, Green was a passionate speaker who could eloquently convey the basic teachings of Islam in clear English. He was a straight shooter who did not seem to contort Muslim teachings to fit within a Western framework, and this appealed to Ferid's sense that morality was clear and meant to be applied fully and sincerely. Despite the trepidation of some community leaders, the conference itself was well attended and, after the fact, notes of appreciation were sent to Ferid for his hard work. Green spoke on a series of topics, including "Muslim Identity," "Marriage in Islam," and "How to give *Da'wa*" (i.e., how to call people to the Islamic faith). The conference spanned from Friday evening through to late Sunday afternoon.

What concerns us here is a lecture that took place on the Saturday evening, from 7:15 to 8:30 pm. Green took his place at the front of the gym-like room within the Student Union Building at the University of Manitoba. The attendees were in good spirits and somewhat sedate, having just filled their stomachs with a delicious meal. As they sat, preparing themselves for the lecture, Green informed those in attendance that they had with them, through pure happenstance, two audience members who could speak from personal experience about the lecture topic. The two were a husband and wife from Chechnya, a Russian province in the Caucasus mountain range, and the lecture topic was "The Forgotten Brothers and Sisters: Chechnya."[45] Despite its great diversity of Western Muslims, few in Winnipeg had ever met Chechens. The Chechen population is only about 1 million and, while many Chechens live throughout the Middle East as refugees, they are seldom part of the Canadian immigrant population—and certainly not in the middle of the prairies.[46] Though most of the audience would not have had Chechen friends, they nonetheless knew more about Chechnya than the average Canadian. Many knew Chechens were Muslims and that they had sought their independence from Russia after the fall of the Soviet Union. Many also knew that the Russian military asserted its control over the region through indiscriminate bombing. The husband, Yahyaer Ibrahim, was paralyzed, in a wheelchair, and appeared to manifest the scars of war on his body. The couple were middle-aged: the husband was likely in his late fifties, though his poor health made it difficult to know for sure, and his wife, Fatima, appeared to be in her late forties. The crowd waited for them to provide an insider's perspective on the Chechen conflict. They looked at them with care and empathy.

Green then began his lecture. If the audience knew something of Chechnya and cared about the plight of its people, Green's lecture was nonetheless going to remind them that they knew and did too little. "Quite rightly," Green stated, "we remember Palestine, Kashmir, Iraq, Darfur, but how about Chechnya? It is genocide on our doorstep. But no one seems to care." He spoke about the history of the Chechens as proud Muslims who contributed to Islamic scholarship and resisted Russian imperialism: "In 1944, Stalin deported the entire Chechen population. He deported them to Siberia. It is said that a third of the Chechen population died. The Red Army, when they were taking the Chechens from the mountains, the people who were too old or too young to be taken into the cattle trucks, were simply thrown off cliffs into the ravines. Whole villages of people were summarily executed in that manner."[47] Green then described details about the violence of Russian troops who had killed more than 250,000 people in the past decade. He concluded by censuring Muslims for only being preoccupied with the political events on their TV screens or those that concerned their own ethnic groups. Green's lament was that the remoteness of the conflict from Western concerns should not therefore make it remote to Muslims. Moreover, Muslims needed to raise the profile of the Chechen cause within their nation-states so that the Russian government would feel greater pressure to end their aggression. Following his lecture, Green invited the Ibrahims to speak to the audience about the plight of their people. As Yahyaer sat in his wheelchair, Fatima detailed how she cunningly concealed from Russian authorities photographs documenting the war. A collective sadness shot through the audience; several were in tears. The next day, the couple brought their pictures and shared them with those interested in seeing how the Russian military had created a population of amputees and mangled bodies.

Ferid, Miawand, and Muhanad attended that evening, but the message was nothing unique for mosque-going Muslims. A pervasive feature of North American Muslim community life was the constant concern with the suffering of the *umma* (the global Muslim community).[48] Decades ago, Middle Eastern historian Nikki Keddie saw the modern umma as the Muslim equivalent of what the West has called a "nation."[49] In her recent monograph, the sociologist Tahseen Shams defines the umma as "the imagined worldwide community of Muslims that transcends borders and connects all Muslims via shared beliefs, rituals, duties, and a sense of membership." "A religious framework of this sort," says Shams, "can invoke a sense of community and collective identity that people can then use to make sense of their world and relationships, to create group boundaries between an 'us' and a 'them' that transcend state borders."[50] The Middle East historian, Cemil Aydin, has added historical specificity to the modern construction of the umma by tracing it to Ottoman attempts to create a pan-Islamic coalition in the face of nineteenth-century European imperialism.[51] Aydin shows us that the concept of the umma is as historically rich as that of the "West." But the umma in the North American context is not simply an "imagined community" in the sense that the noted theorist of nationalism Benedict Anderson used the term to speak of the nation.[52] It is not simply a community premised on shared identity markers like common beliefs or rituals. Instead, it should also be understood as a community of mutual care that demands and is constructed through ethical practices instructing its members to love their brothers and sisters in faith.[53] For North American Muslims, deploying the concept of umma became the way to shape one's relationship to a "Muslim East"—the place where most Muslims lived, where Islam originated, and from where many had immigrated.[54] This discourse assumed a deep and enduring relationship between North American Muslims and their wider global community. By the time Green delivered his speech, a set of assumptions about the proper degree of love and concern one should cultivate for an international Muslim community had been developing among Winnipeg Muslims for some decades.

The concept of love for the umma was a constant within Friday sermons and community lectures. It appears too in the scriptural sources that often inspired sermon topics. The popularly invoked collection *Forty Hadith*, compiled by the thirteenth-century Syrian scholar Abu Sharaf al-Nawawi, is replete with statements attributed to the Prophet Muhammad about the necessity of Muslims loving, caring, and defending each other. For instance, Nawawi relates a *hadith* (tradition) in which Muhammad states, "None of you truly believes until he loves for his brother what he loves for himself."[55] Although grammatically gendered, this hadith was understood as applying to both genders; quoted often, it is meant to impart upon a Muslim an empathy for their fellow worshipper. If they hate poverty, hunger, or pain for themselves, they must also hate it for their brother and sister. Conversely, if they love wealth, food, shelter, and happiness for themselves, then they must wish the same for their sister or brother. By extending feelings of empathy, those using the hadith often sought to galvanize Muslim masses into action. It could thus be employed in charity or disaster relief efforts organized by mosques. And, as with Green's speech, it could be used when one needed to encourage action aimed at those outside of one's natural circle of concern, i.e., those who were not family, friends, members of one's ethnic group, or part of the local community. For instance, the notion of brotherhood and sisterhood motivated three separate Winnipeg Muslim bodies to organize fundraising initiatives for the 2005 tsunami that hurt many of their brethren in countries like Indonesia and Malaysia.[56]

Supplementing the concept of love was the concept of rights. The Prophet had articulated that Muslims possessed God-given rights, saying that "The entirety of the Muslim is sacred to another Muslim: his life, his property, and his dignity."[57] Winnipeg Muslim community members often invoked this hadith to cement solidarity and encourage mutual respect between Muslims. But they also invoked it to explain the need to respond to the violation of Muslim rights abroad. Examples in the 1980s and 1990s included the Soviet invasion of Afghanistan, the Bosnian Civil War, the occupation of the Palestinian West Bank and Gaza, and the Indian occupation of Kashmir. All of these occurred before 9/11 where Muslim sisterhood and brotherhood meant caring about defending Muslims' lives, property, and dignity.[58] The overriding metaphor for the Muslim umma was one that Green himself invoked in speaking about Chechnya: "The Muslim nation is as one body."[59] This concept came from an oft-quoted hadith in which the Prophet states that "when part of the body suffers, the entire body feels its pain." The imagery is striking and the takeaway is clear: Muslims have an unmitigated duty to alleviate the suffering of their brothers and sisters abroad, regardless of whether they have met or will ever meet. Likewise, it does not matter whether they share a language or race: Their rights are God-given and must be upheld.

Love and care for the umma was not simply talk. Rather, it was an aspiration, and as such it conformed to what several anthropologists of Islam have termed Muslim self-cultivation.[60] Self-cultivation uses disciplinary practices that eventually equip the self with deep dispositions, proclivities, and sensibilities—what is often encapsulated in the Aristotelian ethical tradition as *habitus*.[61] Fraternal love, like piety or reliance on God, becomes a goal to achieve. We see this in Green's exhortation to Muslims to care more about Chechnya. The means of cultivating this love were many. One was through constant exhortations like Green's; another was through collective prayer—typically during Friday sermons, asking God to relieve the plight of Muslims suffering calamities. Another was through rallies. In my time with the Winnipeg Muslim community, I witnessed or heard advertised marches or protests on a monthly, sometimes weekly, basis. Some notable examples include protests against President Bill Clinton's 1998 bombing of Iraq, the Israeli occupation of Gaza and the West Bank, the invasion of Afghanistan, the invasion of Iraq, the occupations of Afghanistan and Iraq, and the 2006 Israeli bombing of Lebanon.[62] There were also rallies in support of asylum seekers in the Muslim community.[63] These protests found allies among non-Muslim, typically leftist Canadians. But Muslims often came out as a dominant presence. Those who did not attend heard about the causes in the mosque or the MSA prayer room. Providing money for refugees or rebuilding destroyed infrastructure and schools was another way to discipline the self into caring for one's fellow Muslim.

The care for the umma could not be divorced from the community's social context. The minority and immigrant status of many Muslims helped reinforce their Muslim identity and their affiliations to Muslim-majority countries. Several studies have highlighted how Canadian Muslim identity is crafted in relation to a non-Muslim majority,[64] pointing to the commonality between community members and the socialization that it provides them in the absence of other bonds like language, ethnicity, or culture. Certainly, many of the Muslims I knew during this eight-year auto-ethnography expressed how their Muslim identity helped them situate themselves within a larger Canadian context. Several immigrant Muslims spoke of how they "found Islam" or became "more practicing" once they left Muslim-majority countries.[65] For Canadian Muslims who either grew up in Canada or had been immersed in Canadian culture since a young age, their relationship to Islam and to the umma provided a counterpoint, even if only in their imagination, to a Canadian racial and cultural majority to which they did not fully belong.

Crucially, Canadian Muslims' privileged position as citizens of an affluent and influential country impelled them to do what they could to change policies that harmed Muslims abroad. A concrete example was a February 2001 conference organized in collaboration with the Canadian Mennonite community about the harm caused by US-imposed sanctions on Iraq after the First Gulf War.[66] The conference aimed at highlighting a decade of lost life and suffering for the Iraqi people. It was meant to show how policies designed to prevent Saddam Hussein from developing dangerous military capacities had impacted the Iraqi population instead. The UN estimated that, tragically, more than a million Iraqi children had died because of the sanctions, as a ban on importing basic medicinal products caused children to die from illnesses that were otherwise easily curable. Muslim community members sought to change public perceptions and state policies by raising awareness of Iraqi children's plight. All this was part of manifesting love and care for one's brothers and sisters of the worldwide umma.

The notion of sisterhood and brotherhood in Islam can be jarring for its exclusivism. Certainly, several scriptural sources in the Islamic tradition support dignity and rights for all humans regardless of religious affiliation.[67] But among my Winnipeg interlocutors, the emphasis on the *Muslim* sister/brother in many prominently invoked scriptural texts inevitably placed love and concern for the non-Muslim on a lower rung. Such particularism runs up against a post-Enlightenment tradition that speaks of human rights for all. However, there are two points to note if we are to fully appreciate the contrast between these two discourses. For one, the *human* in human rights discourse has only recently become generalizable.[68] It has historically been the white, cisgender male, heterosexual property owner.[69] Others have had difficulty having their rights recognized without political mobilization. Moreover, as the political philosopher Hannah Arendt has pointed out, humans have rarely seen these rights enforced without the protection and willingness of a strong nation-state.[70] Arendt made this claim after witnessing the destitution of refugee populations at the end of the Second World War. In contrast, the discourse of the umma in North America was aimed specifically at helping humans of foreign nationalities. Within this discourse, guaranteeing the rights of foreigners depended upon affective ties cultivated on an ongoing basis rather than reliance on the legal recognition of the state. Indeed, this affective self-cultivation set Muslims apart from other Canadians who protested the War on Terror. Many—and at times most—Canadians believed the War on Terror was a mistake.[71] This became clear when Canadian citizens supported Chrétien's decision to bow out of the US invasion of Iraq.[72] It was a rare instance in which the will of the people was so explicit that proceeding with the intended plan to support Canada's primary military ally would have been politically unwise.[73] However, this opposition, which included anti-war sentiments, should not be equated with the affective care held by my Muslim interlocutors in Winnipeg. For these Muslims, the bonds with the victims of the War on Terror were deeply personal and, therefore, more immediately injurious.

Second, my Winnipeg Muslim participants often saw their role not as caring for their own but as caring for humans neglected by "the world community"—a euphemism for states with military and economic power. This view is what prompted Ismael Mukhtar, a respected senior community leader, to quote the Egyptian scholar Muhammad al-Ghazali during one of his Friday sermons: "The cheapest blood on the planet today is the blood of a Muslim." The community leader's point was to highlight how Muslim suffering is rarely the focus of media or political attention—as in the cases of the Chechens, the Iraqi children suffering under sanctions, or the Oruzgan wedding bombing. The trend of focusing on neglected populations has continued more recently with the Winnipeg community sharing news of the Rohingya genocide in Myanmar much earlier and with more sustained attention than the Western media. For many, caring about the umma overlapped with the discourse of human rights by seeking to make these rights a reality for those deprived of them. In short, despite its limitations, the notion of sister-/brotherhood among the Muslim community could do what human rights discourse often could not: generate concern and mobilize action to support a sizable population from the formerly colonized world.

But at the same time, the notion of the umma has tended to reduce political complexity. Conflicts around the globe followed a typical script within the Winnipeg Muslim community: Muslims were suffering and their antagonists were at fault. Often, this narrative provided an important counterpoint to what could be found in the Western public sphere. In the example of sanctions in Iraq, it diverged from the narrative that Saddam Hussein's military capacities needed to be stopped at all costs, asking instead if it was right for a million children to die as a result.[74] But it could also prevent constructive dialogue on a fraught political issue. This became all too apparent in global flashpoints that involved two Muslim parties. For instance, it was rare for Muslims to speak up for the rights of Kurds whose antagonists were other Muslim-majority countries, i.e., Turkey and Saddam Hussein's Iraq. Darfur was perhaps the prime example of this discomfort with intra-Muslim strife (even though, to his credit, Green listed Darfur in his lecture on Chechnya).

News of the Darfur genocide became prominent in Western media in the summer of 2004. Two years later, the director of an influential local Muslim organization named the Islamic Social Services Association, chastised Winnipeg Muslims for staying conspicuously silent about the conflict. She intimated that race might matter in this instance, since the government sponsoring the Darfur genocide comprised an Arab Sudanese leadership. In advertising a pro-Darfur march, the director wrote, "Can someone please take [the] lead in informing people we are clear [that] Islam does not condone this [violence] or that it [i.e., the conflict] is [not] Arabs against Blacks. There is no place for racism in Islam and we cannot be divided across racial lines."[75] These cases highlight the simplistic nature of Muslim solidarity and the lack of political nuance in Muslims' many conversations around politics.

Love for the umma necessarily shaped the place of the United States and its Canadian ally within the post–9/11 political imaginary of Canadian Muslims. The United States increasingly became the primary antagonist in military activities that took heavy Muslim casualties abroad. By the time Green delivered his lecture, the list of US military engagements was lengthy: Afghanistan, Iraq, Somalia, and Pakistan (Yemen would soon be added to the list). Moreover, military campaigns were pursued spectacularly, with extensive media coverage of military advances. The fact that each campaign was part of a supposed larger War on Terror made the violence continuous with no apparent end in sight. Before 9/11, mosque-going Canadian Muslims sometimes strongly backed US military efforts. The US support for the rebellion against the Soviet-backed Afghan government in the 1980s is a good example. This was a period in which both US and broader Anglophone media supported the Afghan resistance.[76] Likewise, the 1990s saw US-based NATO intervening to save Muslim lives in both Bosnia and Kosovo. If many mosque-going Muslims were suspicious of US foreign policy owing to its support of dictators, its weapons funding to Israel, and its ongoing military and economic violence in Iraq, they were nonetheless selective in their opposition. After 9/11, their objections were more persistent and pervasive.[77] They could point to an overarching military policy that potentially positioned the entire Muslim world as a battlefield. The loss of life that mosque-going Muslims witnessed during the War on Terror produced what we might call an affective injury. By using this term, I seek to highlight the visceral pain and wounded feelings produced from knowing that bombs were raining down on their Muslim brothers and sisters abroad and that bodies were piling up.[78] To know that countless people lost family members, were orphaned, killed, maimed, or made refugees was not only a point of political disagreement or rational objection; it was also a lived hurt.

FERID'S DILEMMA: THE AFFECTIVE VERSUS THE LEGAL

With the preceding in mind, we can begin to analyze Ferid's comments anew. To recall, Ferid expressed that he could not bring himself to care about terrorist victims. The statement is bold and seemingly heartless. It was, to be clear, an opinion that few mosque-going Canadian Muslims I knew would have echoed. In this sense, it was radical. But it came from a place that Canadian Muslims understood. It stemmed from a place of care and concern for fellow believers. Ferid had watched, over several years, the American state and its allies kill and maim innocent civilians in Afghanistan, Iraq, Pakistan, and Somalia. These were people he never met but with whom he shared mutual rights of sister-/brotherhood: Their lives, wealth, and property were inviolable. They were people toward whom Ferid had cultivated affective bonds of love since coming to Canada as a child. In the mosque, he heard of the need to care for and love them: "Love for your brother what you love for yourself." They were part of a countless mass for whom he prayed on Fridays. When calamities had hit them, he had joined collective prayers asking God to help them and to improve the lot of the weakest and most destitute among them. He had prayed that their hardship should soon turn to ease. The violence perpetrated against them in the context of the War on Terror was therefore unconscionable to him. Whatever policy objectives North Atlantic states had in mind were not worth the loss of life that he witnessed. But to add insult to injury, the state and public sphere did not even mourn their lost lives—at least, not in the way he would have done. It appeared his brethren could be sacrificed with little concern. What Ferid rebelled against was the duplicity of his state and the public sphere it dominated, which demanded that he grieve for others even as his brethren were leaving this world unrecognized. In the wake of this duplicity, he chose not to care. In some ways, it was a tit-for-tat move: If you don't care about our lives, don't ask me to care about yours. But it was also a self-sacrificing move. Ferid knew well that he was different from Muslims abroad. His passport made him a privileged participant in this war to defend civilization. He could continue to live a life of security and comfort; all that was expected of him was to periodically demonstrate his loyalty by asserting his opposition to terrorism and his sympathies for its victims. Ferid's comments showed his refusal to put himself over his sisters and brothers.

Of course, Ferid did not need to choose between callousness toward terrorist victims and betrayal of his brethren. There was another way. Ferid could have mourned victims of terrorist attacks and worked hard to expose the military ideology that had devalued his brothers' and sisters' lives abroad. In this way, he could have assumed a principled stance against the unjust taking of all lives. Indeed, many Muslim social justice activists at the time recognized that violence is violence no matter who perpetrates it. They performed what Omid Safi calls multiple critique (a term taken from feminist scholarship), leveling critique against both Western violence and jihadist groups.[79] In many ways, their pain at witnessing the War on Terror called upon them to find a greater sense of justice and purpose in the world. Many of these social justice activists have emerged from the War on Terror seeking to find allies across the spectrum of marginalized communities, whether it be with Black and Indigenous communities fighting racism and settler colonialism, feminist groups, or LGBTQ groups.[80]

Before closing the door on Ferid's comments, we must ask two questions. What role did religion play in his utterance? And did his statement truly show that he was on the road toward joining a terrorist organization? On the one hand, we could say his religion played an important part in his sentiments. It was his love for the umma that led him to show apathy for terrorist victims. But what is easily missed in Ferid's jarring statement is his acknowledgment that his religion might very well condemn his apathy. To recall, Ferid expressed the idea that terrorism might indeed be prohibited in the religion, but held that he personally could not bring himself to *feel* empathy for terrorist victims. In other words, Ferid faced a dilemma between his affective, or visceral, feelings and the legal injunctions of his faith. Here we find that his religious faith made him question his emotive reaction and concede that perhaps God wanted him to care about the suffering of terrorist victims. Whereas Islamophobes often blame the Islamic religion as being responsible for violence, in the case of Ferid, it was his faith that prevented him from condoning violence. In short, we are far from seeing Ferid as set on the path to terrorism. Instead, we see a disheartened young man who cannot bear the violence perpetrated against his fellow believers, and finds the posture of grieving some lives more than others insulting and painful.

CONCLUSION

In this chapter, we have used Ferid's inability to express sorrow for the victims of 9/11 to shed light on Muslims' affective injury at the ungrievability of lost Muslim life abroad. What appears at first blush to be sympathy with terrorists ends up, on closer examination, to be feelings of hurt stemming from a nation-state's lack of concern for Muslim suffering during the War on Terror. This hurt was widely felt among my interlocutors. What was different was that Ferid's hurt led him to protest by refusing to go along with public forms of mourning that he felt made him complicit in devaluing his brothers' and sisters' lives. In contrast, most Muslims I knew and interviewed spoke of the Islamic duty to mourn all loss of life. Thus, Ferid's sentiments reveal a key part of the Muslim experience of the War on Terror. His sentiments are also essential to understanding why he, Miawand, and Muhanad left. If the three men all felt this affective injury, then they would be more likely to have sought a means to end the violence that caused it. Unfortunately, their search for a solution to this violence would eventually take a dark turn, which we will examine in the next chapter.

But I want to end here with something perhaps counterintuitive. Do Ferid's comments only shed light on mosque-going Muslims? Or could Ferid's words also teach us about ourselves as citizens of Canada, the United States, and other Western nations? Could it be that Ferid's injury reveals something about our social imaginary that is hidden but that should give us serious pause? To recall, Ferid's hurt was based on the lack of parity with which we treat human life. During the last two-plus decades, the War on Terror has been a testament to our inability to mourn Afghan villagers, Baghdadi children, or Somali peasants in the same ways that we mourn the victims of the World Trade Center attacks, the French Bataclan attacks, or the London train attacks. And yet we claim that all humans have the right to life and freedom. What Ferid's comments highlight, then, are our self-delusions. We have been duplicitous with our claims to care about our fellow humans. Our assessments of violence—at least in our public sphere—have been inevitably tied up with the notion of righteous violence. It matters to us who kills and who is killed. When this contradiction is brought to light, we brush it off: Our violence is self-defense and, besides, it will eventually benefit its victims.

Was Ferid, then, not simply mirroring our own callousness? If his apathy for the innocent revolts us, should we not also be disgusted by our own apathy? Is the difference the deliberate targeting of civilians? We do it by mistake; they do it on purpose? Perhaps. But the question of the difference between the terrorist's violence and our own is one that Talal Asad has explored in some depth through his engagement with philosopher Michael Walzer's argument for the legitimacy of the War on Terror. Showing the various ways Walzer's theory could also be invoked as self-justifications by the terrorist, Asad concluded that "however much we try to distinguish between morally good and morally evil ways of killing, our attempts are beset with contradictions, and these contradictions remain a fragile part of our modern subjectivity."[81] I am therefore less inclined to pursue the question of the ways in which terrorists' violence renders ours righteous.

Rather, this chapter has shown that we might care more if "they" were our own. If the casualties of the War on Terror were our citizens or belonged to our imaginary Western Civilization, then would we grieve their lives more? And if we did, would we still justify our military actions? Ferid's protest shows us what it would mean to treat swathes of the previously colonized and savage world as part of a human family. If we all possessed his level of love for others and indignation toward their deaths, what type of world might we be able to build? What new forms of international relations could be disclosed to us? Perhaps this Ferid from 2005 could have gone on to help us learn this lesson. But, alas, things unfolded differently.

3

THE EMERGENCE OF THE HOMEGROWN JIHADIST

Our group tent awaits us in Mina, a region on the outskirts of Mecca. Ferid, Sabir, Miawand, Muhanad, and I are walking toward our destination after a long day. We have completed the central rituals of our pilgrimage. Though it has been arduous, we feel spiritually uplifted. It has been a week since we arrived in Mecca. We had been anxious then. We did not know what would await us once we began the rituals of our pilgrimage. Now, after our day in 'Arafa, our night in Muzdalifa, our casting of stones at the *jamarat*, and our circling of Abraham's temple, we are embraced by a sense of accomplishment, peace, and contentment. That day we had shaved our heads as a sign of rebirth: The one who completes the hajj is said to be as pure as the day his mother gave birth to him.

Miawand is walking to my right. I see his tattoo on his left shoulder. I know he is ashamed of it; it is a relic of a past life he wishes to forget. I have barely spoken to him this trip. I cannot seem to connect with him: He always has his guard up and I find him hard to read. I approach him, wanting to share the joy of our recent accomplishments.

"What are you listening to?" I ask.

He is wearing headphones, as he has been for most of this trip. He is dedicated to listening to new lectures on various aspects of Islam. "It's a talk about the Taliban," he says. "The media lies about them. They portray them as the bad guys but they are really the good guys."

The statement is simplistic, but I am less than shocked. I assume it stems from common Muslim frustrations about the War on Terror. Still, it doesn't countenance the complexity of politics in Afghanistan. My experience tells me that Muslims in science and engineering know little about politics or history. I see the exchange as an opportunity for a discussion on the topic. "Miawand, the situation is a bit more complicated. For sure, the media vilifies the Taliban, and sometimes unfairly, because the US is at war with them. But even before the US invaded Afghanistan, the Taliban was one warring faction among others. Some Afghans appreciated the stability they brought to their war-torn country and some strongly opposed them."

Miawand suddenly seems upset. He shakes his head and looks at me squarely in the eyes: "You can't say that. You can't say that about any mujahidin [fighters of jihad]." The increasing harshness of his tone begins to feel threatening. "You can't question their motives. That's *haram* [religiously unlawful]."

Before I can say anything more, Miawand walks away abruptly. What just happened, I ask myself?

* * *

Somebody must have known, right? If the three men were radicals, then their friends must have seen it coming. No, not really. Not even a little bit. This was my only tangible clue that something might be amiss among my pilgrimage companions. And even then, though I thought Miawand's political sympathies were ill-informed, I had no idea that they might translate into criminal activities. In hindsight, I wish I had offered Miawand help or sought the guidance of a community elder. But hindsight is always 20/20, and this was long before the appearance of ISIS. Worries about homegrown jihadists were just beginning to emerge in Canadian Muslim communities. It had only been a few months since the arrest of the Toronto 18 had revealed that some Canadian Muslims thought violence was the correct solution to the War on Terror. As in the Toronto 18 case, and so many cases since 2007, one man played a disproportionate role in pushing Miawand, Ferid, and Muhanad to violence. Not Osama bin Laden, whose flowery Arabic went over the heads of Canadian-raised Muslims; nor Abu Musʿab al-Zarqawi, the ruthless leader of the al-Qaeda insurgency in Iraq, who seemed to communicate only through grisly televised acts.[1] No, it was a man who spoke both English and Arabic perfectly, a man who was born in New Mexico, attended university in the United States, and became a spokesperson for peaceful and moderate Islam in the months after 9/11—even giving a luncheon talk at the Pentagon to an audience that included the hawkish defense secretary Donald Rumsfeld. This man, Anwar Al-Awlaki, had since decided that America and Islam might not be so compatible after all. It appears his change of heart had something to do with FBI threats to unveil his double life as an imam and a generous patron of prostitutes in the Washington, DC, area.[2] In 2006, when we were in Mecca, Al-Awlaki was languishing in a Yemeni prison a few hundred miles south of us. But his sermons were beginning to attract attention among English-speaking Muslims. "Finally," some of them thought, "a Muslim scholar unafraid to speak about the US's brutal and unjust invasion of Muslim lands. Finally, a scholar telling us the truth about our religious duty to fight back."[3] Al-Awlaki would continue to preach violent resistance to the War on Terror until the Obama administration had him assassinated in 2011.

If we are to grasp what happened to Ferid, Miawand, and Muhanad, Al-Awlaki is the final and most important piece of the puzzle. But to fully grasp Al-Awlaki's impact, we must place him within a wider history of thought on war and peace in Islam. To this end, we begin this chapter by reviewing the classical doctrine of jihad in Islamic thought. We will see how premodern Muslim jurists had a highly pragmatic view of politics. They conceived war as a mechanism that should serve the imperatives of Muslim empires seeking to extend their territory and maximize their strength while maintaining internal stability and prosperity. In contrast, Al-Awlaki's vision of jihad marked a departure from the pragmatism of premodern Muslim jurists. Al-Awlaki was a proponent of what I call "utopian jihad"—a term that signifies the hope that an ideal state of affairs might come about through military combat, even while recognizing the seeming implausibility of such an outcome. The modern discourse of utopian jihad can be traced back to thinkers of the 1970s and 1980s. But Al-Awlaki's version of jihad was also a response to the War on Terror. My contention is that the influence of Al-Awlaki on Ferid, Miawand, and Muhanad was a product of his ability to offer a solution to the violence being committed against Muslims around the world—a problem that, as we have seen, deeply impacted the three men. I support this claim by tracing when and how Ferid, Miawand, and Muhanad began to gravitate toward Al-Awlaki's ideas. If my analysis is correct, it leads to an unexpected and disturbing conclusion: The ideology of jihad that has led so many Western Muslims to join terrorist groups and commit terrorist acts came into existence *after* 9/11. This conclusion not only shows that Islamic thought around war and peace continues to be refashioned by political circumstances, but it also highlights the limits of secular governance in regulating the proper expression of religion by showing that privately cultivated religious passions sometimes give rise to unpredictable political commitments.

THE PRAGMATIC JIHAD OF THE PREMODERN PERIOD

We begin with an exposition of premodern jihad doctrine. The focus on the premodern is prima facie not obvious: Why should writings from centuries ago tell us anything about the disappearance of three young men in 2007? There are two reasons to focus on the past. The first is that Muslims today continue to reference the past ideas of their tradition to make sense of the present. Their grappling with past ideas on jihad therefore matters in explaining the ideology to which the three men subscribed. Second, a key contention of this chapter is that the jihadist ideology of al-Qaeda represents an important rupture with the past, characterized by an abandonment of Sunni jurists' pragmatic considerations when advocating for war or peace. This in turn shows that there is nothing intrinsic to the Islamic tradition that would lead its followers to violence today; the same break between Sunni thought and al-Qaeda's ideology also explains why most of my Winnipeg Muslim interlocutors knew next to nothing of the latter before 9/11.

To understand premodern jihad doctrine, it is necessary to say something about the nature of Islamic law. At its essence, Islamic law was the product of an academic exercise conducted by a class of jurists.[4] Islamic law therefore existed first and foremost as an ideal rather than as any given state's actual law. Moreover, there were as many versions of this ideal as there were jurists. Premodern jurists, particularly from the eighth to the thirteenth centuries, debated what the law should be. They recognized this law to be religious in nature, and most agreed that revelation (*al-shar*ʿ) is the basis upon which the law should be derived. But they also agreed that determining God's law based on scripture is an exceedingly subjective task.[5]

Scripture could always be interpreted in divergent ways. Premodern jurists therefore accepted their peers' right to divergent interpretations. After all, they could be wrong and their peers could be correct.[6] Nonetheless, by the tenth century, jurists typically labored as part of legal schools, each with its own set of legal positions developed over generations. The jurists' academic pursuits mattered to the lives of Muslims in two ways. First, the state would hire some jurists to serve as judges. As in today's courts, Muslim judges settled disputes among plaintiffs or imposed penalties for actions considered injurious to the public welfare. Second, jurists served as consultants to the lay Muslim population. Lay Muslims recognized that the law is a complex subject that they could not hope to study themselves.[7] They therefore petitioned Muslim jurists when they needed guidance on implementing the dictates of religious law. The answer of a jurist was called a *fatwa*. Today, Islamic law plays only a modest role in most Muslim-majority states, and yet many Muslims see the law as a normative source for determining their conduct.

Premodern jurists wrote magisterial manuals of law documenting their reasoning on a set of standard legal questions. One of these manuals can fill bookshelves in its contemporary printed multi-volume edition. Chapters on the laws regarding war and peace were staples. They often carried the title *kitab al-siyar* (the book of conduct [in war]) or, more rarely, *kitab al-jihad* (the book of jihad).[8] It is here that we can locate premodern legal views on jihad. Although the term *jihad* is a complex one in the Islamic tradition (the word literally means "struggle," and Muslims often use it to refer to the spiritual struggle against the base desires and whims that distract the self from mindfulness of God),[9] when jurists used the term in their manuals of law, they unequivocally referred to military combat (*qital*). As Khaled Blankinship argues, jurists' treatment of jihad is equivalent to Aquinas's and Augustine's theory of just war in the Christian tradition.[10] Theories of just war generally tackle three questions: When should war occur, how should it be waged, and how should peaceful relations be established? While theories of jihad rely on the Qur'an and Muhammad's example to flesh out the laws of war, they are also clearly a product of jurists' own assumptions about the harms and benefits that war brings to Muslim-governed lands.

Chapters on jihad are implicitly addressed to state rulers. They inform these rulers of their duties as military commanders—though historically, the degree to which rulers conformed to jurists' ideas in practice varied greatly from one era to the next. And the jurists' formulation of these laws of war and peace was profoundly influenced by their historical context. The jurists' treatment of jihad first took shape in the second half of the eighth century, when the ʿAbbasid dynasty had taken control of Muslim-governed lands and moved the Muslim capital from Damascus in Syria to Baghdad on the banks of the Tigris River in Iraq. The Muslim conquests of the prior century had succeeded in completely overtaking the Sassanian Persian Empire and large swathes of the Byzantine Roman Empire, bringing immense power, prestige, and wealth to the Muslim community. Muslim jurists continued to see this expansion as an ideal to which rulers should aspire, even after the ʿAbbasid rulers stopped prioritizing conquest and began to busy themselves instead with the social, economic, and intellectual prosperity of their realms.[11]

By the ninth century, jurists across legal schools asserted that territorial expansion was a communal duty for Muslims (*fard kifaya*). These jurists did not justify conquest as a means to impose conversion upon non-Muslim populations, at least not directly. Rather, they claimed that territorial expansion was part of establishing God's glory on earth. For instance, some jurists spoke about how territorial expansion strengthened God's religion (*iʿzaz din illah*),[12] by inviting new populations into the Islamic faith and subjugating those that refused Muslim rule. Thus, chapters on jihad speak about the necessity of inviting a population to convert before any fighting could commence. The early Hanafi jurist Abu al-Hasan al-Shaybani, for example, quotes the following prophetic statement: "If you meet an enemy from the polytheists, call them to Islam. If they convert, then accept their conversion and refrain from showing them aggression . . . if they refuse, then invite them to pay a poll tax [*jizya*]. If they do so, then accept it from them and refrain from showing them aggression."[13]

The jurists were aware that war brought hardships to humankind. In fact, they did not praise war itself: The Hanafi school spoke of war as a form of corruption on earth because it destroyed God's creation.[14] Their ambivalence followed the Qur'an, which speaks of war as a burden,[15] and which commands Muslims to accept peace if their enemies call them to it.[16] But the jurists nonetheless saw the final years of Muhammad's life as establishing an imperative to further conquest. During these final years, Muslims demanded the surrender of non-Muslim populations across the Arabian Peninsula. Taking a cue from the early Muslim community's dedication to territorial expansion, the Shafi'i school insisted that a ruler attack enemy territories at least once a year; this way, his focus on conquest would be maintained.[17] The jurists' portrayal of jihad as a war of Muslims against non-Muslims, though, distorts the messiness of politics during the premodern era. In reality, as 'Abbasid strength waned and new Muslim states emerged, wars over territory frequently pitted Muslim rulers against each other. But intra-Muslim wars were not easy to justify theologically: They were always seen as a failure of the Muslim community to establish unity among its ranks. Thus, while jurists did theorize rules for cases of internecine strife in their treatment of war and peace, they never glorified intra-Muslim wars.[18]

The juristic ideal of conquest was a product of the international politics of the era. Muslim and other empires, like the Byzantine Roman Empire, deemed territorial expansion a good and considered peace with neighboring states always fragile. The jurists' world lacked our contemporary international treaties that establish normative behavior for interstate interactions. It thus mirrored an extreme version of the dominant "Realist" approach taught in courses on international relations, which views international politics as an anarchic realm devoid of a sovereign authority.[19] In such a context, jurists saw wars of conquest as inseparable from self-defense. The eleventh-century Shafi'i jurist Abu Ishaq al-Shirazi explained that rulers' raids on enemy territory prevented enemies from coveting Muslim lands: "Jihad must be fulfilled at minimum once a year . . . because in forsaking it for more than a year, the enemy will covet the Muslims [i.e., their lands and possessions]."[20] Likewise, Hanafi jurists like 'Ala' al-din al-Samarqandi affirmed that the purpose of jihad was not only to strengthen the Islamic religion but also to repel the evils that war brings to a population.[21] These evils included death, enslavement, and the destruction of property. Muslim jurists therefore reasoned that waging war against enemy states served to protect the lives, freedom, and property of populations living under Muslim governance. Simply put, they considered the best defense to be a good offense.

While conquest was an ideal, jurists were also pragmatic. This pragmatism is evident in the limits they set on pursuing conquest. The jurists desisted from calling upon all Muslims to join military efforts. The tenth-century Baghdad jurist Abu Bakr al-Jassas explained that if all Muslims partook in conquests, then other aspects of life—such as education, the economy, or raising families—would be neglected.[22] Jassas noted that an excessive focus on war would lead to self-destruction because Muslims would lack the resources that support their armies and repel attacks from foreign enemies. Jassas' reasoning reveals that jurists saw territorial conquest as one among many goods. A ruler raising an army hence had the duty to weigh the good of conquest against other goods. He needed to consider whether spending money on war was more important than patronizing colleges or supporting trade.

The jurists also revealed their pragmatism in their debates over the legitimacy of pursuing peace treaties. On the surface, jurists presented peace treaties as a temporary delay on the path to ongoing conquests. Thus, early Hanafis legitimated peace treaties only when a Muslim army was too weak to face its foes.[23] Likewise, the Shafi'is stipulated that a peace treaty could not exceed a ten-year period, citing a historical treaty between Muhammad and the Meccan tribe of Quraysh.[24] And yet jurists also recognized that normalizing relations between imperial powers was sometimes mutually beneficial. They affirmed, for example, that peace treaties gave subjects of foreign kingdoms rights to enter Muslim-governed land for trade or other purposes (in a manner resembling modern-day visas).[25] The normalcy of these peace treaties is evident in jurists' lengthy debates about the rights of foreigners on Muslim territory and the duties of Muslims in foreign lands. For instance, jurists debated whether Muslims should be subject to Islamic laws of commerce while trading abroad. They also argued over the proper heirs of a foreigner who dies while legally residing in Muslim-governed lands. The attention that jurists gave to laws regulating cross-border interactions between subjects of different territories is a recognition of the normalcy of peace treaties.

The ideal of conquest thus easily gave way to accommodating a political reality in which Muslim states and non-Muslim states continued to exist side by side. Even the tolerability of long-term peace became more widely accepted within legal discourse. By the late twelfth century, the central Asian Hanafi jurist Burhan al-Din al-Marghinani no longer made the weakness of Muslim armies a condition for peace.[26] As long as peace treaties protected life, property, and freedom from slavery, Marghinani believed they were justified; this position became common among later jurists of his Hanafi school. Moreover, jurists increasingly recognized that peace might serve God's religion better than war. Some spoke about how the peace of Hudaybiyya became a means for non-Muslim Arabs to get to know Muslims and see the "beautiful aspects of Islam" (*mahasin al-Islam*).[27] The key criterion for the Hanafis was that peace should bring about a benefit (*maslaha*) for the population of a Muslim-governed state. The Qur'anic exegete, Abu al-Qasim al-Zamakhshari, summarized this position, stating, "The issue of war and peace depends upon what the ruler sees as beneficial for Islam and Muslims and there is neither a definitive imperative to always fight nor to always [respond to an invitation to a peace treaty]." The centrality of the concept of maslaha in decisions regarding war and peace would shape the way the Ottoman Empire envisioned international politics in the early modern world.

Recognizing this pragmatism is important in thinking about the genesis of jihadist groups. On the one hand, the premodern vision of jihad fits oddly within the modern world where an aspiration to increase territorial control is no longer the norm and where religious differences between rulers do not lead to a presupposition of enmity. On the other hand, premodern jurists' pragmatism can easily be extended to support a modern vision of international relations in which state sovereignty is respected and cooperation is promoted. This is because juristic pragmatism places considerations of war and peace squarely within the ambit of state leaders' decision-making and asks them to weigh the benefits of peace against those of war. Indeed, the problem with the application of premodern doctrines of jihad today is not the fanaticism of its authors but its anachronistic assumptions about imperial rivalries. Unsurprisingly, some contemporary Muslim thinkers have drawn on premodern juristic thought to advocate peaceful relations rather than war as the norm.[28] Contemporary jihadist thought, as we shall see, emerges from elsewhere.

But what relationship did premodern doctrines of jihad have to the Winnipeg Muslim community? To recall, many Muslims still take an interest in learning and applying their religious law. We might then expect mosque-going Muslims to have engaged with the premodern tradition on war and peace. However, the answer is otherwise: Not much of a relationship existed between these premodern doctrines and the Winnipeg Muslim community. I only knew of one person who took an active interest in understanding the rules of jihad. Even he had little knowledge of the premodern discourse of jihad, being more interested in contemporary articulations of the doctrine that emerged after the Soviet invasion of Afghanistan. My time within the Winnipeg Muslim community suggests that premodern ideas on jihad were seldom known and seldom relevant to North American Muslims. Despite my many hours at the mosque and in learning gatherings, I was only exposed to these doctrines years later when I consciously studied them in books of law whose authors most of my interlocutors had never heard of. My sense that Winnipeg Muslims knew next to nothing about the premodern discourse of jihad was confirmed when I began to ask my interviewees what they understood jihad to be. For instance, my engineering friend Sabir answered that jihad was not something he grew up hearing about in multiethnic and religiously diverse Trinidad. He emphasized how his family and community had more of an attitude of "letting people live their lives as they wanted to." In saying this, Sabir clearly linked jihad to a politics that undercut cooperation and coexistence among peoples of different faiths. Likewise, Nabeel, an Arab immigrant and former international student who attended the University of Manitoba alongside Ferid, Miawand, and Muhanad, felt that jihad today is simply "a power grab" in which some groups try to impose their will upon others.

This ignorance about classical jihad doctrine is easily understandable. War was too distant from people's spiritual lives or social roles to warrant much theoretical attention. The concept of jihad surfaced only on rare occasions. One was when Muslims sought to defend the concept against widespread media portrayal. In these cases, they might seek to reclaim the term by affirming its distance from the actions of terrorist groups like al-Qaeda. The second case was in reference to fighters in a foreign land defending their homes. Thus, Abdurraheem Green had spoken of the Chechen resistance to Russian invasion as a jihad during the conference discussed earlier because he wanted to underscore its legitimacy. But Green notwithstanding, referencing jihad became far less common after 9/11, when Winnipeg Muslims were increasingly careful about endorsing military struggles. When Muslims did speak of jihad, their reference point for a just war was not the legal debates of the eighth to the thirteenth centuries. Rather, it was the life of Muhammad and his companions whose military struggles were understood as part of a unique historical triumph in which Muslims defended themselves against religious persecution. Winnipeg Muslims might consider this reference point a source of moral lessons for today, but they did not care about developing or understanding systematic rules of war and peace. Of course, this should cause no more surprise than discovering that most Christians do not bother to learn St. Augustine's ideas on war and peace, or that most liberals do not seek to learn Michael Walzer's contemporary theory of just war.[29] The consequence of this absence is important for the analysis that follows. Neither Ferid, Miawand, nor Muhanad knew the classical theory of jihad. Instead, they would obtain their teachings on jihad from a new and innovative source. To be convincing, this new source would need to present a vision of jihad that made sense to them. This vision needed to explain why the world is as it is today and how military combat might make the world a better place. But first, let's look at how this source initially earned the three men's trust.

AL-AWLAKI'S FOOT IN THE DOOR

The first time I heard Anwar Al-Awlaki's voice was in the winter of 2006—a month or two before we left for hajj. The story of that day sheds light on who Al-Awlaki was and the appeal he possessed for Ferid, Miawand, and Muhanad. I had been invited to the home of a Sri Lankan Muslim alongside four friends. Our Sri Lankan host, Rashid, was a gentle and kind man in his thirties, married with two children. He had decided that we would spend part of the afternoon together listening to a religious lecture. Anthropologist Charles Hirschkind has shown how audio lectures were immensely popular in the 1990s among Egyptian Muslims,[30] and Winnipeg Muslims in the 2000s were no different from Hirschkind's subjects. Many listened to renowned preachers to better learn their faith. Sometimes they listened to lectures alone in the comfort of their homes or in their cars. But they also listened to lectures in a group. When they did, the religious learning of the activity gained a social dimension: Learning about God with others built a sense of community.

On this day, Rashid put on a new favorite of his: *The Lives of the Prophets* by Anwar Al-Awlaki.[31] The CD was part of a long set—approximately twenty-one hours, in fact—and traversed the biographies of the twenty-five prophets mentioned in the Qur'an, a number that includes many biblical figures such as Abraham, Noah, David, and Jesus. As the CD began, Al-Awlaki introduced the purpose of sharing these prophetic stories by quoting a Qur'anic passage in its original Arabic that translates as "Relay the stories to them, perhaps they will reflect upon them." In a steady and confident voice, Al-Awlaki then explained, "These stories are not to entertain us. These stories are for us to derive lessons and reflect, and to contemplate. And to think about. To deeply reflect on them, that is what we need to do."[32] He continued, again quoting from the Qur'an, "They are those who are guided, so follow their guidance." In a borderline informal English and with references to common Western ideas about the need for role models, Al-Awlaki explained this second Qur'anic verse, characterizing the prophets as "the ones who are guided [by God], and [God] is instructing [the Prophet Muhammad] to . . . follow their guidance, because they are the best. . . . It is very important for the human being to have models, especially in the early stages of our life."

The lecture then explained the story of creation, in which God tells the angels he will place a vicegerent on earth—a Muslim equivalent to the Christian notion of stewardship. The lecture itself was nothing novel. Al-Awlaki relied heavily on the writings of the thirteenth-century jurist Ibn Kathir.[33] I had seen Ibn Kathir's book *Qasas al-Anbiya'* (*Stories of the Prophets*) sold in every corner of Damascus when I had been there a few years prior. Moreover, it was one of the few classical texts translated into English and widely accessible to Muslims.[34] Al-Awlaki consciously appealed to past authorities; quoting them was a common means for Muslim preachers to gain legitimacy by placing themselves within a lineage of thought.[35] Yet, although they relied on the past, Al-Awlaki's lectures addressed modern social issues that he knew would resonate with his audience. For instance, he sought to inform his audience of the need to trust in God rather than fear financial instability: "We worry about *rizq* . . . *rizq* is our sustenance [in the Arabic language]. We always think about tomorrow. We are sustenance-phobic . . . how will we make it tomorrow? But listen to this: [God] wrote down the sustenance of creation fifty thousand years before the heavens and the earth were created . . . it's a done deal. What you will get is already written down, are you still going to be very concerned about it?" I would later see this as one of Al-Awlaki's common rhetorical moves. He relied on scripture or past authorities to derive new teachings for social and political problems of the present.

The lecture was not much of a hit with those in attendance. Two of the guests, Jaan and Faysal, sat reclined against the basement wall looking listless. They listened, politely obliging their host. But for those in attendance, these stories were well-trodden ground; they had heard or read them countless times. When the pizza arrived and Rashid stopped the CD, the attendees were happy to engage in more mundane discussions about our community, work, and social lives. But having now heard Al-Awlaki, I understood the buzz around him. He was one of the few able to combine Arabic and English effortlessly. Arabic provided credibility for a Muslim preacher.[36] It allowed the speaker to quote the Qur'an and to cite authoritative *hadith* to argue for a position. No serious authority within the Sunni or Twelver Shi'a community could do without it. But most Muslims, in Canada and abroad, do not understand Arabic beyond a few expressions. Like Rashid, they had few resources for learning their religion in the 2000s. They were accustomed to hearing immigrant imams delivering Friday sermons in broken English. More importantly, these Friday preachers had difficulty relating to the cultures of native English speakers. Although originally from Sri Lanka, Rashid had been schooled and immersed in an Anglophone context for years. This is what distinguished him from many of his guests that day. Most of those present were young

Arabs who had access to other oral and written religious sources. But if Rashid differed from his guests, he had much in common with Ferid, Miawand, and Muhanad. Muhanad alone among them knew Arabic, and his Arabic was only colloquial, as he had had almost no schooling in classical Arabic. Al-Awlaki not only spoke the cultural language of Anglophone Muslims but did so with eloquence and charisma. He was a storyteller, someone who could create a vivid picture in the minds of his listeners. I had heard Muslims in the Muslim Student Association (MSA) mention Al-Awlaki in passing before that day. His lectures were becoming quite popular and were making the rounds among students.

The mass following that Al-Awlaki gained was initially innocuous. Thousands of Muslims would listen to him for religious knowledge. To the *Stories of the Prophets*, one could add the equally popular *The Life of Muhammad*: fifty-three-hour-long lectures on the life of the Prophet, covering both his initial years in Mecca and his later years in Medina.[37] Al-Awlaki produced these and other lectures when he was as mainstream as any other Muslim. The lectures did not incite violence (despite the later attempts of terrorism experts to find evidence of Al-Awlaki's radicalism within them).[38] In fact, Al-Awlaki condemned terrorism in unambiguous terms at the time. He believed that Muslims in America could be the bridge between the East and the West: Muslims had a duty to show America a different face of Islam from the one they associated with the September 11 attacks.[39] For months after 9/11, Al-Awlaki was a darling of US television networks as a spokesman for moderate Muslims.[40] His moderate lectures made him a trusted figure among the Muslims who listened to him. He had crafted an audience of loyal listeners. In short, should he wish to shape their religious views, he already had a foot in the door. However, Al-Awlaki's lectures soon underwent a momentous political shift. This seems to have coincided with his return to Yemen in 2004, though traces can be heard in lectures produced the previous year while he resided in the UK.[41] I knew Ferid, Miawand, and Muhanad were listening to Al-Awlaki, but neither I nor most Muslims at the time knew of Al-Awlaki's violent turn.

There were nonetheless whispers throughout the hajj trip. During a car ride, the three men mentioned a lecture they had listened to that transgressed mainstream norms. Ferid, Miawand, and Muhanad characterized it only as Al-Awlaki's "jihad lecture" and they jokingly told each other to be quiet about it, as though to indicate that authorities would not want them listening to it. Those of us who heard them speak of this lecture had little reason to suspect that it could be dangerous. Again, this was long before ISIS and we did not know of Canadian Muslims leaving to fight overseas.[42] Like me, many had heard bits and pieces of Al-Awlaki's mainstream lectures but did not know of his new affiliation with al-Qaeda's branch in the Arabian Peninsula. However transgressive Al-Awlaki's lecture might have been, I had assumed it grappled with jihad from a historical and doctrinal perspective. I knew that all three men were interested in learning Islamic law, and jihad was a part of this legal discourse. Their joking attitude was less telling of the radicalism of the lecture than of the public suspicion that talk of jihad, however historical, could arouse.

My only solid clue was that night at hajj when Miawand rudely and abruptly scorned me. It took me several years to understand why Miawand had acted the way he had—thirteen to be exact. In 2020, as I prepared to research the now notorious ideas of Al-Awlaki, I listened to a lecture series titled *Constants on the Path of Jihad*. I soon realized that it was the lecture Miawand had been listening to that evening. What made this clear was the lecture's ending, when Al-Awlaki praises the Taliban just as Miawand had. The lectures rebuke any Muslim who denies the necessity of jihad today as a *munafiq* (a hypocrite). Miawand had no doubt viewed my pushback as a sign of hypocrisy, which was why he refused to listen to any criticism of the Taliban. In his phase of convert-like zeal, he understood his moral obligation to be to reprimand me lest I lead him astray. *Constants*, then, was the infamous "jihad lecture" that the three men spoke about in hushed tones. And it is *Constants*, in the end, that holds the key to understanding the three men's eventual disappearance.

UTOPIAN JIHAD

Al-Awlaki's *Constants* departs from the classical juristic theory of jihad. In the lecture, Al-Awlaki rarely refers to the great jurists of the past, and his ideas are largely alien to theirs. Instead, his theory of jihad belongs to a more recent tradition of thought. This genealogy is sometimes attributed to the Egyptian thinker Sayyid Qutb, who believed Muslim societies had gone astray by Westernizing their laws.[43] Qutb himself had very little to say about jihad, but his ideas were used by later jihadists.[44] Among them was bin Laden's right-hand man, Ayman al-Zawahiri, who supported the overthrow of secularist Arab regimes. However, the most influential thinker within Al-Awlaki's tradition of jihad would be the Palestinian-Jordanian theorist ʿAbd Allah ʿAzzam. With the help of the Saudis, ʿAzzam had called for the international jihad in Afghanistan against the Soviet Union in the 1980s—the first such mobilization in modern times. His ideas have been instrumental to jihadist thought ever since.[45] ʿAzzam popularized the notion that invasions of Muslim-majority lands necessitated the widespread mobilization of Muslims worldwide. He considered the defense of Muslim lands to be a religious obligation upon individual Muslims and encouraged all Muslim males to abandon the comforts of their homes to join the fight in Afghanistan.[46] He defended his stance by citing copious post–eleventh century Egyptian and Syrian jurists who also saw the defense of one's homeland against invading forces as a religious obligation. ʿAzzam largely quoted these thinkers in ways that oversimplified their ideas on jihad and stripped them of historical context. Nonetheless, by using past authorities he gave the impression that his theory of jihad was so widely accepted that no Muslim could seriously doubt its claims to orthodoxy. ʿAzzam died in 1990, but his theory has had a long afterlife. Jihadists have invoked ʿAzzam's theory in military conflicts in Bosnia and Chechnya in the 1990s and Iraq and Afghanistan in the 2000s. It has inspired a variety of groups, including al-Qaeda, al-Shabab, Boko Haram, and ISIS.

Since the 2010s, the compound term *Salafi-jihad* has become a popular designation for the ideology to which Al-Awlaki would contribute.[47] The term has its virtues: It identifies the brand of Islam to which al-Qaeda, ISIS, and like-minded groups belong; it excludes local or national jihadist groups such as the Lebanese Shiʿa group Hezbollah or militant groups in Kashmir;[48] and it distinguishes Salafis who embrace violence for political ends from the politically quietist Salafi majority. However, the term also has its limitations. For one, it overlooks the fact that the architects of this jihadist ideology were not Salafis. This is true of Abdullah 'Azzam, who was trained within classical law and relied heavily on premodern authorities to develop his theory of jihad.[49] It is also true of Sayyid Qutb, whose rationalistic engagements with the Qur'an were rejected by leading Salafis.[50]

For our purposes, the greatest drawback in speaking of Salafi-jihad is that it tells us very little about what is most distinct about this jihad in comparison to classical law. The characteristic feature of modern jihadist thought is its utopian character. I use the term *utopian* to highlight how ideologues, beginning with 'Azzam, themselves recognize the seeming impossibility of their military victory. For utopian jihadists, two factors dictate their commitment to war: first, the vision of a better world, regardless of the immense obstacles in achieving it, and second, the belief that God demands that they fight to make this better world a reality. For instance, 'Azzam championed fighting against the Soviet Union, despite knowing that his enemy possessed disproportionate military strength. He acknowledged that Muslims would have their work cut out for them but insisted they could emerge victorious if they all took up their duty to fight.[51] Likewise, ISIS's dream of establishing a Caliphate was rationally difficult to justify. The international community would not allow such a state—with its avowed enmity toward the world's leading powers—to endure. Yet ISIS contended that all Muslims had a duty to immigrate to its lands and that it was ushering in an apocalyptic battle in which it would emerge victorious against the West.[52] Whereas classical Muslim scholars believed that the religious duty to make war or peace followed from a judicious assessment of means and ends, utopian jihadists affirm that obeying God can bring about the miraculous.[53] 'Azzam's utopian theory of jihad has greatly influenced many jihadist thinkers and groups in the last four decades.

Al-Awlaki belonged to this tradition of utopian jihad. His lecture series *Constants on the Path of Jihad* is easily traceable to 'Azzam and those he influenced. The lectures comment on a book written by a former Arab-Afghan fighter named Yusuf al-'Ayayri. Al-'Ayayri was a Saudi who joined bin Laden in Afghanistan in 1992 at the age of eighteen. He returned to Saudi Arabia but continued to be part of al-Qaeda, and was jailed in 1996 following the Khobar tower attacks.[54] Two years after his arrest, he was released and began to organize al-Qaeda in Saudi Arabia. He was killed in 2003 in a shootout with Saudi forces. After his release from prison, though, al-'Ayayri had become a prolific writer. Al-Awlaki gravitated toward one of his books, *al-Thawabit 'ala Darb al-Jihad* (*Constants on the Path of Jihad*), which would become the title of his own lecture series. Al-'Ayayri's *Thawabit* argues that jihad possesses constants that are immutable regardless of time and place. He contends that Muslims have forgotten these constants and have come to see the obligation of jihad as contingent. Al-'Ayayri tells us some of their justifications: "they say that jihad is only defensive, that jihad should only be to liberate lands, that jihad depends upon the guidance of a ruler . . . and others say that jihad has ended since the time of the prophet Muhammad or that jihad is not suitable for our day and age in which we have a 'new world order.'"[55] Thus, al-'Ayayri seeks to set the record straight by arguing that jihad remains an obligation today.

Al-'Ayayri wrote several books in the six years between his release from prison and his death. *Constants* could have met the same end as his other writings, which are virtually unknown among Anglophone Muslims today. But instead of being relegated to the vast dustbin of humanity's historical ideas, *Constants* found a new life through Al-Awlaki. Al-Awlaki made al-'Ayayri's ideas legible to those who lived halfway across the world and did not know Arabic. In some ways, Al-Awlaki expanded upon both 'Azzam's and al-'Ayayri's ideas about jihad as an individual obligation today. Al-Awlaki asserts that jihad is an obligation in all times: "an obligation until the Day of Judgement." He states that jihad is part of *da'wa* (calling people to Islam), a point that resembles the classical view that the Islamic faith is strengthened through jihad. Like 'Azzam, Al-Awlaki divides jihad into "offensive" and "defensive" variants. Whereas Al-Awlaki considers offensive jihad to be a communal duty that only some need to carry out, he contends that the invasion of Muslim lands renders the participation in jihad obligatory upon each and every able-bodied Muslim (*fard 'ayn*). He quotes a metaphor from the thirteenth-century jurist Ibn Taymiyya to explain why: One must protect one's financial capital before seeking profit. In this metaphor, the financial capital is the land of the Muslims and the profit is conquest. As we have seen, this division of the world was part of an imperial vision in which conquests were a coveted good. Yet even in the twenty-first century, Al-Awlaki continues to imagine that conquest and missionary work go hand in hand.

Also like ʿAzzam and al-ʿAyayri, Al-Awlaki provides decontextualized scriptural evidence to affirm the obligation of jihad. He presents Qur'anic verses in which God commands Muslims to fight. These verses originate in the conflict between Muhammad and the Arab tribes who opposed him. We have seen that premodern jurists did not believe the Qur'an sanctioned unbridled war. Rather, they interpreted verses addressing war in ways that fit within their international context of rival empires. In contrast, Al-Awlaki reads these verses as needing no historical contextualization: Jihad was, is, and will continue to be an obligation. To support his interpretation, Al-Awlaki relies heavily on one verse: "*kutiba ʿalaykum al-qital*" (fighting has been prescribed for you). Al-Awlaki notes that the wording of the phrase mirrors the Qur'anic command to fast during Ramadan: "*Kutiba ʿalaykum al-siyam*" (fasting is prescribed for you). He takes these two phrases to show parity between the two obligations. In fact, he includes prayer too, stating, "There is no difference between jihad, fasting, and *salat* [prayer]. Fasting is prescribed upon you and jihad is prescribed upon you." The statement is important in two respects. First, the obligations of prayer and fasting are widely recognized as pillars of Islamic practice. Muslims worldwide pray each day and fast in Ramadan. To place jihad at the same level as these obligations is to assert its foundational importance to Muslim piety. Second, and most important, Al-Awlaki uses the comparison to refute claims that considerations of war are contingent. For instance, he refutes Nasir al-Din al-Albani, one of the foremost Salafis of the twentieth century, who had spoken of the need for Muslim education (*tarbiyya*) as having priority over jihad. Only after Muslims have corrected themselves spiritually should they think about political matters like jihad, al-Albani claimed. Likewise, Al-Awlaki rejects claims that Muslims today live in the equivalent of the Meccan period of early Muslim history during which the Prophet Muhammad peacefully preached his religion, a claim the Sudanese thinker Hasan al-Turabi had popularized decades earlier.[56] By focusing on these objections, Al-Awlaki placed in relief his claim that jihad was an obligation like fasting and praying: "Would anyone today say to a convert that we are in the Meccan period for fasting? They would not. It's a joke." In making this equivalency, Al-Awlaki elides the fact that jurists historically considered prayer and fasting immutable rituals, while jihad had always been linked to contingent political considerations. "Does *salat* [prayer] change?" he asks. "Can we argue today because we live in the twenty-first century, people should pray differently? There's no need to argue this." "So jihad is *fard* [obligatory]," Al-Awlaki concludes. "Full stop."

However, in other ways, Al-Awlaki departs heavily from the rhetorical style and arguments of 'Azzam, al-'Ayayri, and other Arab ideologues of utopian jihad. To understand why, we must recall that Al-Awlaki knew his Anglophone audience well. The claim that jihad is necessary for da'wa would not have had much effect on Western Muslims who had deep friendships and amicable relations with non-Muslims. When I asked my interviewees about the link between the two concepts, they thought it strange to believe violence would bring people to Islam. Thus, as we will see, Al-Awlaki's lectures focus primarily on jihad's role in ending the War on Terror. He knew that his Anglophone audience experienced the War on Terror as an unjust war and a problem that needed to be solved. He understood the affective injury many Muslims experienced as a result of casualties in Afghanistan and Iraq.[57] He knew how the US government had placed Muslims under a microscope. And he knew what Muslim leaders were saying in mosques to accommodate themselves to the scrutiny of the state. After all, he had been one of them. Thus, it would be a mistake to consider Al-Awlaki a mere translator into English of the ideas of his utopian predecessors. Al-Awlaki appropriated and transformed the thought of these predecessors for a Western audience. Figures like 'Azzam and al-'Ayayri knew very little about the West. Their audiences were Arabs, and Saudi Arabs in particular. They spoke to their own. In contrast, Al-Awlaki's utopian jihad was distinctly North American.

AL-AWLAKI'S CRITIQUE OF WESTERN MUSLIMS

What appeal did Al-Awlaki have for three young men with promising lives ahead of them? Why would they heed his message of war? At the time, the public poorly understood Muslim fighters' motives.

Crass explanations—"they hate our freedoms" or "they want seventy virgins in Paradise"—passed as profound commentary. This last explanation tapped into older racist tropes about Arabs and Orientals as sexual deviants with pent-up frustrated desires. Since then, radicalization studies has made great headway. And yet even our best narratives—those that avoid presenting Islam as intrinsically violent and instead seek to historicize what is often called "political Islam"—are still too simplistic in many regards. For one thing, they miss how religion is always political. Even when a religious community does not formulate a specific political agenda, the sensibilities and aptitudes one cultivates within community contexts are inextricably linked to public commitments, shaping in turn one's evaluation of the state's domestic and foreign policies.[58] Seemingly private practices of piety can indirectly impact citizens' interactions with each other and with the state.[59] For another, it misses how religion is always politicized by the state. Scholars of religion such as Hussein Agrama, Mayanthi Fernando, and Saba Mahmood have all noted how secularism involves the active management of religion, thereby making a purportedly private domain a focus of state intervention.[60] In the context of the War on Terror, we see a series of policy initiatives promoting religious interpretations deemed tolerable to the state—what political scientist Elizabeth Shakman Hurd calls "good religion." Today, good Islam is typically associated with Sufism, an Islam that allegedly remains focused on the spiritual. Yet Noah Salomon has shown how in nineteenth-century Sudan the British saw Sufism as excessively political and sought to promote more modern forms of religion that today have become suspect. Thus, if we wish to understand why the men left, we must look beyond claims that they were misled into letting religion dictate their politics. Rather, we will need to pay attention to why jihad—the call to arms—made sense to them as Muslims with distinct sensibilities and commitments living in Canada in the early 2000s. Put another way, why would jihad, defined as an armed military struggle against an antagonistic non-Muslim party, seem like a suitable mode of politics for them to engage in?

Al-Awlaki's *Constants* sought to answer two questions that would have resonated with North American Muslims living through the War on Terror: First, why have Muslims abandoned jihad at a time when Western powers have invaded Muslim lands? And second, why is jihad against the United States and its allies the only solution to the suffering of Muslims today? I should note that Al-Awlaki is not explicit in his aim of tackling these two questions. He was not an academic, and the listener will have trouble identifying a thesis statement in his lectures. Above all, he was a rhetorician who was well-versed in the art of convincing his audience. His answers to these questions are nonetheless intertwined throughout *Constants*' six lectures.

The first question takes for granted Al-Awlaki's listeners' sense of injury over the violence suffered by Muslim populations. Al-Awlaki knew the loss of Muslim lives was weighing on the minds of Western Muslims (he had expressed as much in an interview with PBS in 2001).[61] In *Constants*, Al-Awlaki explains why Muslims have abandoned jihad by quoting the same Qur'anic verse that affirms their duty to engage in it: "Fighting is prescribed for you *though you dislike it*" (Qur'an 2:216). He notes that the reality of war "is horrible" and that for this reason Muslims find a means of "bailing out of jihad."[62] He considers that disliking war is normal and embedded in people's *fitra* (natural disposition). He even contends that the early Muslim community also experienced this dislike. For Al-Awlaki, Muslims today who abandon jihad permit their dislike of war to overtake them and to prevent them from fulfilling their religious duty. One can easily grasp the salience of this claim for young Muslim men like Ferid, Muhanad, and Miawand. Al-Awlaki offered these men an explanation for the inaction of their community in the face of the seemingly gross injustice of the War on Terror: They were afraid. Muslims had become cowards. Al-Awlaki identifies the root of this fear as attachment to the *dunya. Dunya* is an Arabic term that literally means that which is lower or lowly. It is used to speak of this world in contrast to the heavenly life of the hereafter. I previously used the term in speaking about the hajj as an occasion to leave worldly preoccupations behind and focus on one's essence as a spiritual being. To say that Muslims are attached to the dunya is to assert that they privilege material wealth, social status, or even personal relationships with friends and family over religion. In Islamic thought, this is an unhealthy attachment because the dunya is an illusory good. It is ephemeral and short-lived. Those who are wise invest in the eternal life to come. They engage in pious deeds and good works for which God will reward them. "Accumulation of wealth preoccupies you," the Qur'an states. "But soon you shall know; soon you shall know with certainty" (Qur'an 102:1 and 6).

Al-Awlaki spares only jihadists from this damning judgment of cowardice. They belong to what Al-Awlaki calls the saved sect (*al-ta'ifa al-mansura*).[63] This notion goes back to a prophetic tradition in which Muhammad foretells that his community will become divided into a multiplicity of sects, only one of which is correct in the guidance it follows. Al-Awlaki does not quote this tradition but notes how Muslims often wonder which Muslim organization or movement they should follow. He describes Muslims appealing to him, "Shaykh, it's so confusing . . . there are so many different Muslim groups, which one should I join? Everyone claims that they have the solution for the *umma*. . . . Every *jama'a* [group] claims to represent the true religion." Al-Awlaki answers these questions by quoting a Qur'anic verse that praises Muslim fighters:

> O you who have attained faith! If you ever abandon your faith, God will in time bring forth [in your stead] people whom He loves and who love Him—humble towards the believers, proud towards the disbelievers: they fight in God's cause, and do not fear the blame of blamers: such is God's favour, which He grants unto whom He wills. And God is infinite, all-knowing. (Qur'an 5:54)

Al-Awlaki interprets the verse as meaning that the "saved sect" is the one engaged in jihad.[64] This interpretation was a departure from classical understandings of the Qur'an. In fact, the tenth-century Qur'anic exegete Muhammad ibn Jarir al-Tabari understood the verse as a reference to the period immediately after Muhammad's death when a group of Muslims abandoned their faith. He understood the verse's reference to the "people whom [God] loves and who love Him" to refer to the first Caliph, Abu Bakr, who fought the tribes that rebelled against Muslim authority in Medina after abandoning Islam.[65] By departing from historical interpretations, Al-Awlaki appropriates the verse to raise the status of jihadists as the true believers.

Most important, Al-Awlaki's interpretation also links being a true believer to the defense of Muslim communities under attack. It is worth quoting him on the subject in full because this is the argument that resonated most with Miawand, Ferid, and Muhanad:

> They're "humble towards the believers." What does that mean? It means they are concerned about the believers, they love the believers. They care about what happens to the Muslims. They follow the news about what is happening to the believers around the world. They feel that the Muslim in the East is my brother. And the Muslim in the West is my sister. And if that Muslim in the East is killed, it is my responsibility to defend him. And if my Muslim sister is hurt, it is my responsibility to defend her. Who are the brothers who are so concerned about the Muslims that whenever they hear that Muslims somewhere in the world are abused or oppressed, they immediately go to help them? And they respond to the call? So they are humble towards the believers, they are willing to give their lives to defend the believers, they are willing to give their money to defend the believers. So they are humble towards the *mu'minin* [the believers].[66]

True Muslims according to Al-Awlaki are those who not only care about the plight of their fellow Muslim brothers and sisters, but also are willing to do something about it. They are willing to fight back militarily if needed. His exegesis had appeal for a Muslim audience who purported to care for their co-religionists but felt powerless to help them in practice. In short, Al-Awlaki uses the verse to cement his claim that the Muslim masses have fallen prey to their worldly attachments and have for this reason remained largely passive when confronted with the War on Terror.

Al-Awlaki then uses a latter passage within the verse—"and [they] do not fear the blame of blamers"—to push back against common discourses in North America that disparage jihadists as evil: Al-Awlaki explains to his Western Muslim audience that the discourse of the War on Terror is a distortion of the truth. "The *kuffar* [non-Muslims] are going to blame them," he states. "But do these brothers care? As long as it pleases [God], that's all that matters." The claim was powerful because it tapped into the awareness of many Western Muslims that the discourse of the War on Terror often masked violence by legitimating the taking of life abroad. If this discourse served to hide the truth about the killing of innocent people, could it not also hide the righteous nature of the jihadists' struggle by portraying them as terrorists hell-bent on destroying the world? Could Western Muslims not be under the spell of an illusion? And could those who rebelled against this illusion not actually be the just ones? In an attempt at ideological subversion, Al-Awlaki tells his audience: "Every time you hear the word 'terrorist' replace it with 'mujahid' and every time you hear the word 'terrorism' replace it with 'jihad.'" Thus, Al-Awlaki seeks to play the role of truthteller in the face of a Western world that broadcasts lies in order to perpetuate injustice.

But Al-Awlaki does not simply attempt to uncover what he sees to be Western lies. He also sets his sights on Muslims who decry jihad today. He sees these Muslims as hypocrites seeking to please non-Muslims out of cowardice, and claims that there is nothing new about Muslims kowtowing to powerful enemies. It happened at the time of the Prophet Muhammad, he avows, just as it happens today. The idea that cowardice has driven Muslims to hypocrisy throughout Muslim history is a theme that Al-Awlaki emphasizes repeatedly throughout his lectures. In particular, the second lecture dwells on the historical battle of Uhud to exemplify this point. The battle of Uhud took place in 625 CE, three years after Muhammad and his followers had migrated from Mecca to Medina to escape the religious persecution of their fellow tribesmen of Quraysh, who resented Muhammad preaching a monotheistic faith that disparaged their ancestral beliefs. The battle was the second military encounter between the Muslims and Quraysh: The first had gone in the Muslims' favor, the second not so much. At a certain point in the battle, the Quraysh managed to break through the Muslim ranks and attack Muhammad. They believed they had killed him. News of his death spread through the battlefield, eliciting different reactions among Muslims. Al-Awlaki explains that some Muslims affirmed that Muhammad's death signaled the end of Islam. They encouraged their tribesmen to return to their ancestral polytheistic religion. Al-Awlaki contends that these hypocrites never sincerely subscribed to the Islamic faith. A second group remained

Muslim, but feared that their lives and property would be lost if they continued to fight. With Muhammad gone, they reasoned that there was nothing left for them to do but to retreat in haste. Al-Awlaki also reproaches this group for wavering in their faith. Their obligation to God was to continue to fight despite the death of Muhammad. Finally, Al-Awlaki notes a third group of Muslims whose faith remained strong despite the discouraging state of affairs. This third group is represented by one of Muhammad's men who says, "If Muhammad is dead, then let us fight until we also die for the same cause as he."[67] Al-Awlaki criticizes the first two groups for "judging results on their outcomes." They abandoned Islam because they lost faith in God. He states that these two groups represent the position of most Muslims today: "A lot of Muslims today are saying if the Taliban and the Muslims with them are correct, they wouldn't have lost, and gone to the mountains." Al-Awlaki sees Muslims as shifting their assessment of jihad depending on momentary fortunes rather than firm principles.

Al-Awlaki reserves his harshest criticisms for Muslim religious leaders. He contends that these leaders support non-Muslims in their oppression of Muslims by giving religious support to the War on Terror. In his commentary on the Qur'anic verse quoted above, Al-Awlaki states that some Muslims have "the opposite of [the] trait [of humility toward Muslims]."[68] They are harsh toward Muslims because they provide justifications for their imprisonment, their interrogation, and their surveillance. "You find that they are willing to stand with the kuffar [disbelievers] to fight against Muslims." Again, Al-Awlaki finds a historical precedent for this position, invoking the Third Crusade in which the alliance of Richard the Lionheart, Philip of France, and Frederick Barbarossa mobilized massive numbers of troops to conquer Jerusalem. He explains that several Muslim jurists despaired when they heard of the number of troops gathered and encouraged Muslims to withdraw from their territory to avoid fighting. Al-Awlaki's attempt to undercut Muslim religious leadership is of crucial importance in understanding his lectures' effectiveness on Anglophone Muslim audiences. These audiences were accustomed to deferring to their religious leaders as authorities knowledgeable in religious duties to God. For instance, Ferid, Miawand, and Muhanad all showed great deference to the MIA mosque imam: They took religious classes with him and they frequently sought council from him. But Al-Awlaki had shown through example that these religious authorities might not be fully trustworthy when it came to matters of politics. Moreover, Al-Awlaki further undercut their authority by telling his audience that following these scholars will not save them from God's punishment on the day of judgment: Now that they know the truth about the obligation of jihad, he asserts, they must follow through.

In sum, Al-Awlaki's answer for why Muslims have abandoned jihad set out to provide an explanation for Muslim inaction in the face of the War on Terror. It imagined that Muslims were too afraid to stand up against US aggression in Afghanistan and Iraq. In particular, their religious leadership continually sought to appease non-Muslims even at the cost of betraying their brethren. This cowardice had led Muslims to abandon an act of worship on par with prayer or fasting. Just as prayer and fasting are historical constants, so too is jihad. For Al-Awlaki, God has commanded Muslims to fight when Muslim lands are attacked. Only those who surmount their cowardice and engage in jihad are on the right path. Only they truly love God and are loved by him.

JIHAD AS THE SOLUTION

Al-Awlaki's accusations of Muslim cowardice left him open to a counter-critique: Might the tactics that Al-Awlaki would dismiss as cowardly actually be more effective in preventing Muslim suffering? A Western Muslim would naturally wonder why it is cowardice to use non-military means to fight against an unjust war, especially when one has freedom of expression, freedom to protest, and the ability to vote. Moreover, why would the strategy of Western Muslim leaders to "show people the beauty of Islam" not work as a means to foster coexistence between religious communities?[69] In other words: Why is jihad the solution to the War on Terror? Al-Awlaki answers this question indirectly in the first three lectures of *Constants* and in a more sustained manner in his last three lectures. He does so by reconceptualizing the notions of victory and defeat, contending that they are not limited to the battlefield. He lists eleven different forms of victory that jihad brings about, only one of which is military.

Al-Awlaki's treatment of these victories centers on two claims. The first is that jihad is itself a victory even if Muslims lose on the battlefield. He contends that the jihadist wins because he overcomes his own love of this world.[70] For Al-Awlaki, the act of jihad is the ultimate sacrifice. It involves giving up material comforts and security. It involves leaving family and surrendering one's wealth to the cause. All this is done because the jihadist places his obligation to God before all else. Unlike the Hanafi jurists of the past, Al-Awlaki sees war not as a necessary evil in the world but rather as part of a divine test of faith. God made jihad an obligation to test the Muslims. Only those willing to respond to God's call pass that test. Like Abraham, who proved his faith through his willingness to sacrifice his beloved son, the jihadist proves that God matters more to him than anything else.[71] Moreover, the jihadist becomes an example of faith for all Muslims. Cowardly Muslims now see a group of people who are unwilling to compromise in their beliefs. The jihadist therefore achieves a moral victory, in which the principles of the fighter endure long after the fighter himself dies. Al-Awlaki invokes a variety of stories within Muslim history to support his claims. Foremost among them is a Qur'anic story about Moses, Pharaoh, and two magicians. In the story, Pharaoh challenges Moses to defeat his court magicians and prove the veracity of Moses' claims to prophethood. As in the biblical story, Moses defeats the sorcerers by turning his staff into a snake. But Al-Awlaki is most interested in what happens next in the Qur'anic version of the story. The two magicians recognize that Moses is not a sorcerer. His power comes from elsewhere and they therefore embrace his religion. Pharaoh is shocked and angered. He threatens them with the most gruesome of deaths: cutting off their limbs and crucifying them. But the two magicians hold fast to their faith.[72] They know the truth and will not abandon it despite the threat to their lives. Al-Awlaki sees modern jihadists as fitting within the mold of the two sorcerers: They are willing to persist in obeying God regardless of the consequences to their lives. Al-Awlaki views this commitment as a supreme victory. And the victory is not only against non-Muslims: it is also against those Muslims who "water down the religion" because of their love of worldly comforts. The jihadist upholds and exemplifies religion. In contrast, defeat is compromising one's faith. Muslims who decry jihadists allow the principles of their religion to be changed. They are not only turning their backs on a central obligation of their faith, but also opening themselves up to imitating Western culture. Al-Awlaki states that the War on Terror is not only a war on the battlefield. It is also ideological: The "US is attempting to win the hearts and minds of Muslims." He contends that the West is happy when Muslims abandon their faith, giving the example of France's ban against the hijab in public schools.[73]

For Western Muslims seeking to end the War on Terror, Al-Awlaki's claim that military defeat constitutes a victory for jihadists appears painfully unsatisfying. It leaves untouched the lamentable suffering jihadists meant to correct. But Al-Awlaki adds a second claim: namely, that jihad *will* produce victory.[74] He contends that if jihadists do their part, God will do the rest. Al-Awlaki knows that a victory would be nothing short of miraculous. But he also presents copious scriptural and historical sources to support his claim. Among prophetic stories, he again appeals to the story of Moses, in which Pharaoh and his army are drowned after Moses miraculously parts the sea. Among historical examples, Al-Awlaki appeals to the victory of the 1980s' mujahideen against the Soviet Union. The Soviet Union was a superpower similar to the modern US Army. It possessed immense military resources and nuclear weapons. The ability of the mujahideen to force its withdrawal in 1989 was testament to the ability of God to support the faithful. Al-Awlaki gives his listener reason to believe the same victory could be imminent today: "There was a report in which Secretary of Defense Donald Rumsfeld noted how no matter how many people they kill, the troops of the enemy are not being depleted. Mr. Rumsfeld, the reason is because you are fighting the *ta'ifa mansura* [the saved sect]—no matter how many you kill, no matter how many you arrest, you can never win this war."[75] Al-Awlaki seeks to give his listeners confidence that the jihadists will win because God is on their side. Thus, together, Al-Awlaki's two claims suggest that Muslims who give up their lives in what appears to be a hopeless cause are part of a larger divine plan leading to eventual triumph.

Al-Awlaki's two claims function to refute those who see engagement in war and peace as part of a pragmatic calculus that takes into account the complexity of human life. As we have seen, this is the heart of the classical juristic understanding of war. Correct decisions about war and peace for classical jurists depend on assessing *maslaha* (benefit). But Al-Awlaki presents his utopian jihad as the authentic reading of the religion. He explicitly denounces "the logic of people who always say 'let's weigh the benefit and let's weigh the harm' until everything in the *shari'a* becomes a vegetable soup and everything is lost."[76] Instead, he proffers a vision in which faithfulness in God is measured by one's willingness to engage in jihad, and faithfulness can produce God's intervention in history. This was what made Al-Awlaki's jihad utopian: He presented a vision of a world in which Muslims might bring an end to the War on Terror and argued that they had a duty to God to fight for it despite its seeming impossibility.

To return to our initial question: Why would this utopian vision of jihad resonate with our young men? The answer to this question necessitates a further examination of their lives in the year before their departure. In the next section, we turn to this period of their lives. But one point already stands out. Al-Awlaki gave the three men a cogent explanation for the inaction of Muslims around them during the War on Terror. Muslims were afraid. They clung to their lives and comforts even as their brothers and sisters suffered oppression abroad. Only jihadists grouped under the banner of al-Qaeda or like-minded organizations seemed to care. Only they fought to help end the injustice. Though rationality made it seem as though they fought a lost cause, at least they died trying to do something. The rest was in God's hands. And perhaps they would pave the way for a movement strong enough to eventually defeat their enemies.

RADICALIZATION

On March 16, 2006, I received an email in my inbox. It was from Ferid. He had sent the email to twelve young Muslim students who frequented the University of Manitoba prayer room. There was nothing odd about this. Ferid often sent mass emails about Islam to those he thought would benefit from them. Typically, the emails contained links to websites. Examples from my inbox are varied. One addresses proper interactions between unmarried Muslim men and women;

another provides a link to a Qur'anic recitation Ferid found beautiful. Nor was Ferid the only one to do this. Dawud (my friend who moved to Toronto), Sabir (my travel companion during the hajj), and Eric (a student my age majoring in political science) also regularly shared email links with fellow University of Manitoba Muslims. But this time, something was different. At the end of the email's subject were four exclamation marks; Ferid was clearly enthusiastic. The subject line read, "Anwar Al-Awlaki!!!!" The message was terse:

> Assalaamu-alaikum Everyone!!
> This is a very good lecture I found on Aswatalislam titled
> "It's a War against Islam"
> Insha-Allah [God willing] we'll all benefit from this . . .
> Wassalaam [Peace],
> Ferid[77]

It was Ferid's first exposure to the American imam, and his attraction to Al-Awlaki was instantaneous. The lecture itself is short, running about twenty minutes. It was recorded in 2003, when Al-Awlaki was still the imam of the Falls Church mosque in Virginia.[78] It was a Friday sermon that Al-Awlaki delivered to his congregation in the aftermath of FBI raids on a number of Muslim charities, businesses, and educational associations.[79] In the lecture, Al-Awlaki critiques what he calls the "dangerous turn" of the War on Terror. What had begun as a legitimate cause to protect America from terrorist attacks has now in his estimation morphed into a campaign that directly attacks American Muslims. Al-Awlaki mentions that law enforcement held the family of a "respectable member of the community" at gunpoint for hours as they searched his home.[80] He claims that no Muslims are safe from government suspicion and potential violence. Even a liberal Muslim organization that had given its wholehearted support to the invasion of Afghanistan in 2001 was targeted. According to Al-Awlaki, the US government is preaching freedom to the world while denying its own Muslim citizens freedom at home. Its raids have fanned the flames of anti-Muslim bigotry by treating mainstream Muslim organizations as suspect. Al-Awlaki links the raids to a wider trend in which the US government lies to gain public support for unjust acts. Significantly, he accuses the US government of lying about their goal in invading Iraq, claiming that their real motivations were geopolitical and economic gain. The Bush administration's actions could therefore no longer be seen as a war against terror. The war was against Islam and Muslims. "Who is next and who will be safe?" "Maybe congress will pass a bill that outlaws Islam."

Ferid found in Al-Awlaki the preacher of the truth that he had been yearning for. He had long felt that the War on Terror was unjust. He felt frustrated with the pervasive stereotypes and anti-Muslim sentiments in the media and public sphere. The situation had become even more dire in the months prior to hearing this lecture. In the fall of 2005, Danish cartoons depicting the Prophet Muhammad as a sexually perverse and bloodthirsty terrorist had unleashed protests among Muslims worldwide. In the wake of this event, Ferid expressed his consternation that the Danish cartoons were treated as a question of freedom of expression. He saw their publication as an expression of pervasive anti-Muslim sentiment within Western society.[81] Since Muslims typically see Muhammad as an object of emulation, likening him to a terrorist is equivalent to saying that Muslims, not al-Qaeda, are terrorists.[82] Ferid was not the only one to feel this way. An email thread about the injury of Muslims over the Danish cartoons circulated among the Muslim students at the University of Manitoba.[83] These students included Muhanad and Miawand. All three men therefore found in Al-Awlaki someone who spoke to their lived experiences at a time when most North American religious leaders shied away from directly critiquing the state for fear of unwelcomed scrutiny.

But at the point when Ferid, Miawand, and Muhanad started listening to them, Al-Awlaki's lectures remained within acceptable limits of dissent. Despite its provocative title—"It's a War Against Islam"—Al-Awlaki explicitly cited civic activism as the solution to anti-Muslim government policies. "There are no rights unless there is a struggle for rights," he states. "The history of America is very clear: African Americans in this country had to go through a struggle." What was initially attractive about Al-Awlaki was not his radicalism but his relatability. He understood the difficulties of being a Western Muslim. In the following months, the three men began listening to his lectures regularly.

They sometimes made a social event of it, at least once gathering at the home of a fellow student named Ramy to listen to Al-Awlaki.[84] They listened to the *Lives of the Prophets*, *The Life of Muhammad*, the biography of the Second Caliph 'Umar, and the *Hereafter* series, which examines the eschatological events of the Last Days.[85] Then, in the fall of 2006, they discovered Al-Awlaki's *Constants*.

Constants showed up at a time when Canadian and US military action was intensifying in Muslim-majority countries. In 2006, the Canadian military announced that it was moving away from its nation-building activities toward combat operations in Kandahar province, Afghanistan.[86] The result was increased support for militarism within the Canadian public sphere. The strong Canadian critique of the War on Terror in Iraq began to recede. Coupled with this were international headlines on Somalia as a new front in the War on Terror.[87] In 2006, the Islamic Courts Union (ICU) took control of the Somali capital, Mogadishu. Until then, Somalia had been immersed in two decades of civil war. The United States saw the ICU ideology as a mirror of al-Qaeda and supported Ethiopia's invasion of Somalia. Soon, al-Shabab formed as an ICU splinter group and became the object of US aerial bombardments. Finally, the Iraqi insurgency continued unabated. Al-Qaeda in Iraq, the forerunner to ISIS, continued fighting US troops despite the loss in 2005 of its leader, Abu Mus'ab al-Zarqawi. The violence often grabbed international headlines. These new developments had the effect of reinforcing Al-Awlaki's thesis that the War on Terror was a war against Muslims.

In November 2006, a month before we left for hajj, Ferid sent out an email with a link to an *Al-Jazeera* article. The article concerned the reelection of George W. Bush. Ferid found one passage within it noteworthy. The passage makes two claims: first, that the reelection of George Bush was a war crime, and second, that the US electorate had failed to recognize the dangers of US foreign policy to world security. "The ball is now in the court of ordinary citizens of the west," the author writes.[88] It would be wrong to read Ferid's email as support for violence against civilians.[89] As we shall see, the three men did not believe terrorist attacks on civilians were lawful when they left Canada. But it does show that Ferid was increasingly bothered by what he saw as popular acceptance of the War on Terror.

When we returned from hajj in January 2007, the three men were rarely around campus. During the following months they researched the legal obligation of jihad in greater depth. Miawand attempted to locate ʿAzzam's writings, and both he and Muhanad watched videos produced by al-Qaeda in Iraq. All three men planned for a journey from which they had no intention of returning. *Constants* had changed their perception of their community, of their national belonging, and of the War on Terror. They now believed that they had an individual duty to fight back. To do otherwise was to disobey God. But this belief in a religious obligation to wage war was not rooted in scripture alone. They did not hear the Qur'an for the first time when Al-Awlaki began reciting its verses. Rather, it was the product of an interpretation of scripture that made sense of their lived experience. It was an interpretation that offered a solution to a state of affairs that they felt was intolerable: the devaluation of Muslim life abroad coupled with the passivity of Muslim leaders worldwide. Al-Awlaki provided the three men with a means to reclaim their agency by changing the narrative: The jihadists, in this story, were the good guys, and both history and scripture showed that they would eventually emerge victorious.

Then, on March 7, Miawand sent a letter to his family. It was meant to be a farewell letter, explaining why the men had left and hoping that his mother would forgive him for breaking her heart:

> As-salaam-alaikum my dear family.
> I know this is going to hurt the family but I chose the path in which Allah SWT [*subhanahu wa-taʿala* (may God be exalted)] guided me.
> I have left the country already with two of my friends to help my brothers and sisters. We live in a life of ease while our brothers and sisters are suffering so much without food, shelter and so on. They have a shortage of food while we throw food away when we feel like it. Why is it that we do this, do we have to be in their place to understand the reality. These were the things that were stressing me out. Education is very important, but also we have to understand that when our brothers and sisters are in need we have to leave everything to

> help them.
> I know Abi [mother] loves me so much, and tell her that I'm very sorry for not informing her about my decision and left the country without her blessing.[90]

Miawand never mentioned jihad in his letter. His family and community would wonder what he meant by "the path in which God has guided me." But one thing was quite clear: Miawand felt convinced that the life of ease that his family and other North Americans lived blinded them to the reality of the suffering of his brothers and sisters abroad. He also felt convinced of his duty to do something about it.

THE LIMITS OF SECULARISM

As we have seen, in examining the ideas of Al-Awlaki and their reception among the three men, an unexpected conclusion emerges: The three men's jihadist ideology could only have taken shape *after* 9/11. This is because the most important aspect of Al-Awlaki's theory of jihad was neither its embrace of ʿAzzam's claims about defending invaded Muslim lands nor its adoption of al-ʿAyayri's position that jihad is global and ongoing despite changing conditions. Rather, it was the diagnosis of—and the solution that it offered to—the War on Terror, i.e., the military campaigns in Afghanistan, Iraq, Somalia, and soon, Pakistan and Yemen. Thus, it is a mistake to see the emergence of the homegrown radical as the outgrowth of a continuing battle between radical Islam and the West that predates 9/11. Rather, the jihadist ideology of the homegrown radical was an effect of the War on Terror. The War on Terror had produced a fertile ground from which a new theory of jihad would take shape—one that was indebted to al-Qaeda's utopian jihad but was distinctly Western nonetheless. There are obvious conclusions that follow from this finding. For one, it refutes claims that something intrinsic about Islam gives rise to violence. Those who since 9/11 have sought to understand jihadism by picking up a Qur'an or classical legal text (one recalls how the Qur'an became a bestseller after 9/11) have missed the ways in which our political landscape shapes Muslim beliefs about war and peace. For another, it is a clear indictment of the War on Terror for producing the very violence it sought to eliminate. The War on Terror's casualty count not only fueled recruitment for jihadist groups in Afghanistan, Iraq, Yemen, and Somalia, but also produced the ideology that encouraged North American Muslims to rebel against their own states. Beyond these fairly straightforward conclusions, though, we can also consider what this historicization of Al-Awlaki's doctrine of jihad tells us about Islam's relationship to politics and the limits of secular governance in liberal democracies.

First, the analysis suggests that Muslim political discourse today is neither a site of systematic elaboration within North American mosques nor a site of significant consensus-building. The Winnipeg Muslim community largely eschewed normative claims about the nature of proper political authority and just war. This reluctance to develop a political theory, crucially, fostered the conditions that made new theories of jihad possible: The absence of active discussions on the nature of war and peace in Islam created a vacuum that Al-Awlaki filled. It is telling that the American Muslim scholar Yassir Qadhi, speaking with the *New York Times* in 2011, described his desire to refute Al-Awlaki by speaking more, not less, about jihad in his seminars—a move he felt powerless to make considering the state's scrutiny.[91] Although it is impossible to know for sure, I cannot help but think that if Ferid, Miawand, and Muhanad had delved into the complexity of the Islamic tradition, they would not have left. They would have found in the history of their faith too much diversity and nuance to take Al-Awlaki as an uncontested speaker of truth. They would have recognized that Islamic political thought today draws eclectically on a vast and contradictory archive.

Second, the analysis shows that successful Islamic political claims depend on their ability to speak to Muslim audiences' embodied sensibilities, ethical commitments, and theological beliefs. The three men's active cultivation of care for their brethren, their deployment of a legalistic framework to evaluate religious obligations, and their belief that divine agency intervenes in human history formed the grounds with which Al-Awlaki's theory resonated. My point here is not to raise the specter of dangerous Muslims whose religion might at any time cause them to adopt violent politics. Quite the contrary: North American Muslims overwhelmingly ignored or dismissed Al-Awlaki, at least partly because his theory offended their sensibilities about the sanctity of life, the rule of law, and the injunction against transgression in the pursuit of justice. But the analysis does have something to teach us about the limits of secular governance.

In the last decade, anthropologists of Islam have theorized secularism as a regime that sees the state continually intervene within the lives of religious communities in order to redefine the boundaries between the public secular sphere and the religious private sphere. Although influenced by Asad, Agrama's *Questioning Secularism* is the starting point of this understanding of secular governance, and Mahmood and Fernando have made impressive use of it in their ethnographies of Egyptian minority governance and French laïcité. However, this chapter's analysis shows the limits of secular liberal governance by emphasizing how passions cultivated in the private sphere can give rise to actions that threaten the state in unpredictable ways. After all, the men's ethical commitments and beliefs had once fit comfortably within a Canadian secular liberal democracy. Until they discovered Al-Awlaki, these commitments and beliefs had helped them contribute to their Muslim community and broader Canadian society. The possibility of private passions threatening the state is true of all communities within liberal democratic societies,[92] religious or not. Recall how the passions of young men formed through online discussion forums on sexual seduction methods became dangerous the moment a self-declared "incel" in Toronto intentionally drove a van into pedestrians, killing ten, on a sunny fall day in 2020.[93] Or consider how evangelical Christian passions harnessed in support of American military campaigns abroad turned dangerous the moment they were directed at the US Capitol building in January 2021.[94] Moreover, the evangelical example suggests that liberal democracies seek less to eliminate the passions that can cause violence than to direct them toward the state's ends.[95] The story of Ferid, Miawand, and Muhanad teaches us that as much as modern liberal states seek to regulate, define, and control the acceptable expression of religion, privately cultivated passions can always manifest in unexpected political actions that threaten state stability.

CONCLUSION

In the spring of 2006, Ferid, Miawand, and Muhanad discovered a little-known preacher named Anwar Al-Awlaki. With his perfect English and his ability to effortlessly quote Arabic scripture, Al-Awlaki became a favorite resource for the three young men seeking to better understand their faith. They listened to his lectures on the prophets, the life of Muhammad, and the hereafter alone and together at friends' houses. They came to trust the American preacher for his seeming erudition. But from the beginning, they also admired something else about him. They saw in Al-Awlaki a speaker of the truth. The young preacher was not afraid to call out the United States for its duplicity during the War on Terror: Whereas the United States claimed to be fighting terrorists, they often targeted ordinary Muslims or symbols of Islam (e.g., Abu Ghrayb, flushing Qur'ans down the toilet, or raiding Muslim American organizations). His claim that the United States was attacking all Muslims and even Islam itself resonated with the three men, who had witnessed increasing anti-Muslim racism in Western states.

Then Al-Awlaki's *Constants on the Path of Jihad* appeared. The three men gravitated toward it, listened to it several times, and discussed it among themselves. *Constants* spoke to their lived experience in a way that no mosque leader had previously been able to do. It addressed the madness that the War on Terror had created around them. How was it that Afghans, Iraqis, and now Somalis were being killed and occupied and Muslims worldwide remained inactive? The best of their Muslim leadership claimed that Muslims simply needed to show non-Muslims the true face of Islam, and the worst sided with the United States and its allies against Muslims. Al-Awlaki's claim that all of them were cowards attached to the dunya resonated deeply. More important still, he offered the men a solution to the devaluation of Muslim life abroad. God had promised the Muslims victory if they gave themselves wholeheartedly to his cause. Scripture and history were replete with examples of the prophets and the righteous miraculously defeating stronger foes. But even if they did not win on the battlefield, they would be victorious in another way. They would surmount their own attachment to this world and die doing what they knew was right. According to Al-Awlaki, God had commanded them to fight back, full stop. He enjoined them to die fulfilling their duty. In the spring of 2007, one year after they discovered Al-Awlaki, the three men left Winnipeg to fight jihad.

If Al-Awlaki offered a vision of the world that resonated with the three men, it was also a significant departure from the premodern legal theory of jihad. The premodern theory of jihad was based on pragmatic considerations of imperial states. To be sure, it belonged to an international order that encouraged and praised territorial expansion, but only insofar as the state was able to secure other beneficial ends for the Muslim community. Neither war nor peace were to be pursued without thinking of the consequences each would bring. In contrast, Al-Awlaki attacked contemporary Muslims who thought of war in terms of cost and benefit, denouncing their attempts to "water down" God's religion. Instead, the genealogy of his thought belonged to a modern current that saw jihad as a means to bring about a utopian or seemingly impossible victory against a disproportionately powerful opponent. This current of thought saw the obligation of defensive jihad as unconditional. For Al-Awlaki, God had commanded Muslims to pursue this utopian end. Despite its seeming impossibility, God could bring Muslims victory if they did their part.

But Al-Awlaki's vision of jihad was not simply a rehashing of the ideas of previous utopian jihadists. Even al-ʿAyayri, whose texts he comments upon, had little chance of impressing North American Muslims. His text was too removed from their lives and concerns and amounted to a stale affirmation that jihad was an obligation for all times. It failed to answer "why?" in any compelling way. Al-Awlaki not only made utopian jihadist ideas accessible to Ferid, Miawand, and Muhanad, but also shaped these ideas to resonate with their lived experience as North American Muslims living through the heyday of the War on Terror. This fact raises a troubling consequence: The discourse of jihad that led them to leave in March 2007 did not exist when al-Qaeda hijacked four airplanes on September 11, 2001. Al-Qaeda's own ideology resonated mostly with Saudis and other Arabs. As we shall see, the three men did not yet know or sympathize with much of al-Qaeda's ideology when they left Canada. Al-Awlaki had produced a distinctly North American jihadist discourse for a distinctly North American Muslim predicament.

Of course, there is nothing new in the claim that the War on Terror produced more terrorism. As war casualties increased abroad, some pundits complained that US foreign policy was driving people to support terrorism. But there is a difference between stating that the War on Terror drove people to an enemy's ideology and saying that it created this ideology itself. In the case of North American Muslims who have radicalized, the facts point to the latter. In the years after Al-Awlaki's *Constants*, several Anglophone Muslims either engaged in or attempted terrorist attacks in the United States, Canada, and the UK. When ISIS emerged, many more flocked toward it. From the Toronto 18 to the 2013 Boston Marathon Bombers, Al-Awlaki has been the constant variable connecting them. But without Bush's War on Terror, Al-Awlaki's ideas lose all salience. We must therefore conclude that the fight against homegrown terrorism is not a continuation of our fight against the September 11 hijackers but a product of the world we helped shape in its aftermath. The history of homegrown terror not only tells us about how certain political discourses came to resonate with Muslims, but also highlights the limits of secular aspirations to regulate violence in modern liberal democracies.

4

UNDER SUSPICION

TARGETING, HARASSMENT, AND ABUSE OF POWER

Jaan looks happy. Only a few months have passed since his marriage to Melanie. They met while volunteering as student peer counselors at the University of Manitoba. Melanie is from British Columbia. The daughter of an RCMP officer, she came from a practicing Evangelical family before converting to Islam in the spring of 2006. Jaan is Turkish and is from a religious upper-middle-class family in Istanbul. They were married in November. Now, it is late March 2007, and Jaan is hosting a large gathering at Melanie's house in St. Boniface to say goodbye to the Muslim friends he has made over the last four years. The couple will soon leave for Toronto. Among those gathered are University of Manitoba students and fellow Turkish friends.

I notice a group of about five or six students outside on the front porch. The porch is small, part of an older house design, common in the French quarter of Winnipeg. I join them, but the atmosphere is odd. The mirth and joyful tone that characterized the inside of Melanie's house is gone. Instead, the students are serious. Mahdi is there; so are Dawud and Sabir.

"What's going on?" I ask.

Mahdi looks at me diffidently: "Ferid, Miawand, and Muhanad left. They're gone."

"What do you mean they left? Where'd they go?"

"They've just disappeared, no one knows where they are." He pauses. "But there's suspicion that they left for jihad."

My expression changes to one of concern. I feel shaky. How can that be? I think back to four years ago, when I was studying Arabic in Syria in 2003. Stories circulated around the city about Muslims who had crossed Syria's Eastern border to fight American troops in Iraq. But I had never heard of a Canadian doing something similar. "Why do you suspect that?" I ask.

"I've been contacted by CSIS and the RCMP. They told me that Miawand left a letter to his family. He says that he's leaving because Muslims are suffering around the world. His family was worried so they contacted the police."

I keep pressing him for more info. "I don't know anything more," Mahdi tells me.

* * *

On March 6, 2007, Ferid, Muhanad, and Miawand disappeared. Where to? Initially, no one knew. The men's families and friends were perplexed and concerned. Their immediate response was a blind trust in the Canadian legal system. If some harm had come to the three men, then the police would help them as best they could. If, alternatively, they had indeed left to fight in a war zone, the police would conduct a thorough investigation and charge them for their crimes. This is how the men's families and friends understood the law to work. But as it turned out, the state did not interpret the case within conventional parameters pertaining to missing persons. Before even gathering evidence about the men's motives, the RCMP and CSIS deemed the case to be a matter of national security. In particular, CSIS (the Canadian Secret Intelligence Services) swooped down on the University of Manitoba campus to further investigate matters. They were afraid—not only of Muhanad, Miawand, or Ferid—but of the Muslims who were left behind. What if they too were radicals? What if they were part of a larger cell seeking to inflict harm on Canadian or American soil? In this chapter, we will analyze CSIS's investigation into radicalization at the University of Manitoba. But I tell the story from the perspective of the targeted Muslims, not the law agencies who investigated them. The image that emerges is one of harassment, intimidation, dissuasion from seeking legal counsel, attempts at recruitment, and punitive measures against vulnerable young Muslim men, despite a lack of credible evidence of intent to commit a crime or even sympathies with violent political groups. CSIS's tactics caused significant harm to my interlocutors without providing greater security to Canadians. As will become clear, there is reason to doubt that the experience of my interlocutors is unique. Rather, I claim that the surveillance of minorities deemed threats to national security breeds faulty intelligence and abuse of power. By *abuse of power*, I here refer to one of two things: (1) clear violations of Canadian law, and (2) actions that are difficult to justify considering the basic values of privacy and freedom expected in liberal democracies. The chapter therefore reveals the perils to rights and freedoms that result when security agencies are given a green light to pursue with abandon a possible domestic threat.

CONDITIONS RIPE FOR ABUSE: CSIS BEFORE THE WAR ON TERROR

CSIS was formed in 1984 as a response to the discrediting of an RCMP (the Royal Canadian Mounted Police) spy division. The RCMP had come under heavy scrutiny for intrusions into civilian life; among their offenses were investigations of well-established and popular political parties like the NDP and the Parti Québécois, the former for its socialism and the latter for its commitment to Quebec separatism.[1] The Macdonald Report of 1981 made several recommendations to curb abuses when gathering national intelligence. Among them was that Canada's spy agency be removed from the ambit of the RCMP and be civilianized.[2] The consequences would be twofold. First, the intelligence agency would be led by career bureaucrats rather than trained police officers. Second, the agency's mandate would be limited to intelligence gathering, being now stripped of the authority to make arrests. Another recommendation was the creation of an independent oversight body that would monitor the agency's activities and ensure it did not trespass on Canadians' rights and freedoms. The Liberal government of the time used Macdonald's recommendations to pass the CSIS Act, giving birth to a new spy agency. But despite these changes, CSIS ended up largely being a continuation of its RCMP predecessor. Historians Reginald Whitaker, Gregory Kealey, and Andrew Parnaby characterized Canada's new spy agency as "old wine in new bottles."[3] Part of the reason for this continuity was that the same individuals who had led the RCMP's spy division were now appointed to senior roles inside CSIS.

These officials traded in their police uniforms for civilian garb, but the institutional culture they knew and promoted in the RCMP came to CSIS with them—including its tendency to countenance abuse of power.

A prominent example of this abuse is the case of Suleyman Goven.[4] Goven was a Kurdish refugee who settled in Toronto in 1991. Shortly after his arrival, he co-founded and became president of the Toronto Kurdish Community Centre, which generally had favorable views of the PKK, a Kurdish organization seeking independence in Turkey. CSIS accused Goven of belonging to the PKK and of supporting its violent tactics. But it also approached Goven with an invitation for him to work with them as an informant. They threatened to have his immigration application denied if he refused. Goven rejected claims he belonged to the PKK and turned down CSIS's offer to become an informant—and, true to their word, CSIS ensured that Goven's immigration application was denied. Goven fought for many years to have his name cleared and obtain Canadian citizenship. His case became well known to the body created to oversee CSIS's activities, the Security Intelligence Review Committee (SIRC). In 2000, SIRC found that there was no credible evidence Goven was ever part of the PKK. Had the story ended here, we might conclude that SIRC provided the necessary oversight to prevent CSIS's abuses of power. But despite being proven wrong, CSIS continued to harass Goven and place considerable roadblocks on his path to citizenship. In short, CSIS attempted to coerce a vulnerable individual to become an informant, and they were vindictive when the individual refused.[5]

In the early 2000s, journalist Andrew Mitrovica expressed doubt that CSIS could successfully defend national security while respecting Canadians' rights in the new era of the War on Terror.[6] Mitrovica had extensively interviewed a former agent turned whistleblower. His informant painted a picture of an agency that was both inept and deeply corrupt: He reported that illegal searches of property were a standard agency practice and attested to intelligence leaks, also noting that the agency would use its funds for private ends.[7] Further, Mitrovica rejected contentions that SIRC or the Investigator General (also charged with overseeing CSIS activities) could effectively monitor CSIS, claiming that these oversight bodies were only privy to information that CSIS's director volunteered. Had history unfolded differently, perhaps CSIS's abuses and corruption in the late 1990s and early 2000s would have sufficiently worried the public to push elected officials to further restructure the agency. But after September 11, politicians and the public saw CSIS as more important than ever before, and thus, sizable amounts of money were directed to its coffers. By the time Ferid, Miawand, and Muhanad disappeared, CSIS's budget had more than doubled.[8] Part of that budget went to recruiting several hundred new agents, many of whom were in their early twenties and had only recently completed their undergraduate degrees. Thus, 9/11 created a perfect storm in which an agency with a questionable track record for respecting citizens' rights was given copious public funds and the state's confidence to protect Canadians against foreign and domestic threats.

It is no surprise, then, that troubling reports about CSIS's conduct during the War on Terror have emerged over the years. Judges have rebuked CSIS for seeking the detention and deportation of permanent residents based on flimsy evidence.[9] Journalists and historians have identified instances in which CSIS's information-sharing has led to the imprisonment and torture of Canadians on foreign soil.[10] And recently, former CSIS employees have sued the spy agency for the pervasive anti-Muslim racism they encountered while at work. One former employee told Canada's national broadcaster, the CBC, that her colleagues treated her as an internal threat while she performed her duties.[11] She reports being questioned on why she wore hijab and being asked to undergo a lie detector test and to cut ties with her community. We also possess SIRC reports around the time of the disappearance of Muhanad, Miawand, and Ferid that document Muslims' experiences of feeling physically threatened, abused, and intimidated during their interactions with CSIS.[12]

CSIS's attitudes toward Muslims in the post–9/11 era cannot be divorced from widespread anti-Muslim racism in North America. Scholars of Islamophobia have taught us to see anti-Muslim racism as both structural (a product of deeply entrenched social norms rather than individual belief) and systemic (embedded in social and political institutions). Legal scholar and theorist of Islamophobia, Khaled Beydoun, roots Islamophobia in the long-standing orientalist tropes that have circulated in Europe and America in different shapes and form since the nineteenth century.[13] Today, anti-Muslim racism is fueled by American and Canadian foreign policy.[14] State policies that positioned Muslims as outside enemies before and after 9/11 are responsible for producing disparaging representations of Muslims. Erik Love notes that, like other forms of racism, Islamophobia involves subjecting Muslims to essentializing traits.[15] Popular TV shows like 24 or *Homeland* and movies like *The Kingdom*, *Zero Dark Thirty*, and *American Sniper* reflect the cultural nexus between foreign policy and Islamophobia.[16] While politicians emphasized that domestic Muslim populations were not the enemy, the state nonetheless gave its security agency the power to go out and find the bad Muslims wherever they might be. Stated differently, the state gave CSIS carte blanche to live out a heroic narrative of locating the terrorist threat among a suspect Muslim population.

But what were Muslim communities' experiences with CSIS? How did CSIS's surveillance impact them? Sociologist Baljit Nagra gives us insight into Canadian Muslims' experiences with CSIS from 2004 to 2008. In her study of educated Muslim youth, she highlights young Muslims' pervasive sense of being unfairly targeted. Following the lead of studies by critical race theorists Razack and Sunera Thobani, Nagra interprets this surveillance as part of a state of exception imposed on Muslims post–9/11. Muslims, according to Nagra, were unable to fully benefit from rights afforded to fellow citizens, instead being forced to mobilize so that they might claim equal access to the Canadian nation. In her recent study of Islamophobia, *Under Siege: The 9/11 Generation*, Jasmin Zine documents the extent and impact of CSIS surveillance of campuses: "surveillance campaigns," she writes, "have targeted university campuses in ways disproportionate to demonstrated threats from these sites." Zine documents the fears, anxieties, and self-policing that CSIS surveillance of Muslims produced. She contends that Muslims who grew up in the shadow of 9/11 came to experience their presence in Canada as "a problem" for the Canadian multicultural nation.[17]

In the next two sections, we will focus on a scenario that has not drawn much attention from fellow scholars, exploring what happened when CSIS shifted from a general suspicion of Muslim communities to a state of heightened and anxious vigilance regarding a subsection of a Muslim community. What particular forms of intrusion and violence were rendered acceptable in the name of safeguarding the nation? And what long-term consequences did these forms of violence have on targeted Muslims? In pursuing this line of inquiry, my goal is not merely historical. I am interested in showing how the modern liberal state creates tolerance for intrusion and violence against citizens who are deemed threats to national security. To the extent that this is the case, perhaps CSIS's abuses of power in the last decades are not exceptional. Perhaps they are an inescapable part of the work of modern security agencies. I also want to raise the possibility that these forms of intrusion and violence are intended to reassure the nation more than actually protect it. As we shall see, CSIS did great harm to my interlocutors without the payoff of being able to say that Canadians were made safer from acts of terror.

FROM WITNESSES TO SUSPECTS

The Muslims on the University of Manitoba campus were shocked and perplexed. Most had no idea what had happened to Ferid, Miawand, and Muhanad. Then CSIS came calling. It all started in the third week of March 2007, when some students found strange cards at their doorsteps—just a name and a number, no credentials or affiliations. Others received "cold knocks" on their door at any and all hours of the day. It was the beginning of a series of persistent attempts from CSIS to gather intelligence on the Muslim campus community. I heard accounts from my friends and community members about their encounters with CSIS and saw my already marginalized and racialized community become increasingly distressed. At first, there seemed to be goodwill among the Muslim students. None of them knew anything of use in locating the three missing men, and only Mahdi and Tariq had any clue as to the three men's criminal motives. Still, campus Muslims were willing to provide CSIS with whatever information they could.

A CSIS agent named Nick showed up unannounced on campus one day to meet Dawud (the close friend and community member introduced earlier). He insisted they go out for coffee. He took Dawud to the Tim Horton's in the Student Union building. There, they sat on the greyish-white chairs attached to plastic tables in the food court, surrounded by students eager to take in a few calories before their next class. The area was open and offered little privacy from curious ears. Dawud felt uncomfortable speaking in public with a CSIS agent about possible radicals.

"How did you know the three men?"

"Mostly through the MSA [Muslim Student Association]. Miawand was my roommate last year for some time."

"Where do you think they went?"

"I don't know."

"Did you see anything suspicious?"

"No, nothing. I mean we haven't seen them around campus much in the last three months or so. But when I did see them, there was nothing strange."

Dawud, like other young Muslim men, was under the mistaken impression that CSIS's questions were aimed at uncovering the mystery of the men's disappearance and thus, despite his discomfort, he cooperated with them. In reality, CSIS was less interested in the three men than in the interviewees themselves. After the first two meetings, Nick stopped asking Dawud about Ferid, Miawand, and Muhanad. He now focused his attentions on Dawud himself. He wanted to know if Dawud was like Ferid, Miawand, and Muhanad—a Winnipeg radical. "He would start off being friendly," Dawud recalls, "and then after casual conversation, he would try to hit me with a question to throw me off. He would ask me, 'What do you think about the war in Iraq?' 'What do you think about al-Qaeda?' 'What do you think about jihad?'"

CSIS had begun to subject Dawud to what the agency calls "targeting." As the Canadian national security expert Stephanie Carver explains, CSIS's activities are structured around the practice of targeting. Targeting refers to a process by which CSIS identifies a person of interest and begins to investigate them to determine whether they constitute a threat. Carver notes that targeting can take place with or without a court warrant, depending on the level of surveillance CSIS deems necessary, e.g., wiretapping, intercepting emails, etc.[18] If CSIS comes to believe that a target has broken the law, the RCMP takes over the investigation. Carver's exposition of CSIS practices makes clear that targeting takes place *before* the threshold of suspicion needed for law enforcement to investigate the commission of a crime has been reached. Unsurprisingly, then, targeting leads to a high level of intrusion into the lives of a number of targets who justifiably feel that such attention is unwarranted. Dawud, for his part, felt judged and unfairly treated. "I was not the one who left or did anything illegal," he reflects. "Why are they suddenly assuming that I condone violence?"

But CSIS's targeting of Dawud was also instrumental. Nick saw Dawud as a means to target Winnipeg Muslims more generally. Nick subsequently turned to asking Dawud about the wider Muslim community. "They tried to turn me into an informant. They started asking me, 'Do you know so and so? What do you think about them? Have you heard anything strange about them?' They asked me to attend conferences for them and to sit in on the Friday prayer and pass on the contents of what was said." Respected community leaders were often objects of questioning, seemingly targeted for their prominence within the Muslim community. This did not sit well with Dawud, who knew that service to one's Muslim community could not be equated with potential radicalization. At one point, CSIS explicitly crossed the line into illegal activities by asking Dawud to steal a cell phone belonging to another community member so they could scan its contents. Dawud's experience highlights how CSIS's investigation into the three missing men really became an investigation into the Winnipeg Muslim community, and particularly its campus population.

Depending on one's perspective, CSIS's actions can be considered either unfair or necessary. On the one hand, collective suspicion can subject a community to unmerited scrutiny.[19] Why would the actions of three individuals place the entire Muslim community under the microscope? On the other, it is easy to rationalize the agency's new focus on young Winnipeg Muslim men. If radicalization involves the sharing of an ideology, then national security agencies must ask who transmitted this ideology to the three men, who shares this ideology, how widespread it is, and whether there are members of this community who are trying to put this ideology into action.[20] Layth, a long-standing member of the Winnipeg Muslim community and an annual youth camp organizer, endorsed the legitimacy of intelligence-gathering: "I believe in the mandate. Intelligence gathering keeps us safe. Every community has its radicals and we're no different. So it's important [CSIS] investigates."

But through my research, I identified a disconnect between those Muslims who have interacted with CSIS and those who have had the luxury of remaining off its radar. CSIS had not contacted Layth at the time of my conversation with him, but has frequently contacted Layth's close friend Kareem. Why? Was Kareem a particularly shifty person? No, rather, Kareem has held official positions within the structure of the Manitoba Islamic Association and has often delivered Friday sermons to the congregation. His prominence made him a person of interest. Kareem told me how CSIS would encourage him to cast doubt upon members of his community. "They just did not accept when I told them I don't know much about a person. [I told them,] 'Unless you want me to break into his house looking for clues, I've already told you what I know.'" After several meetings, Kareem felt compelled to break off ties with CSIS: "They were becoming too pushy, insisting I rat out people that haven't done anything." The perception that CSIS's tactics are harmful to Muslims without being useful to national security is pervasive among Winnipeg's Muslims. Zayd, a former president of the Manitoba Islamic Association, reported that when he was first elected, his fellow Board members dissuaded him from speaking to CSIS, citing the agency's ill-will toward their community. "When I asked them if I should help CSIS, someone told me, 'Why bother? We have the police. If I see something suspicious or illegal happening in our Muslim community, I'll go straight to the police, but I wouldn't go to them.'" Zayd's story reflects a common sentiment among Winnipeg Muslims that there is a chasm between the ideal of national security, meant to protect us all, and the reality, which has harmed Muslims often without increasing Canadians' security.

This chasm should elicit little surprise when we factor in two considerations. First, national security work seeks to *prevent* rather than prosecute crime. But as Arun Kundnani explains, a preventative model of policing relies less on evidence than on projections: It depends on profiling what type of person would have a propensity to commit a particular crime.[21] The margin of error is therefore much greater than in conventional police investigations.[22] Second, and closely related, my data suggest that association was the foremost means by which CSIS identified potential Muslim suspects. In particular, young Muslim men who were friends, roommates, or collaborated in community events with one or more of the three young men were scrutinized. The closer CSIS thought that an individual was to Ferid, Miawand, and Muhanad, the more intense its scrutiny. But it takes little reflection to see that association is a problematic basis for discerning wrongdoing, relying on an assumption that only radicals work, live with, or befriend radicals.[23] It is unsurprising that association as the basis for determining guilt has long been rejected in Anglo-American law. Our legislation is cautious not to convict individuals based on mere association.[24] Typically, helping in some way to commit a crime, like aiding and abetting, is necessary to arrest someone. Even Canada's anti-terrorism legislation requires an individual's participation in activities that further the ends of a terrorist organization to secure a conviction. Thus, while association might be cause for some investigation, it more often than not leads to dead ends.

Indeed, none of my interlocutors were ever charged with crimes. The RCMP, who ran its parallel investigation with immeasurably greater restraint and, to use my interlocutors' terminology, "professionalism," would eventually claim that Ferid, Miawand, and Muhanad acted alone and were not "radicalized" through their Muslim acquaintances. CSIS seemed to overlook that Muslims in Winnipeg had various reasons for associating with the three men. Some simply wanted to partake in a Muslim community on campus. Others lived by an ethos of sister- and brotherhood wherein they showed basic courtesy and care to all Muslims they encountered. I know of only three individuals who were even exposed to the men's growing affinity for Al-Awlaki's theory of jihad. Ferid, Miawand, and Muhanad guarded that information from others, knowing that their community would oppose the theory. Thus, CSIS's methods showed an inability to appreciate the different ties that bind Muslims together. In the end, their assumptions led to the targeting of vulnerable racialized young men rather than advancing national security.

But how then did CSIS's investigation impact young Muslim men on the University of Manitoba campus? In the next section, we turn to the story of Mahdi. I show that CSIS tactics involved harassment, intimidation, and punitive measures. These tactics severely affected young Muslim men's livelihood, social ties, mental health, and mobility.

THE CONSEQUENCES OF TARGETING: MAHDI'S STORY

Mahdi came to the University of Manitoba in 2005 to pursue an undergraduate degree in science. He arrived with dreams of someday studying medicine. Mahdi is Somali, and like many Somalis, he came to Canada as a refugee from a war-torn land.[25] His family settled in Toronto; they rented an apartment on Dixon Road, an area known as Little Mogadishu. I can only imagine how much Mahdi's family sacrificed for him to attend a university in the middle of the prairies, or how difficult it was for Mahdi to work his way through university. In the years between his arrival at the University of Manitoba and the departure of the three men, Mahdi became very close to Muhanad. It was not hard to see what they would like in each other. They both liked movies, the latest electronics, and loved to laugh. They were both "goofy," for lack of a better word. They became roommates and even traveled to China together in the summer of 2006. In the months before March 2007, Mahdi lived with Muhanad and Miawand. More than anyone else, Mahdi was privy to the men's increasing interest in Al-Awlaki's lectures on jihad. But even still, he never thought this interest would translate into action. Perhaps he was naïve at the time, but he saw their interest as the result of their opposition to the War on Terror and their curiosity about the legal tradition of jihad. When the three men left, Mahdi was devastated.

Mahdi's closeness to Muhanad raised suspicions among CSIS officers. CSIS agents interviewed him throughout March and into exam season in April. Mahdi answered their questions as best he could. He soon left for Toronto, where he hoped he would find solace with his family after the pain of losing a close friend. But this search for solace was interrupted: CSIS agents soon began to visit Mahdi once more. They believed that Mahdi was concealing information and feared he might be a threat to national security. As a result, they sought to pressure him into revealing what he knew about the three men and divulging his own radical ideas. But these tactics made Mahdi's life very difficult. CSIS agents began interviewing Mahdi's neighbors and fellow Somali community members. The Somali community on Dixon Road, which was associated with drugs and gang violence, was already heavily policed. The community did not want this additional scrutiny. Through their questioning, CSIS cast doubt on Mahdi's moral character. They intimated that he was a radical and could not be trusted. Fairly soon, Mahdi was ostracized: "They turned my community against me," he says. It is difficult to imagine that CSIS did not recognize the social vulnerability of Somalis in Little Mogadishu. More likely, they tried to use this vulnerability for their own ends. By showing Mahdi their ability to tarnish his reputation among his community, officers hoped to pressure him to talk.

The persistence with which CSIS targeted Mahdi overwhelmed him. He remembers that CSIS agents often parked in front of his apartment building, waiting for him to come out. He lived with the anxiety that every time he left his home, CSIS agents might approach him. He began to feel watched at every corner. "One time, I went to my aunt's home. A man and woman came into the elevator with me but left on a different floor. I had a strange feeling they were following me so when I got into my aunt's apartment, I looked through the peephole. Sure enough, they were there waiting for me." On another occasion, Mahdi was going out with a group of friends when CSIS intercepted them and announced they would join the group for dinner. At the restaurant, Mahdi had to listen to CSIS questioning his friends about his character.

Another of CSIS's tactics was to threaten Mahdi's livelihood. CSIS agents came to know of Mahdi's aspiration to study medicine. They therefore contacted the dean of the faculty of medicine at a university in Ontario and asked him to speak to Mahdi on their behalf. The request must have seemed odd. Mahdi was still an undergrad and had not yet applied to med school. But the dean obliged and called Mahdi. The dean asked Mahdi if he could facilitate a conversation between Mahdi and CSIS agents. Mahdi, immensely embarrassed, politely declined. He understood CSIS agents' attempts as intimidation, as though they were telling Mahdi, "Cooperate or we can derail your future."

But Mahdi's most painful memory was when CSIS agents decided to escalate their interview methods. Mahdi recalls how CSIS agents pulled up on the sidewalk and aggressively told him to get into the car. Mahdi complied, feeling he had no choice. The agents took him to a hotel where several CSIS agents were waiting in a boardroom. They had determined that this would be the day that Mahdi would finally tell them what he knew about the three missing men. As the questioning progressed, Mahdi's answers did not satisfy them. He did not know where the men were or why they had gone. Eventually, the agent interviewing Mahdi stood up, towering over the twenty-year-old, his face red and his fists pounding the table: "How do you not know anything?!" His body language and demeanor became increasingly threatening and Mahdi began to fear for his safety as the agent pounded the table and advanced toward Mahdi. "You're going to tell me! You're going to tell me!" Feeling afraid and alone, Mahdi began sobbing and buried his face in his hands. The man's peers eventually asked him to step outside. Reflecting back on this experience as a mature adult, Mahdi wondered, "How could they feel proud of themselves doing this to a kid? I was nineteen or twenty years old. I knew nothing about the world and these grown men felt they had the right to pick me up, isolate me in a location of their choice, and intimidate me."

Hearing Mahdi relay this story today is not easy. Mahdi exudes simultaneously an air of bravado and vulnerability. He characterizes the agent as having lost all dignity even as his voice betrays the painful memory of the fear and intimidation he felt himself. We may wonder why Mahdi did not seek legal counsel throughout his ordeal. Had he done so, he would have likely been spared some of his hardships. But lawyers are expensive, and twenty-year-old children of refugee communities are not in a position to easily hire one. Besides, Mahdi was not charged with a crime. What could a lawyer do for him, he thought to himself.

At some point during the summer, Mahdi could tolerate no more. He learnt that he could call the police if CSIS harassed him. He mustered the courage to go downstairs and speak to the agents parked in front of his building. He told them he was done talking to them and would call the police if they did not leave him alone. The agents grudgingly obliged, but not before uttering some final haunting words: "Just wait. You'll see what will happen."[26] What did the officers mean by this, Mahdi wondered as he regained his composure and went back inside. A few months later, Mahdi decided to travel to the state of New York on vacation. The border is not far from Toronto and he intended to cross it by car. As Mahdi pulled his vehicle up to the border, he handed his passport to the US customs officer. "As soon as he scanned my passport," Mahdi recounts, "a group of officers surrounded my vehicle with their guns drawn." Mahdi was then placed in a small room where he was strip-searched and held overnight. "I was brought back to Canada in handcuffs." He continues, "Do you know what something like that does to a person? Especially at that age?"[27]

Mahdi's experience with CSIS left him with deep scars: "I was depressed for years." Mahdi had lost the support of his Somali community, he no longer wanted to associate with a Muslim community, and he still had deep trust issues, worried that any friend, old or new, might be recruited by CSIS to monitor him. He constantly worried that CSIS agents would reappear. It took years of therapy for Mahdi to get back on his feet. And, despite expending great resources, CSIS abandoned their interest in him. It seems Mahdi really was not a threat or a relevant source of information after all. Mahdi has never been charged with a crime and today would be considered a productive member of society.

In presenting Mahdi's story, my aim has been to convey a picture of CSIS tactics and their impact on Muslim Canadians. Among my interviewees, CSIS's attention to Mahdi was exceptionally intense, likely a product of his closeness to Muhanad and his socioeconomic vulnerability. Nonetheless, many discussants reported encountering similar tactics from Canada's spy agency. They spoke of threats to their livelihood when CSIS would show up unannounced at their workplace. They spoke of being dissuaded from seeking legal counsel. They spoke of CSIS agents' attempts to embarrass them in front of their family, friends, peers, and roommates. They spoke of harassment. Importantly, this language of harassment was not only theirs. It was also the word that CSIS's then director Jim Judd employed to describe his agency's behavior. A Wikileaks cable reveals that in speaking to the US Counsellor to the Department of State, Eliot Cohen, in 2008, Judd had affirmed that "CSIS had responded to recent, non-specific intelligence on possible terror operations by 'vigorously harassing' known Hezbollah members in Canada."[28] Harassment is here a badge of honor for Judd. The director presumes that it is directed at suspects so loathsome that they are not to be afforded their typical legal rights. In fact, Judd complained to his American counterpart about the roadblocks that Canadian courts had created during the War on Terror. For Judd and his subordinates, the law was not the source of proper parameters for ensuring fair treatment of citizens while pursuing national security. Nor was the law a means of making certain that evidence against a possible terrorist suspect could actually withstand scrutiny. Rather, the law was a lamentable impediment to finding those who would want to harm Canadian interests. Judd's attitude reveals two things: first, the confidence with which CSIS deemed the people it harassed national security threats, and second, the desire to push against the customary boundaries that limit state intrusion in people's lives.[29]

CONCLUSION

This chapter has used the investigation of Winnipeg Muslim men in the wake of Ferid's, Miawand's, and Muhanad's disappearance to shed light on CSIS's surveillance tactics and their impact on Muslim communities during the War on Terror. Past academic studies have shown that CSIS generally saw the Muslim community as an object of suspicion. CSIS sought to monitor community leaders and recruit informants within the Muslim community. But an event like the disappearance of Ferid, Miawand, and Muhanad triggered a heightened state of disquiet that manifested in what the agency called the "targeting" of young Muslim men. In particular, CSIS's method was to identify possible threats on the basis of association: Closeness to a radical was interpreted as a sign of radicalization. A few Muslims in Winnipeg approved of CSIS's work. Investigating radicals keeps us all safe, they told me. But these interlocutors rarely had much contact with CSIS. In contrast, those who encountered CSIS were typically critical of their tactics. They felt harassed, willfully embarrassed, and threatened. We have seen a prominent example of these tactics in the case of Mahdi.

Though the tactics deployed against young Winnipeg Muslim men had a severe impact on the lives of my interlocutors, they did not make Canadians safer, as the RCMP would later confirm. This lack of payoff for intrusion into citizens' lives is not surprising. As we have seen, association is often a shaky basis for suspecting wrongdoing, particularly when security agents have little familiarity with the ties that bind a community's members together. Moreover, CSIS's mandate to prevent crimes before their commission gave it wide latitude to continue targeting individuals long after the trail of evidence had run dry. In fact, those I spoke with often told me that it seemed as if CSIS had developed a desire to punish its Muslim suspects. It is difficult not to see CSIS's actions as reflecting a culture in which all Muslims were perceived as enemies of the state, deserving of ridicule and hardship. Considering that abuse of power has been endemic to CSIS and to its RCMP forerunner, it is plausible that this abuse is an inescapable feature of national security work in modern liberal democracies. By granting these security agencies a mandate to continually surveil communities without evidence of wrongdoing, liberal democratic states create conditions for abuse. And this abuse takes place despite the existence of oversight bodies like SIRC or the Inspector General who are sometimes kept in the dark about the details of investigations and sometimes accept CSIS tactics for the security of the nation. Thus, although the state apparatus imposes nominal guardrails against certain abuses of power, that same state apparatus also enables the wide array of abuses of power that occur within its prescribed limits. It is difficult to imagine that such intrusions and violence against Canadians would be accepted if they could not be circumscribed by race or religion. So long as other Canadians could feel immune from the forms of intrusion that Muslims suffered, the narrative that CSIS tactics made us all safer was sufficient to create general public acceptance that they should continue.

POSTSCRIPT: BORDER WOES

I did not know Mahdi's story until I interviewed him in the winter of 2021. But throughout the spring of 2007, I did see my fellow community members become increasingly troubled by CSIS's interviews. I remember receiving an email from one of them attempting to alert fellow campus Muslims of their rights. The tone was one of panic. Throughout this period, I watched from the sidelines, never suffering the indignities of my peers. I was privileged in ways I did not recognize back then. When Nick eventually called me asking for an interview, I had resources others did not. For one, my brother was a police officer. He advised me to decline to speak to the agents:

"You're under no legal obligation to speak to them," he told me. "Doing so will needlessly create a file on you." For another, my family possessed social capital. My mother came from a family of lawyers and my father was a university professor. I told Nick over the phone that I did not know anything and could not help him. For the next year, I went on with my life. No harassment, no intimidation, and no threats to my livelihood. That was that. The end of a sordid episode that did not concern me. Or so I thought.

* * *

July 2008. Aziza is crying. This isn't right, I tell myself. She's only fifteen years old. The US Customs officers are going through our luggage. I am seated with Sadaf in a waiting room. I look across the room: My eyes meet those of Sadaf's father, then Sadaf's mother. They are confused and worried. They don't understand what is happening. But I have no answers. I don't understand either. Sadaf and I had collected our tickets from the KLM booth and made our way to US Customs. I gave my passport to the customs officer, but something was off when he scanned it. The customs officer had suddenly become very aggressive, his voice betraying a mixture of anger and suspicion. "Wait in here," he told us. "Are you traveling with someone else?"

"Yes. My wife's parents and sister. They're waiting for us at the boarding gate."

The customs officer turned to his colleagues: "Go get them. Get their luggage. We'll check it all."

A few minutes later, Sadaf's parents and sister entered the waiting room, a concerned expression on their faces. "Sit over there," they were told coldly. Three customs officers began to go through our luggage.

As time passed, I watched Officer Smith, the customs officer who scanned my passport, talking about me to his superiors on the phone. He read information from his computer. I looked at the clock: 2:30 pm. Our flight was to leave in twenty-five minutes. I started to worry. Sadaf's parents had organized a special two-week trip for the family. We were to land in Istanbul and spend a few days in Turkey.[30] Then it was off to Athens, Santorini, and finally Rome. What would happen if we missed our flight? Aziza must have been wondering the same thing. I saw her stand up to ask, "Excuse me, do you know when we will be able to leave?" Before she could finish her sentence, the customs officer yelled, "Sit back down, or I'll arrest you!" That's when I saw Aziza begin to cry.

I feel intensely embarrassed. My wife's family is being mistreated because my passport was flagged. What will they think of me? I look at the clock slowly ticking. It passes 2:55 pm. Our flight is gone. I contemplate the uncomfortable burden of having ruined our family's vacation. Still we wait. Finally, at 3:30 pm, Officer Smith tells me to follow him into a small office. "Do you know why you've been stopped."

"No," I answer, shaking my head.

"Do you know who Ferid Imam, Miawand Yar, and Muhanad Al Farekh are?"

So this is about them? I say to myself in disbelief. "Yes, they went to my university."

"And why are they in our system?" he asks.

Shouldn't he know? Why is he asking me?

"What do you know about them?" he continues.

"I know that they left Canada last year. From what I've heard they left for Pakistan. The Canadian government is worried that they might have gone to fight US and Canadian troops in Afghanistan." Officer Smith writes down what I tell him. "But what does this have to do with me?" I ask.

"It says here that they traveled to join a terrorist organization. It says that you might have traveled with them. That's why you're flagged in our system."

"Okay, well this is all a misunderstanding then. I traveled with them months *before* they left for Pakistan. We went on a pilgrimage to Mecca. And anyways, I didn't really travel *with* them. We didn't plan or coordinate our travels together. You don't choose who you go to Mecca with. It's like a cruise: If you're on a cruise, you don't choose your fellow passengers. Or a hotel: If you're in a hotel, you don't choose the other hotel guests. The pilgrimage group brought students together from all over Canada. I was one of hundreds to travel with a company based in Ottawa. We all met up in Toronto to leave for Saudi Arabia. If I had truly traveled with them, why didn't we take the same flight to Toronto? Why did I stay overnight at my aunt's house while they all stayed in a hotel?"

Officer Smith registers what I tell him. "It's called the hajj, right? The pilgrimage? I knew people who did the hajj." Officer Smith is Black. As a Black American, he has likely had more contact with Muslims than his white peers have.

"Yes, the hajj," I say.

He continues: "So, listen, this is what will happen. You are not going to be able to fly through the US today. You're not on the no-fly list and we are not officially barring you from entry into the US. But we're going to need to fingerprint you and you're going to sign a form that says that you withdraw your application to enter the US. You can try to apply for a US visa to see if it solves your situation. For now, if you still want to go to Turkey, you'll have to find a different route, one that doesn't involve a stopover at a US airport."

I look at Officer Smith with furrowed eyebrows. I want to say something. I have to say something—anything. My sense of dignity depends upon it. "You know, at the very least, you could have been polite."

"Sorry, I'm not following?" Officer Smith replies.

I continue in a moralistic and indignant but measured tone. "You could have shown us basic courtesy. You didn't need to speak to me and my family harshly. You could have gathered this information by speaking to me normally. You guys made my sister-in-law cry, all because I went on a pilgrimage two years ago and three people who *might* have done something wrong happened to be there?"

Officer Smith reflects on my words. I suspect he's seen this before: Muslims being barred from travel based on suspicions alone. He softens up: "Listen, I got a family too. I got a job to do to take care of them. That's all I'm doing. I'm not here to be polite. I'm here to do my job."[31] Despite defending himself, Officer Smith's tone changes for the rest of our interaction.

Another customs officer enters the room. I see his name tag: "Schumacher." Officer Smith tells Schumacher that we're done. Schumacher radios the RCMP to escort me out. I feel vulnerable thinking about my own country's collusion in my ordeal. I hear Schumacher say into his radio, "I'm escorting the terrorist suspect out now." Schumacher's words sting. Deeply. There is a giddiness in his voice. He's excited to be protecting his country. Getting the bad guy. He lacks Officer Smith's doubts or self-reflection. My family-in-law is waiting outside

US Customs. I don't know what to say. I feel paralyzed, crippled by my thoughts and emotions. What is there to say, really?

We arrive at my parents-in-law's home. I am determined to fix this. Thoughts run through my mind frantically: "The US has the facts wrong because I didn't speak to CSIS. Oh God, I'm so stupid. CSIS wasn't calling me to find information about those three guys. They were calling to find information about me. How could they think I was a threat? Regardless, I gave them no reason to dispel their suspicions. It's okay, the US just needs to know that I didn't make travel plans with those guys. They need to understand how the hajj works."

I call Sabir. "Sabir, I need the contact info for Nick, the CSIS agent. Do you have it? It's urgent." Sabir gives me Nick's number. I hope he'll answer; the work day is already over. The line rings.

"Hello."

"Hi, Nick, it's Youcef Soufi. I don't know if you remember me. You called me last year to discuss Ferid Imam, Miawand Yar, and Muhanad Al Farekh. Listen, I was at the airport today on my way to Turkey. I had a stopover in Minneapolis but US Customs prevented me from flying. They think I traveled with Ferid, Miawand, and Muhanad to Pakistan. It seems you guys have sent the US an unclear message. You know I never traveled with them to Pakistan. I'm happy to sit down with you and give you information. Either way, you've got to communicate with them the right facts about me."

I'm interrupted by Nick's chuckle. "Youcef, sorry, you're on your own with the US. But I'm always happy to get information from you. Any time, man." Nick laughs again. I feel my stomach drop. He doesn't care about my predicament. He's relishing this moment. Is this payback for not talking to him last year? Could he really be that petty?

* * *

That day at Winnipeg Airport is seared in my memory. I had never before, nor have I since, felt so humiliated. My sister-in-law crying. My parents-in-law's concerned expressions. Schumacher's accusatory declaration. Nick's laugh. There was the indignity of being called a terrorist suspect. Then, there was the indignity of CSIS's disregard for my predicament. I could easily prove I had never traveled to Pakistan with the three men, but what did it matter if my own government fed inaccuracies to the United States about me? But the greatest humiliation was the pain the episode caused to Sadaf's family. Sadaf and I had only been married for a year at that point. I still barely knew her parents. I worried about what they would think of me. And I felt horribly about the cost of the tickets they had lost. Eighteen years have passed since that day. It is a sign of their immense graciousness that they have never once reproached me for the money they lost. I don't even know the sum, though I suspect it exceeded ten thousand dollars.

As the years wore on, the humiliation I experienced began to matter less to me than my actual inability to travel to the United States. Initially, I thought I would easily remedy the situation, regardless of Nick's indifference. I contacted a member of Parliament for whom I had interned three summers earlier. I contacted an RCMP officer who had led the investigation into the three men's disappearance. I contacted a lawyer who had experience with Muslims being unable to cross the border. They all tried to help. But ultimately, I was a Canadian citizen and as such I had little recourse against the United States' decision. The United States is a sovereign state and can deny me or any other foreigner entry within its territory without justification. My avenues of recourse ran dry. I had no need to vacation in the United States, but the impact on my livelihood was immense. I was about to apply for PhD programs when the episode at the Winnipeg airport took place. I could no longer consider US schools. During my PhD years at the University of Toronto, I could not attend the annual conferences of large academic associations like the American Academy of Religion or the Middle Eastern Studies Association. Still today, I have not met most US scholars of Islamic law in person, despite the relatively small size of our field. And when I finished my PhD, I was barred from the US market where most of my fellow Canadian colleagues had found employment in previous years.

Throughout this period, I sometimes harbored hopes that my border woes would pass.[32] During the Obama years, the US Department of Homeland Security created a redress process for individuals wrongly prevented from traveling. From 2014 to 2016, I could travel to the United States. I began to attend conferences. I thought my ordeal was behind me. The timing was just right too: In 2016, I was about to defend my thesis and look for employment opportunities across North America. But then the threat of ISIS made the US Department of Homeland Security extra cautious. Terrorist attacks in Europe, followed by those in San Bernardino and Miami, made any security risk unpalatable. And though I had once been cleared to travel, I was now back on one of the United States' watchlists. In the eyes of the United States, I was and will always be someone whose own government found them sufficiently suspicious to share information on them with a foreign state.

I present my experience with travel to the United States for two reasons. First, I want to corroborate my interviewees' experiences at the US border with the greatest possible level of intimacy and detail.[33] Second, I want to draw attention to the broad power and discretion accorded to CSIS and the RCMP in sharing information about Muslim citizens.

For the longest time, I thought CSIS had passed on information to the United States because I had refused to speak to Nick. I kicked myself for listening to my brother. I should have met with CSIS agents rather than leave them in the dark. I might have been within my legal rights, but I gave Nick reason to act vindictively. But then I discovered that others were in the same boat, regardless of their cooperation with CSIS. In particular, Sabir's situation mirrored mine. He too had gone on the hajj trip with Ferid, Miawand, and Muhanad. He too ended up being unable to travel to the United States. He too would face consequences to his livelihood. His willingness to provide CSIS with the information it wanted did not mean the Canadian state would protect him from US-imposed travel restrictions. The context that shaped both of our experiences goes back, predictably, to 9/11 and the War on Terror. CSIS has an obligation under the Smart Border Declaration to share information on security threats with the United States. After 9/11, the US government worried that a terrorist threat could enter American soil through Canada, and the Smart Border Declaration was a means to mollify its anxieties. In principle, the sharing of information makes sense. It can potentially keep both countries safe. But in practice, the lack of oversight meant that there was no standard for determining what was deemed sufficient evidence to warn the United States about a Canadian citizen. In fact, there was no oversight to ensure that the evidence was even correct. Over the course of my research, I would find several other Muslims, some of whom were acquaintances of other terrorist suspects, who were also unable to travel to or through the United States. A pattern emerged in which "association"—sometimes tenuous—acted as a basis for the inability to travel. I also discovered that these discussants were not only barred from entering the United States: For many, US airspace (including emergency landings) was also off limits, making it difficult to travel to any destination outside Canada. There is something deeply disturbing about the ease with which Canadian agencies—both CSIS and the RCMP—could send information to the United States that would place serious barriers on the life pursuits of Canadian citizens.

As the years have gone by, my sense of frustration, powerlessness, and anxiety over border woes has shifted to resignation. I often think about the extreme violence that the War on Terror has caused: the bombing of civilians, the kidnappings of Canadians (euphemistically called extraordinary rendition), the entrapment of young Muslims by security agencies, the torture of innocent people.[34] In a sense, neither I nor my interlocutors have much to complain about. We have succeeded in making good lives for ourselves, despite this hurdle to our mobility. But our experience is not divorced from a larger system of violence. Nick's chuckles, the CSIS agent who threatened Mahdi, the request that Dawud steal someone's phone—all these were rendered possible by the identification of Muslims as a potential fifth column. These examples reveal why more extreme forms of violence against Muslims took place during the War on Terror. They gesture toward the permission granted to security agencies to harm Muslim citizens unburdened by the customary strictures of due process.

5

"I WANT OUT"

DISILLUSIONMENT WITH UTOPIAN JIHAD

2008. The dishes are almost done. I hug Sadaf, holding her tight. She senses something is wrong. "What are you thinking about?" she asks.

"Those guys."

She nods her head, registering my answer. I stare out our basement suite window. They left six months ago. I wonder how they are. I wonder where they are. I believe the RCMP's story that they left to join a militant organization, but I am not sure what happened afterward. I think about how we all left Winnipeg, but under very different circumstances.

"You know, Sadaf, I have these waking dreams sometimes when I see them. I see them as farmers somewhere in Central Asia, maybe Tajikistan. I imagine that when they got to Afghanistan, they saw that things were different than what they expected. They saw that politics is messy and that the war isn't what they thought it would be. I imagine that they sought a way out. But they knew they couldn't come back to Canada. So they crossed a border northward and they found a village where no one would care about state immigration laws or bureaucracies. A little village in the middle of nowhere where people farm and pray and live simply. I see them married with little children with Tajik features. They have lots of kids, of course, to help them plow their fields and pick fruits from their orchards. They are happy among their Muslim brothers and sisters. They found the peace they couldn't have here."

"That's a beautiful thought," Sadaf says.

"Is it?" I sigh wistfully. "I suppose I'm just deluding myself." I pause again. "You know what makes me most sad? I know that Ferid and Miawand must have been committed to going. They were hardheaded, both of them. I know that I couldn't have convinced them to stay. But Muhanad was different. Muhanad heeded the words of others. Had I been able to talk to him, had I known what they were up to, I could have shown him a different path. I know he would have listened. I know he wouldn't have gone. That eats at me sometimes."

* * *

After they left, we were in the dark about what had happened to them. For years, I wondered if we would ever find out. I rarely saw the other guys from the Muslim Student Association (MSA). The summer after Ferid, Miawand, and Muhanad left, Sadaf and I got married and we moved to Victoria, British Columbia, so I could pursue a master's degree in political science. When the MSA group did get together, Ferid, Miawand, and Muhanad would inevitably come up. We shared bits and pieces of news fed to us by the RCMP or CSIS. After a while, though, there was nothing more to say.

When Muhanad's trial took place, the prosecution gathered information on the case from the four corners of the globe: emails to family members, testimonies from al-Qaeda trainees, letters obtained through obscure CIA channels. A reasonably clear narrative of what happened to the three men before Muhanad's capture in 2014 emerged. To my sorrow, the story of the three men did not end with a quiet life in the countryside of Tajikistan. There would be no happy ending to this story. But while Muhanad might never have made it to Tajikistan, we will see that he did want out at some point. He eventually became disillusioned with armed resistance. His disillusionment took place in the context of a recognition that his life hopes and aspirations could no longer be fulfilled by a life in a jihadist organizaton. Muhanad's desire to abandon jihad reflects his realization that ideology could not replace politics. In this chapter, we will trace the journey of the three men in the border region of Pakistan and Afghanistan, from their immersion in jihadist ideology to Muhanad's search for a way out. My aim is to complicate our understanding of jihadist ideology. Against the view that positions jihadist ideology as a type of brainwashing or virus that turns individuals into automatons by indoctrinating them into an extremist worldview, I show that jihadists continue to think through and reassess the merits of the ideology they have come to embrace.[1] As an ideology, jihadism is subject to the same type of rethinking as any other set of ideas. And jihadists are just as vulnerable to amending or abandoning their view of the world as any other human.

BEFORE IT'S TOO LATE: COMPETING VIEWS OF JIHAD

The three men tried to cover their tracks as best they could. But family is family, and they could not leave without saying goodbye and ensuring their closest relatives knew they were well. In this section, we will examine the three men's continued correspondence with their families. In doing so, it will become clear that the men did not yet subscribe to two pervasive claims of the modern utopian ideology of jihad: that Muslims who reject contemporary jihadist groups are deviant or hypocritical,[2] and that all Westerners, including civilians, are enemies of Muslims.[3] Rather, we shall see that the three men expressed a continued sense of responsibility to their families and to the Canadian society they had left behind. This view would eventually change as they immersed themselves in their militant organization.

The week after the three men left, Ferid sent a final message to his family, assuring them that he was safe and affirming his enduring love for them:

> Assalaamu-alaikum everyone.
> Al-hamdullillah [praise be to God] everything is working out well. I am doing fine. Just keep praying to Allah that He accepts from me this effort. I am constantly keeping you in my dua's [prayers] that Allah guides us for the ultimate success, that is Jannah [paradise]. And I hope that you got my letter that I sent you in [a] usb. [Jalal][4] should have received it. If you did not get it please take care of my debts.
> This is probably the last email you'll receive and I ask Allah to make us a family in Jannah like He has made us a family in this life.
> Wassalaam [and peace], Ferid[5]

The tone of the email is heavy and ambiguous. Ferid discloses neither where he is nor what he is doing. All he says about his actions is that his intentions are oriented toward God (using the Arabic *Allah*). Though he is not asking his family's permission for his undertaking, he is nonetheless asking them to pray that God accepts his actions. But why is Ferid uncertain about God's acceptance of his choice? The answer is not evident. Perhaps he has doubts about the religious correctness of taking up arms with a Muslim militant organization. After all, he knows that most Muslims would see him as misguided for doing so. Alternatively, perhaps his uncertainty stems from knowing that he will cause his family heartbreak, or that he might harm innocent people in the pursuit of a perceived higher good. Or, finally, perhaps Ferid is worried about the purity of his intentions in participating in war. Within the Islamic tradition, right intentions are key to the proper performance of pious deeds.[6] If his deed is not done for the sake of God, then regardless of its legitimacy, he may be laying down his life in vain. Whatever his reason, the letter shows that Ferid has no ill-will toward his family. He considers his family good Muslims and asks for their prayers, despite knowing that they will disapprove of his choice. This attitude toward his family reveals that Ferid had not fully accepted Al-Awlaki's disparaging view of Muslims who disagreed with the necessity of taking up arms against the United States and its allies: Al-Awlaki saw these Muslims as cowards who were attached to this life rather than the hereafter; only those who embraced jihad were "the saved sect." But Ferid did not yet have this view of his family. The teachings he had imbibed since childhood about the Islamic responsibility to maintain family relations likely made him reluctant to see his family in a negative light.[7]

Ferid's email did little to dispel his family's uncertainty over his reasons for leaving. It was Miawand who would provide the three men's families with the greatest clue as to the cause of their disappearance. Miawand appears to have felt obliged to stay in contact with his family, and he was willing to jeopardize the secrecy that he and his friends had guarded so diligently to fulfill this obligation. In particular, Miawand's letter would lead the men's families to worry that they might be engaged in something nefarious. We saw the letter earlier. In it, Miawand writes, "When our brothers and sisters are in need we leave everything to help them." This sentence is sufficiently clear to show that the three men intended to help those suffering.[8] But what exactly did this mean? It could mean that they intended to engage in a military struggle, just as it could mean a whole host of other possibilities. Perhaps Miawand intended to join some charitable organization or use his engineering education to help build Muslim societies abroad. After all, the email began with a statement expressing sympathy for material hardship endured overseas: "We live in a life of ease while our brothers and sisters are suffering so much without food, shelter and so on. They have shortage of food while we throw food away when we feel like it."[9]

Miawand had sent his letter before departing from Canada. The letter arrived at Miawand's mother's house on March 10, four days after the men were last seen on Canadian soil.[10] Miawand's mother, an elderly woman whose English remained rudimentary after moving to Canada, did not know what to make of the letter. But Ahmad, Miawand's older brother and father figure, felt apprehensive after reading its contents. Although Ahmad was not entirely sure what Miawand's intentions were, he did know that he was abandoning his studies and his family. As the letter makes manifest, Miawand was about to break his mother's heart: "I know Abi [Mother] loves me so much and tell her that I'm very sorry for not informing her about my decision and left the country without her blessing."[11] She had moved the family to Canada to take her children out of a refugee city and offer them a better life. Miawand joining a gang and selling drugs had been a bump in the road, but his family held out hope that he would turn things around.[12] The last time they had spoken, Ahmad reminded Miawand to focus on his studies and finish his final year with strong grades. The family had a clear view of what Miawand's future would look like: He would finish his studies, find steady employment, and settle down to start a family of his own. Miawand was already engaged, and the family's plans seemed to be coming together. Then this letter appeared, suggesting everything could be derailed.

Two days later, Ahmad received a message on his answering machine. It was Miawand. He told his family that he was well and that he "is where [he] want[s] to be."[13] But this time, Ahmad had a clue as to his brother's whereabouts. The call display showed an area code. The message came from Pakistan.

Pakistan was a country Ahmad knew well. He had lived there for twelve years and he still had relatives there. He called them, hoping

Miawand had turned up. No one had heard anything. Ahmad then contacted the police to file a missing person's report. But he could not leave the matter in their hands alone. He knew his brother was in danger. Kidnappings of foreigners were common in the Pakhtunkhwa region of Pakistan. Ransoms could provide a handsome sum to an unscrupulous group. He needed to find his brother before it was too late, and he began digging on his own. Miawand's letter said he had traveled with two friends. Ahmad came to discover that these two friends were Muhanad and Ferid. He googled Muhanad's last name and found a physician, Dr. Mahmood Al Farekh, working in the UAE. Miawand contacted him. As it turned out, Mahmood was Muhanad's father and he was equally worried. His son had recently emailed him. In the email Muhanad wrote:

> Salam [Peace]. Dad: How are you and how is the family? I hope everyone is doing well. I just wanted to tell you that everything is very good. Pakistan is an amazing country and the people are very welcoming and nice. Insha-Allah [God willing], I'm going to be doing some more sightseeing as well as hiking . . . outdoors. I'll also be looking at universities here, if they are good and whatnot. Send my salams [greetings] to all. I'll see you guys soon. Salam, Muhanad Al Farekh.[14]

Despite Muhanad's assurances, his family was naturally concerned and expressed as much in an email response. Muhanad therefore called his father on March 15. Muhanad told him he was well: He was in Pakistan with his friends and they intended to further their education by joining an Islamic school.[15] Like Miawand's family, Muhanad's father had invested time, effort, and immense financial resources so his son could receive a Western education and gain financial stability. Now, out of the blue, his son told him he wished to pursue a new path in life.

If Muhanad's father was frustrated, he nonetheless had hope. His son divulged his location, letting slip that he and his friends were in Peshawar.[16] Not only that, he knew they were staying at the Lahore Hotel, a medium-sized hotel located near one of Peshawar's highways. This was all the information Ahmad needed to go halfway across the world to find his brother: Ahmad applied for a Pakistani visa; it arrived two weeks later and he touched down in Peshawar on April 4. He went immediately to the Lahore Hotel but the men were not there. Ahmad nonetheless asked to examine the hotel registry. There he saw his brother's name, alongside those of Ferid and Muhanad. Their nationalities were listed beside their names, and stuck out among the other hotel guests: "American," "Canadian," "Canadian." Hotel records confirmed that they had checked in on March 14.[17] They had long since left. But the hotel clerk remembered the three men; he had wondered what they were doing in Peshawar. The three men told him they were joining a missionary group to perform *da'wa*. While *da'wa* typically means calling non-Muslims to the Islamic faith, it can also mean calling Muslims back to their religion, reminding them to be faithful to God.

Ahmad suspected that his brother and his traveling companions had joined the Dawa-e-Tabligh. The Dawa-e-Tabligh, also known as the Tablighi Jamaat, is the largest Muslim organization in the world today.[18] It is centered in the Indian subcontinent and millions of its members flock to Dhaka every year to join the organization's annual gathering. Tablighis are typically conservative in their practice, but largely apolitical. They care more about people's private piety than about determining state policies. The national branch of the Dawa-e-Tabligh in Pakistan was in Raiwind City, about 600 kilometers from Peshawar. Ahmad traveled there the next day. When he arrived at the branch's headquarters, he combed its records to see if the three men had passed through. He found nothing.[19] The trail had run cold. Discouraged, Ahmad returned to Canada with little to no news to report to his worried family. It had been a wild goose chase. Where were the men and what were they up to?

But Ahmad would not lose hope. He continued to email and correspond with his brother. Miawand's emails were more forthcoming than his initial letter about why he had left Canada. Ahmad now knew beyond doubt that his brother and his friends had indeed left to partake in jihad. But for Ahmad, it was not too late for the men to find their way back. He did not see dedication to jihad as the mark of a lost soul. He knew the concept had a deep and respectable history within the Islamic tradition. Ahmad also knew that jihad's meaning was capacious, encompassing more than mere military combat. He saw the potential fulfillment of jihad in the undertaking of any righteous and religious struggle in life. He therefore tried to reason with his brother. He told him that true jihad was to serve his mother who was beside herself with grief, "crying all the time."[20] Miawand knew this and he felt guilty about it. He also knew the high level of importance that the Islamic tradition places on taking care of one's parents, particularly one's mother: When asked, for example, who was most deserving of a man's company, the Prophet Muhammad reportedly answered, "Your mother." When the questioner replied, "And then who?" the Prophet repeated his answer—not once but twice.[21] Miawand had often heard this report, and had indeed learned to live by it. His mother was the matriarch of his household. She had raised and protected her family during their exile in Pakistan prior to moving to Canada. In her family's eyes, she was deserving of the utmost respect. Ahmad tried to appeal to his brother's sense of duty to his mother. In doing so, he sought to teach his younger brother that his jihad was not to be found in the mountains of Pakistan or Afghanistan. It was at home, with his family. Ahmad's appeal to his brother is indicative of lay Muslims' continued debates about the meaning of jihad today. Jihad may be a topic of particular focus for the likes of Al-Awlaki or al-ʿAyayri, but these preachers certainly do not have a monopoly over the term. When lay Muslims do engage with the concept of jihad, it is often to formulate other ways of "struggling in God's path"—struggling to do what they deem right.

Ahmad's appeals to his brother help us think through a central irony of the War on Terror. By virtue of belonging to the same tradition, Ahmad was uniquely placed to argue against his brother's interpretation of the faith. He possessed the discursive resources to speak about an alternative understanding of jihad. He represented an organic means of achieving the state's objective of CVE—counter-violent extremism.[22] But Ahmad's Muslimness also made him a figure of suspicion for security agencies. Soon after his return from Pakistan, Ahmad's family began to be monitored. His sister, who until then had worked in airport security, lost her clearance and therefore her job.[23] Ahmad would henceforth guard many of his correspondences with Miawand from Canadian authorities, afraid that he would draw further scrutiny from security agencies. Those best able to fight the ideology of "radical Islam" were thus also those whom the state most feared. From the state's perspective, although Ahmad could convince Miawand of his mistake, Miawand could also attempt to convince his brother of the correctness of his actions. However little the empirical data supported this outcome, the mere possibility was enough to place someone like Ahmad under the microscope.

When they left, all three men continued to feel a sense of obligation to their families. Miawand wrote to explain his departure. Ferid prayed for his family and asked them to pray for him as well. And Muhanad lied to his father so his family would not worry about his well-being. Moreover, all three men expressed love and affection for their families. They had learned from Al-Awlaki to frown upon Muslims who did not partake in jihad. And they knew that their families would frown upon their new life path. Yet they did not see their families as deviant or misguided. They did not see them as needing moral and religious admonishment and correction. In time this would change.

"PAY MY DEBTS": UPHOLDING THE RIGHTS OF GOD'S CREATION

The men's sense of obligation was not only to their families. It was also to Canadian society. We see this obligation in a request all three made to their families: to pay their student debts. Ferid's last email states, "please take care of my debts."[24] Miawand wrote in his letter, "Also in this letter I've included two papers for the loan that I owe. One is for [a] Manitoba loan. I have about a little over $2500 left and [the other is for] the National Student loan [for which] I have about $4500 or $4000 left. Please pay this for me!! On the orange piece of paper are the numbers for the student loan places. You can call them and find out exactly what I owe."[25] And Muhanad made the same request to his father.

As it turned out, the three men's concern about debts would be interpreted in widely divergent ways. The prosecution in Muhanad's trial took it to be a reference to a Muslim belief that debts must be paid before entering paradise.[26] They therefore considered the requests confirmation that the men were committed to martyrdom. In contrast,

Muhanad's defense claimed that the men's desire to pay their debts undercut the theory that they left to fight in war.[27] Why pay university debts if one is not planning to come back and finish one's studies? Is good credit not irrelevant for foreign fighters?

I want to suggest a third interpretation. The affirmation of the importance of paying one's debts was indeed related to the men's Islamic beliefs, but it was not specific to the possibility of entering paradise. Rather, the obligation to discharge debts was related to Islamic ideas concerning "the rights of God" and "the rights of humans."[28] Whereas the rights of God are usually associated with obligations that benefit society as a whole—for instance, the obligation to devote a percentage of one's wealth to charity—the rights of humans are those obligations that individuals owe to each other. Among them are the fulfillment of financial obligations, including paying debts.[29] Ferid, Miawand, and Muhanad were all committed to fulfilling these obligations. But most importantly, they were committed to fulfilling these obligations even toward non-Muslim institutions, including the Canadian government, which gave loans to students under favorable terms. This concern with their debts is somewhat curious if they were seeking to wage war against the Canadian government. It is especially so when one considers that classical Islamic law denies any financial obligation toward an enemy state. Thus, classical jurists considered it admissible to destroy the property of an enemy if doing so was militarily advantageous.[30]

Perhaps our three men were committed to a romanticized idea of the chivalrous warrior, like Saladin, who famously gifted Richard the Lionheart a horse even as the latter was trying to conquer Jerusalem from him. In this way, they would be showing their enemies that they were honorable men of their word. But I suspect the men's financial commitment had more to do with how they saw non-Muslim civilians. Recall that Ferid had acknowledged the Islamic prohibition against terrorist acts targeting civilians. This perspective had not yet changed when the three men left Canada. If it had, they would not have flown to Pakistan. Rather, they would have plotted in the fashion of the Toronto 18 and targeted locations in Canada itself.[31] The choice to go abroad was like the choice to pay one's debts: Both were part of a commitment to fight soldiers and to refrain from depriving noncombatants of their rights to life or property. In their view, the three men were leaving to protect other Muslims from military aggression, not to fight any and all non-Muslims. Al-Awlaki had convinced them that jihad was the proper means to answer the devaluation of Muslim life abroad, but their commitments were still far from those of the 9/11 hijackers, who were willing to harm civilians. The three men therefore show us that those who "radicalize" do not necessarily subscribe to the ideology of proponents of jihad wholesale. Like all ideas, jihadist ideology is subject to a process of reception, in which followers weigh the ideas to which they are exposed, accepting some and rejecting others. But as we shall see, the more a fighter immersed himself in a jihadist community, the more his views on Islam, politics, and war resembled those of his comrades in arms.

IMMERSION IN AL-QAEDA'S IDEOLOGY

What happened to Ferid, Miawand, and Muhanad after Ahmad came home dejected from his futile search for his brother? Where did they go—physically, but also ideologically? And what did they do? When the three of them arrived in Peshawar, they found men willing to help them join other jihadist fighters. Peshawar had been the center for coordinating foreign fighters since the time of ʿAbd Allah ʿAzzam, and anti-NATO militant organizations still possessed networks there. The population was largely Pashtun—the largest ethnic group in Afghanistan—and was generally sympathetic to the Taliban. But the three North Americans did not fit well within the Taliban. The Taliban was an Afghan and mostly Pashtun group.[32] They emerged in the 1990s, forged from bonds established within Pakistani Islamic colleges that had served Pashtun refugees.[33] The men were told to join al-Qaeda. Al-Qaeda fighters were an international force of Muslims from different linguistic, ethnic, and cultural backgrounds, and the men could more easily function within its chain of command.

From Peshawar, the three therefore made their way south to Waziristan, part of the FATA, a region of Pakistan governed independently by Afghan tribes. The region offered al-Qaeda a sanctuary from the gaze of the Pakistani state and sheltered them, at least up to that point, from US military operations. The men ended up in a training camp near the town of Miran Shah. There, they adopted pseudonyms and were told to hide their nationalities to avoid unwanted attention. They were incorporated into al-Qaeda's command structure under the leadership of a senior figure named Abdul Hafeez. But it is unlikely that the men saw much if any combat. More than a year after arriving, Ferid would tell new recruits that he had yet to engage in military action.[34] Part of the reason was that al-Qaeda had always been more of an ideological than a military force. Even during the anti-Soviet jihad of the 1980s, Arab fighters like bin Laden had little to contribute to the defeat of Soviet troops.[35] Most of the fighting had been undertaken by Afghans themselves, who knew regional tribes and the topography in ways that facilitated their coordination and military success. In the 1990s, al-Qaeda's strength was its ability to undertake and fund spectacular acts of violence, not engagement in ground combat. The situation remained the same after the US invasion of Afghanistan. Al-Qaeda did little to assist in the Taliban's fight against NATO forces. In fact, its military capabilities were quickly being eclipsed by its own Iraqi franchise, which had emerged in the wake of the US invasion of 2003, and by the time Ferid, Miawand, and Muhanad joined, al-Qaeda's strength in numbers and resources were about to be overtaken by its Yemeni branch where Anwar Al-Awlaki was playing a key role.[36] Our three men therefore sought to join a battle whose main protagonists were Afghans not particularly keen on having them. Muhanad would later complain to his senior officer that the Taliban did not really need al-Qaeda's help.[37]

Rather than join an active fighting force, the three men joined a community of shared ideals. These ideals included keeping alive the knowledge of "true Islam" in an era when the Muslim masses had turned their backs on the obligation of jihad. The members of this community lived together and established daily routines. Part of these routines involved engaging in spiritual practices like congregational prayers. Thomas Hegghammer has recently shed light on the prevalence of weeping among jihadist groups engaged in such practices.[38] Hegghammer shows that weeping is a practice of self-fashioning whereby jihadists come to cultivate emotions associated with the ascetic and mystical elements of the Islamic faith. He reminds us that the community that Ferid, Muhanad, and Miawand joined was not only committed to military combat. It was dedicated to spiritual development as well.

The men's daily schedule also involved gaining what they considered proper Islamic knowledge. Thus, they would study the Islamic tradition in the morning with their comrades.[39] Then they would turn to military training. This training included physical exercises to stay fit and weapons training in which the men would learn to maneuver together in various fighting positions. Not everything Ferid, Muhanad, and Miawand studied pertained to jihad. Muhanad might have lied to his father about his desire to enroll in an Islamic school, but he did discover new books from the Islamic tradition. Two months after leaving Canada, Muhanad wrote to his family to tell them his sojourn in Pakistan was more beneficial than he had expected and that he was "learning a lot."[40] He wrote to his family about his study of *Riyad al-Salihin* by Abu Sharaf al-Nawawi and *Zad al-Ma'ad* by Ibn Qayyim al-Jawziyya. The former is a compilation of *hadith*s meant to provide prophetic guidance on how to live righteously,[41] while the latter uses the biography of Muhammad to guide Muslims through various life circumstances. The heavy use of hadith in both texts makes them palatable to Salafi sensibilities. But neither text is part of jihadist canon.

Nonetheless, in the course of living and studying with the other jihadists, the men came to incorporate al-Qaeda's utopian ideology of jihad, which was the culmination of three decades of discursive developments among Arab jihadist writers. We get a sense of the three men's shifting ideas about jihad by reading a letter that arrived at the Yar household in 2009, two years after the men's departure. By then, the email correspondences between Ahmad and Miawand had run dry. The Yar family craved news about Miawand, if only to know he was still alive. On February 2, their wish was fulfilled. A letter from Peshawar arrived at Miawand's mother's Calgary home. It was wrapped in a blue envelope, to which were affixed six stamps picturing Ali Jinnah, the founder of Pakistan, in grey-black with red hues. The letter begins:

> To my beloved family: salam alaykum
> I know it has been a very long time since my contact with you guys and I didn't tell you in detail why I left and where I was going

> to but I swear by Allah (s.w.t. [may he be exaulted]) that I didn't forget you in my du'a [prayers] even though it hurts me so much that you believe that I left because I was brainwashed and didn't know what I was doing.[42]

The letter contains a detailed attempt at legitimizing the Taliban's and al-Qaeda's military struggle. Many of Miawand's claims parrot Al-Awlaki's. But some also incorporate ideas from past ideologues whose writings influenced al-Qaeda. A newfound sense of self-confidence as a religious authority pervades Miawand's writing. He begins by grounding the continued obligation of jihad in scripture:

> The messenger of Allah (p.b.u.h. [peace be upon him]) has said in a hadith "Whoever Allah desires good for, he grants him knowledge in the deen [religion]. And there will always remain a group from [among] the Muslims fighting upon the truth, manifest against those who oppose them, until the Day of Resurrection." This is one of the hadith and there are hundreds . . . more to show you that there will always remain a group fighting jihad against their enemies until the day of judgement.

Miawand then accuses the West and Muslim leaders of hiding the obligation of jihad from the Muslim masses. He directs his greatest opprobrium to the Saudi state for permitting the United States to station its troops on its territory during the First Gulf War, and he accuses their state *mufti* (a legal scholar who issues a *fatwa*) of attempting to change the Qur'an. His contempt for the Saudis follows a familiar script laid out by the Jordanian writer Abu Muhammad al-Maqdisi. In the 1980s, Maqdisi claimed that the Saudi leadership's diplomatic relations with the United States made them apostates. Moreover, Miawand claims that the media lies about al-Qaeda and the Taliban and he characterizes the two groups as "the best of people." But his praise is not because they defend Muslim civilians from the violence of the War on Terror, as we would expect based on Miawand's first letter to his family. Instead, it is because the Taliban and al-Qaeda seek to establish an Islamic state. The commitment to establishing an Islamic state had been central to al-Qaeda's ideology and resulted from its members' agreement with the ideas of Sayyid Qutb, Muhammad ʿAbd al-Salam Faraj, and Ayman al-Zahawiri, all of whom denounced the legitimacy of secular Arab regimes. Now, al-Qaeda's members in Waziristan were passing this commitment on to Miawand.[43] Miawand continues his defense of the two jihadist groups by citing stories of miraculous occurrences (*karamat*) on the battlefield, either reported to him or witnessed firsthand. Among them is the statement that a martyr's blood smells of perfume. Such miraculous tales commonly circulated during the anti-Soviet jihad of the 1980s. Here, we see that their circulation continued in the late 2000s.

In short, Miawand's letter reveals the influence of his comrades on his understanding and defense of jihad. The letter also reveals a hardening of attitudes toward Western society. At one point Miawand states: "Look at all the Muslim countries around you, how corrupt they have become because they chose to follow Western society. If you see Pakistan now compared to the old Pakistan, it is not the same."[44] At another, he explicitly states that the aim of the West is "the destruction of Islam." He even tells his family that they must immigrate to a Muslim country because it is impermissible to live with non-Muslims.[45]

Of course, none of the foregoing suggests that Miawand, Muhanad, or Ferid would have begun to think of all non-Muslims as military enemies. But it shows that they were exposed to deeply antagonistic attitudes toward non-Muslims, particularly Westerners, and that at least Miawand embraced these attitudes. Moreover, the three men were now part of an organization whose leadership had declared US citizens to be legitimate targets. In fact, when three Americans arrived in Miran Shah to join al-Qaeda a year after Ferid, Miawand, and Muhanad, the organization's leadership devised a plan to teach them how to make bombs and carry out attacks in New York.[46] They would likely have asked the same of Ferid, Miawand, and Muhanad had the three men not aroused suspicion when leaving Canada. Ferid met and trained these three Americans in light weapons use before they returned to the United States, where the FBI arrested them. Whatever qualms Miawand, Muhanad, and Ferid previously had about harming civilians, they were now part of an organization that sought to launch attacks on US soil.

NEVER HAVING SAID GOODBYE

On the surface, Miawand's letter is an impassioned defense of al-Qaeda and an affirmation that he was right in leaving his family. Moreover, his newfound sense of religious authority led him to speak condescendingly to his family about their lack of religious practice, providing them lengthy and unsolicited religious advice (*nasiha*). He writes, for example:

> First, I will start with my sisters to please start wearing a hijab, start praying on time, to stay far away from Hollywood [and] Bollywood movies because this is [the] main thing [by] which our ummah [Muslim community] is going astray. To my sister [Sarah][47] to start praying and listening to your mother when she tells you to pray and to stay away from this materialistic life (Ex. fashion . . . etc.). To my [sister Khadija], again I saw you pray but it was usually not on time. So pray on time, stay away from watching those Hindi [and] English movies because there is a brother here that told me a story about a father being punished in a grave regarding Hindi movies and in the dream he was giving advice to his children not to watch those movies.[48]

Gone is the tenderness with which Miawand addressed his family in his first letter. A correspondence between Muhanad and his family the same year reveals a similar condescending attitude toward their watching TV and their insufficient time spent together gaining religious knowledge, suggesting that all three men were taught to see other Muslims as wayward.[49]

And yet Miawand ends on a note that suggests he misses his family and wants to see them. He asks them to join him in Pakistan:

> In Pakistan I can keep contact with you guys and even visit you sometimes. [There are] a lot of other things I want to say but I didn't because I am hoping that you will all move to Pakistan and I will see you there in person; but the decision is in your hands if you love Allah (s.w.t) and his Messenger you will leave that kufar [disbelieving] country. On the end of page 1 is an email address, I

> want you to send a contact [number] of [one of] our relatives and their name, then from there we will keep contact. If I don't receive any email then I will send another letter to you in a few months to try again with a different method.

Miawand's family now had hope. They saw their son and brother as lost and indoctrinated. But his letter gave them renewed optimism. Miawand wanted to stay in contact with them. He missed them. He wanted them to move to Pakistan. He gave them an email address where he could be contacted and where they might touch base. Not only that, but he wanted to speak to them directly, by phone. Finally, after two years, they might hear his voice and communicate directly what they had wanted to say.

Miawand asked his family to send the name and phone number of a relative in Peshawar. They obliged and sent him the contact information of a relative named Naseer. Miawand would contact Naseer to pass on to his family the date, time, and phone number where they should contact him. The day of the phone appointment, the entire Yar family in Calgary congregated together. They huddled around the phone as Ahmad dialed the number Naseer had provided him. From the first words, Ahmad knew it was Miawand. He recognized his brother's voice. Overcome with emotion, Ahmad told him "I miss you . . . [you] still have your place in our heart."[50] Everyone in the family took turns speaking to Miawand. They knew their dreams of seeing him finish his studies, getting married, and starting a home near them were over. If ever he returned to Canada, he would be arrested and jailed, but that did not matter. What mattered was that he was safe, breathing—alive. What they dreaded most was losing him.[51]

At the end of the phone call, Ahmad felt encouraged. Miawand expressed his willingness to meet with him in Pakistan. A few days later, Naseer called again. Miawand wanted to talk. Naseer passed on a new phone number and, again, provided a date and time. This time, only Ahmad and his mother were present for the call. But when Ahmad heard a voice on the other end, it was not his brother's.

"Salam alaykum," a stranger's voice said.

"Wa alaykum salam," Ahmad replied. "Where is my brother? Where is Miawand?"

The next thing the man said shook Ahmad to his core. "Miawand has died."

Ahmad looked to his mother. She asked him where Miawand was. He could not tell her what the man had said. Her health was too poor to handle it. "I want to talk to my brother," Ahmad said in disbelief. "I want to talk to my brother,"[52] he insisted.

"Your brother is no longer alive."

The man hung up. Ahmad felt his heart sink. He did not know if the man was saying the truth. Was Miawand really dead? Did the man want Ahmad to *think* he was dead? Had Miawand gotten cold feet and decided he no longer wanted to meet with Ahmad? Maybe he thought the easiest way for his family to cope was to believe he was dead and to move on with their lives. Maybe this would ultimately dry his mother's tears. If this was the case, it did not work. Ahmad did not give up; he continued to hope that his brother was alive and that he would eventually contact his family. As the months passed, however, his hopes gradually diminished. The Obama administration was intensifying its war in Waziristan. The United States waged this war without boots on the ground. Instead, men in Virginia surveilled the area with predator drones, enabling the United States to target unsuspecting militants. If Miawand was dead, this was likely the way he died.

What made this possibility more credible was the intensity with which Waziristan was targeted that year. As a basis of comparison, the year the three men had arrived in Pakistan in 2007, the Bush administration would order the launch of five drone attacks on the Northern Frontier Provinces of Pakistan. The next year the United States would increase this number to thirty-five, and the year Miawand had contacted Ahmad, the number of strikes increased to fifty-three.[53] Not only did the number of strikes surge, but so did the suspected number of militants killed, up three hundred from the year prior. Moreover, the United States had succeeded in eliciting the support of the Pakistani Army in the struggle against militants in the North Western Frontier Province, and scores of fighters were reported killed the month Miawand last spoke to his family.[54] It is unclear if Miawand actually ever participated in any combat operations, but it is evident from his letter that he had witnessed some of his companions die.

Could Ferid have been one of these companions? A year after Ahmad last spoke to Miawand, Colin Freeze of the *Globe and Mail* interviewed former CIA director Michael Hayden. Hayden reported knowing about Ferid, Miawand, and Muhanad.[55] He recounted how George W. Bush was briefed on their disappearance back in 2007. He worried that the three men knew the West and could use this knowledge to launch attacks against the United States. He also explicitly stated that the United States "had taken care of Ferid." Today, Ferid and Miawand are still officially considered "at large," but Miawand's family has come to terms with their loss. Ferid's family still holds on to the hope that Ferid is somewhere out there, unable to come home but still alive.

Miawand's attempt to contact his family should not be read as a rejection of the life of jihad. But it does show that he tired of the distance between them. He had once decided to leave everything for the sake of military struggle. Now, he wanted something of his old life back. How far might Miawand have gone to see his family? Would he have eventually abandoned al-Qaeda? We will never know, because Miawand died soon after reaching out to his family. However, we do know that this is precisely what Muhanad attempted to do.

DISILLUSIONMENT

It is difficult to know how much Ferid and Muhanad bought into the notion of utopian jihad that Miawand articulated. We must remember that Miawand was less exposed to the complexity of Islamic history and was therefore most likely to embrace wholesale the ideology of fellow jihadists in Waziristan. What is certain, however, is that Muhanad gradually became disillusioned with his life choices. In May 2013, four years after Miawand's last phone call, Muhanad had had enough. Plainly, he wanted out. The reasons for Muhanad's change of heart were many, but he never grappled with them directly in his intercepted letters to his senior commanders, likely out of concern that his leadership would think him a traitor, prepared to abandon the cause. He had come to join a group that promised to usher in a new form of justice. Al-Awlaki had told them that divine intervention was on the horizon. Now, Al-Awlaki was dead; so too was bin Laden, as were so many of the foreign fighters Muhanad had met and befriended. The drone program had not only halted all possibility of combat operations; it also made life unbearable. Muhanad was locked up at home for weeks on end, reluctant to go outside for fear of being targeted in a drone strike. Boredom had set in. The rich social circles he had known upon first arrival were impossible to sustain, and he had run out of new documentaries to watch to pass the time. His only solace was his letter writing. He would correspond with fellow fighters by means of al-Qaeda's internal mail delivery system. In these letters, Muhanad speaks of his fears: "Seeing that the situation here is very confusing, or at the very least, I'm very confused. What I've been seeing in the last . . . amount of years is for brothers that are working, they are getting killed. And for those who are not doing anything, then why on earth are they still here? (Just as extra info, I am in the group that is doing absolutely nothing.)"[56] He speaks of the constant worry about drone attacks: "As for my house, I am not very happy. I don't feel very secure here. And a few weeks back, there was a drone strike quite close. And from the last time I saw you I hadn't gone to the market (It will be almost . . . six months)."[57]

Most of all, we see a clear affirmation that Muhanad and his fellow foreign fighters were of little use to the struggle. "The Taliban themselves," he writes, "don't really have a need for us."[58] He explains that foreign fighters' only serve the symbolic purpose of emphasizing the international dimension of their struggle: "[The Taliban] would much favor a smaller, more symbolic number of fighters from the current amount of foreign fighters currently available." Muhanad was useless to the struggle and he knew it. He lamented this state of affairs, asserting that God does not want Muslim fighters to undertake their struggle if there is no benefit in it or if it brings harm to the Muslim community: "I wouldn't mind to sacrifice my security for the better good of the umma [the global Muslim community], I think almost all mujahedeen do this when they come for jihad but it's not right to sacrifice security for no gain at all, if not even harming the umma."[59] Part of the sentiment is understandable. Muhanad had left because jihad was meant to solve the violence against his sisters and brothers in faith. He clearly saw himself as unable to work toward this solution as long as he was huddled at home sheltering from drone strikes. However, we might ask why the futility of his efforts mattered? After all, Al-Awlaki had taught Muhanad that a Muslim ought to fulfill the obligation of jihad without care for the consequences. His duty was to obey; whether his efforts led to victory or defeat was God's choice. I believe the answer relates to a tension at the heart of the utopian ideology of jihad. The utopian ideology of jihad told fighters to trust in God's power of divine intervention while simultaneously instructing them to develop strategies that would help win their war. Fighters like Muhanad were attracted to the battlefield because they sought to make a difference. They might die, but they needed to see that their cause would be furthered in the process. When this did not materialize, Muhanad began to see his life differently and worried that he had thrown it away.[60]

Wasting his life was all the more unbearable to Muhanad for another reason. Muhanad was now a father. He had married the daughter of another al-Qaeda fighter and by 2013, he had at least two children of tender age.[61] Life was difficult for those under his care, and his family's needs continually preoccupied him. He told his commander that the children were living "mostly on the basics now. This is the price you pay for security."[62] Moreover, their shelter remained precarious. At one point, Muhanad notes their lack of a steady home. On one occasion, they needed to move because their location was becoming too well-known among the local population, who could share this information with either the Pakistani government or NATO forces. After moving, Muhanad's need for discretion became a vulnerability: His new landlord informed him that he was going to evict him unless he provided him with a handsome loan or paid him a higher rent.

Muhanad had virtually no support from his organization when he reached out to his commanders asking for help in protecting his family. Al-Qaeda's rank and file had been decimated by drone strikes. Al-Qaeda mail traveled at a snail's pace and the local leadership was unable—or unwilling, in Muhanad's estimation—to provide funds or help him find a new home. Eventually, Muhanad despaired of receiving help and began to suspect that his superiors were either callous or inept. He became fed up with the state of affairs and bypassed his local leadership by writing directly to a senior leader he had not seen in years who lived outside of the Miran Shah area. This leader possessed a very special skill: He could forge documents.

Muhanad's letter expressed a desire to relocate outside of Pakistan. He needed to submit his request delicately: He could not raise the suspicion that he no longer believed in al-Qaeda's cause, and al-Qaeda's financial and logistical support was essential to making the move possible. This was not the first time Muhanad had tried to leave. He had previously written to a friend named Zuhar, whose daughter was planning to leave Pakistan to join her husband in Syria. After seeking Zuhar's guidance about the possibility of leaving for Syria, Muhanad had suggested that his family could perhaps travel with his daughter there: "My family told me a few days ago that your daughter is making plans to get reunited with her husband. How are the arrangements over there for families? My family was also wondering if they could also travel with your daughter."[63] This first request gives the impression that Muhanad wished to join the efforts of jihad somewhere else. After all, Eastern Syria was on the cusp of becoming the Islamic State of Iraq and Syria (or, more properly, the Levant).[64] Muhanad could join al-Qaeda fighters there in their struggle against the Syrian dictator Bashar al-Assad. But this was not Muhanad's true intention. His later letter to his senior commander makes it exceedingly clear that he had seen enough to make him question the righteousness of his struggle.

It was not simply that Muhanad felt abandoned by his leadership. Unlike Miawand, who affirmed that the Taliban and al-Qaeda were the best people on earth, Muhanad was troubled by what he had witnessed. He wrote to the senior leader in charge of a man who had gained a reputation as a troublemaker among foreign fighters in Waziristan: "There was a brother here that was not quite obedient, he actually started a lot of problems, he seemed to me to be the rebellious type, not quite mature, and I later heard that AQ [al-Qaeda] in Syria put him in a high ranking position. I honestly don't know what to make of it."[65] Moreover, far from seeing Syria as the long-awaited state that would restore Muslim dignity, Muhanad had heard of the battles taking place between al-Qaeda in Syria (al-Nusra Front) and al-Qaeda in Iraq (ISIS): "it has reached the point that brothers are now killing each other." He had also heard about al-Qaeda fighters repressing the population: "another interesting issue I heard from brothers here, how [when] the Syrian AQ [al-Qaeda] are forbidding the evil (wrong doing) they are using force or harsh ways [against] people that are not really religious . . . that makes me worry about their wisdom." In other words, Muhanad could see that al-Qaeda affiliates in Syria and Iraq were likely to alienate the population they allegedly sought to liberate.

In his letter, Muhanad expressed in explicit terms the regret for the course his life had taken. He recognized the wisdom of the educational path his father had envisioned for him years ago. Even beyond material comforts, he saw this path as most likely to benefit the Muslim community whose suffering had motivated the three men to leave: "What I say I believe with a full heart and if I had a chance to go back in time, knowing of course the mujah[i]deen's shortcomings I would give all that I own to study in higher education (a university) in fields that I see my umma is in dire need of today."[66]

Muhanad then made his request to his commander more explicit. He wanted to take advantage of the volatile situation in Syria to start his life anew. He knew of the scores of refugees in Turkey and Jordan. If they could travel there, he believed he and his family might be able to blend in with the Syrian refugees. He knew their Levantine dialect and, as a Palestinian, belonged to the same wider regional ethnicity. Alternatively, he explained, he could assume the identity of one of the fallen foreign fighters from Libya, Egypt, or Saudi Arabia who had come to join the struggle against Bashar al-Assad's regime.[67] Muhanad had access to some international news: He had learned that these countries opposed the Assad regime at the time and financed the rebel opposition. He hoped they would look favorably upon their volunteer fighters returning home after the conflict. This option would have been trickier considering different regional Arabic dialects, but Muhanad knew the Gulf dialect and was willing to try to pull off others if it meant a new life for his family. Both options appear to embody the US State Department's worst fear: an al-Qaeda operative blending in among masses of refugees. This fear has often been bandied about to prevent the accommodation of asylum seekers in Western countries. But this was not Muhanad's intention. He wanted a new identity so that he could silently slip into civilian life, pursue higher education, and earn a livelihood for himself and his family.

Muhanad asked to join his superior in an "intensive study" of document-forging techniques. If his request had been accepted, he would have been able to get himself and his family out of the misery of Waziristan. But Muhanad also knew it was a dangerous plan. His movement could attract attention to the location where the senior leadership resided. He therefore also suggested the possibility of one of the superior's men coming to Waziristan to teach Muhanad. Finally, if his requests were rejected, Muhanad was fully willing to take the plunge and move to Syria without training on how to forge documents. He nonetheless worried for his family if he were to do so. He therefore asked his superior if provisions were made for the families of al-Qaeda men who were killed in Syria. Muhanad's family had become his main concern. He was willing to die if it meant safety for them.

The letter ends with several statements allaying the leadership's fears that Muhanad might be a traitor to his cause. Muhanad asserts his commitment to jihad and couches his requests in deferential language: "I could never leave jihad (I don't feel my life has a purpose without it, I would feel empty and lost) so I ask you do you think if it was possible to study in Turkey if it would be a good idea or something that I would regret in the future?" At times, the veneer of sincerity is exceedingly thin. For instance, Muhanad writes that he wishes to join his superior and learn from his training so as not to drift from jihad: "I worry if I leave the place I am in now, and travel to fulfill what I really feel passionate about (higher education) and I am not under someone's wing, I am scared that in time I might drift away from jihad, and I know then my life would be without a purpose, empty and lost." But he follows this statement with one that reveals his desperation to leave Waziristan: "But if you think that me being close to you would be dangerous for you and others, then what do you think of, if you just help me to setup and then I [do] things on my own [i.e. leave on my own]."

In short, by May 2013, six years after the three men had left, Muhanad wished he could turn back the clock. He was disillusioned with jihad. He had seen rebellious men being promoted to leadership, he knew of violence between fighters, and he felt that his own local leadership was ignoring his family's basic needs. The jihadist ideology to which he had once subscribed depended upon viewing jihadists as the steadfast group of Muslims who were committed to the proper religious path. But Muhanad saw that they could be exceedingly flawed; jihadists could be aggressive and violent to each other and to civilians. They could be venal and would sometimes leave the men under their command in precarious situations. Muhanad was discovering that al-Qaeda's utopian ideology of jihad was no substitute for a pragmatic approach to politics that begins from a sober analysis of the world as it is and devises plausible solutions to perceived problems. Muhanad's disillusionment was also the product of the life he was living. Fear and boredom were his constant companions. The glamour of fighting for the oppressed and for justice had been replaced by the daily anxiety about drones and the loneliness of hiding in his home. More than anything, Muhanad's priorities had changed. He might once have thought he owed everything to Muslims suffering abroad, but now he had obligations to a family. His wife and children shared in his fear and boredom; and as time passed, fear began to overtake boredom. It was not only the fear of drones but also the fear of homelessness. The family lived on scraps, and their landlord was about to repossess their dwelling. Life's real and immediate needs had overtaken the ideology that Al-Awlaki had once proffered. Muhanad wanted out.

What to make of Muhanad's desire to defect from al-Qaeda and return to a civilian life? The Dutch anthropologist David Kloos has suggested that in seeking to understand the evolution of a Muslim's religious commitments, we think about the different stages of their life.[68] Muhanad had left Canada hastily at the age of twenty-one. He had not known a man's love for his partner or a father's for his children. He had a romantic view of fighting for God but had little sense of pervasive fear or war trauma. And he had a rosy view of the courage and selflessness of jihadists and little understanding of how humans in all situations are prone to reject their ideals for heightened reputation, power, or wealth. My point here is not that young men are the most likely and therefore most dangerous jihadists. Rather, my point is that commitments—religious or otherwise—change constantly as individuals are exposed to new life circumstances. Changing empirical realities lead individuals to question their previously held beliefs about the world, and new desires and aspirations are at odds with old ones. Talal Asad has recently suggested that faith is not something one either has or does not have: It is often something one possesses in degrees.[69] But faith is also something that undergoes qualitative changes. To have faith meant something different to Muhanad at the age of twenty-eight than it did six years earlier. And thus Muhanad's interpretation of Islam increasingly pushed jihad to the margins of his religiosity. His priorities had changed.

CONCLUSION

I have tried to trace what happened to Ferid, Miawand, and Muhanad in the seven years after they left Canada. I have shown that they joined a community whose fighting capacities were limited and whose utility to the war in Afghanistan was largely symbolic. This community was dedicated to learning about "true Islam" just as much as it was to fighting militarily. And so our three men studied classical texts and began to see themselves as authorities on a religion whose followers worldwide had become misguided. In studying alongside al-Qaeda fighters, Ferid, Miawand, and Muhanad increasingly absorbed al-Qaeda's ideology. The love they had initially expressed to their families shortly after their departure turned to worried admonitions about their parents' and siblings' waywardness. Their sense of responsibility for upholding the rights of all humans, including the non-Muslim Canadian government, gave way to an acceptance of al-Qaeda's terrorist attacks on Western soil, even as it remains unknown whether they would have agreed to undertake these attacks themselves. Ferid and Miawand likely died in or about 2009 from drone attacks, two years after leaving their family, friends, and community. But Muhanad survived. He married and fathered children. As the years passed, he became disillusioned with his life and his comrades in arms. He sought a way out that would provide a better life for his family.

The shifts in the three men's ideology reveal that a jihadist's commitment to jihad is not so different from any other person's commitment to unremarkable beliefs or practices. The commonly used metaphors of a person being "infected" or "brainwashed" by jihadist ideas only make sense insofar as the ideas are seen as nonsensical and dangerous by those who invoke these metaphors. But in terms of a person's capacity to reason, assess, reconsider, amend, and reject received ideas, jihadist ideology is not qualitatively different from other beliefs. As life circumstances change, so too do all ideas. But even as beliefs change, we cannot always escape the consequences of our actions. As much as he tried, Muhanad's fate had already been determined thousands of miles away in meetings among powerful politicians in Washington, DC.

INTERLUDE

April 2017. I feel nauseous. I need food. Food always cuts the nausea. But I don't have much of an appetite after the chemotherapy. Nothing tastes good anymore. Oh God, how long will this last? I'm just at the start of my treatments. At least the day is nice. The spring sun is a relief. I wait for Sadaf outside a strip mall where she is getting groceries. My phone rings. It's Dawud.

"Salam ʿalaykum, bro, how's it going?" I say.

"Wa ʿalaykum salam," answers Dawud, but I sense something is wrong. His voice is heavy, slow, pained.

"What's up, Dawud?"

"It's my brother, Salman. He's . . . he's dead."

My heart sinks at Dawud's words. I think warmly about Salman. I remember his intrepid attitude and youthful energy at Islamic camp fifteen years earlier. That was before his ordeal. Before the imprisonment. Before the torture.

I think about when Dawud first confided in me about the nightmare his family was going through. It was back in 2013 as we sat eating supper on the rooftop patio of our condo building in Toronto. Dawud told me about how the Ethiopian government had imprisoned Salman. Until recently, Salman went back and forth between Canada and Ethiopia, selling cell phones in the East African country. Dawud explained that Salman was imprisoned after a disgruntled customer accused him of being a terrorist. At the time, the Ethiopian government was particularly suspicious of Salman's Oromo community, which for decades had a well-organized secessionist movement. They imprisoned Salman without a fair trial. But what I found most disconcerting was that the Canadian government led by Stephen Harper's Conservatives had told Dawud's family not to publicize Salman's case in the media. They told the family they would have better luck getting Salman out if they spoke discretely to the Ethiopian government. And yet, in effect, they abandoned Salman and left him languishing in the most abject of conditions for the next four years. By the time he returned to Canada, his mental and physical health had severely deteriorated. In the end, his body collapsed. But what I found out with time was that Salman was also told by his Ethiopian captors that CSIS had requested he be detained. The claim fits well with a pattern of CSIS using foreign governments to pressure Muslims who refused to cooperate with their investigations.[70]

As I register Dawud's words, I think again about his family. I feel overcome by a sense of sadness.

6

PROSECUTING TERRORISM

NATIONAL SECURITY, TREASON, AND THE IMPOSSIBILITY OF JUSTICE

September 12, 2017. I look out the Brooklyn courthouse window. Two witnesses—a man and a woman—are behind me. They are sitting comfortably in the hallway. The woman is chatting on her phone and seems to work for a tech company. They are calm. I'm not. My nerves are shot. And I feel cold, the effects of my recent cancer diagnosis and treatment. I grip my coffee cup. My thoughts are racing. The cars below look like little toys moving slowly as they turn toward the Brooklyn Bridge on their way to Manhattan. Staring at them is calming.

I am about to see Muhanad for the first time in ten years. Part of me is eager to see him in the flesh, out of a desire for some closure. Perhaps if I see him, I can really believe the government narrative. I can really believe that he left to join a jihadist group. That the three of them did. And maybe with his trial, this story that seems too wild to be real will finally have an ending. But another part of me can't stop thinking that I'm doing the wrong thing. "You believe in the rule of law," I tell myself. "You're here to contribute to a justice system. You will only testify truthfully and honestly. Besides, you don't actually know anything incriminating about Muhanad. The prosecution just wants you to provide information about Muhanad's time at the University of Manitoba. John, the FBI agent, said that I'm giving them one piece of a wider puzzle." But my body viscerally disagrees. Something is wrong with this situation, with me being here. Am I contributing to a show trial? Everything I've experienced in the previous days tells me Muhanad can't get a fair trial. I'm still struggling with my conscience when I hear a voice: "Youcef, you're up."

* * *

Muhanad's trial presented me with a question: Can Muslim citizens accused of terrorism receive a fair trial in liberal democratic states, and if not, why not? Since then, I have reviewed the happenings of the trial in detail. The data seem to indicate that the answer to the first part of my question is no, they cannot receive a fair trial. I have come to recognize that I was naïve in my belief in the rule of law. In what follows, I show that terrorism cases depart from other trials because of the ambiguous position of the accused. The Muslim terrorist straddles two irreconcilable positions in the state's bureaucracy: citizen and enemy. Consequently, the state deals with the Muslim citizen accused of terrorism in conflicted ways, bringing the machineries of both the military and the justice department into an uneasy tension. Soldiers kill, lawyers try: Which should prevail for the citizen-terrorist? My contention is that even when Muslims accused of terrorism have their day in court, the imperatives of national security shape court proceedings in ways that act to make a fair trial an impossibility.

The legal scholar Wadie Said has shown the myriad ways that terrorism cases depart from standard criminal law trials. Said cautions championing criminal courts as a remedy against the abuses of military tribunals in prosecuting accused terrorists.[1] By examining the process of evidence collection through spying and informants, irregularities in the application of miranda rights, the use of prejudicial evidence at trial, the use of dubious radicalization experts, and the severity of sentencing, Said exposes how the criminal justice system adopts conditions that render due process questionable in terrorism trials. Said's dexterous analysis is the product of an expert in Anglo-American common law who understands the criminal legal system, and Muhanad's trial confirms many of his troubling revelations about the course of terrorism trials. However, I depart here from his analysis in two ways. First, I seek to provide a framework that explains why national security shapes terrorism trials by paying attention to the bureaucratic and political context in which Muhanad's trial took place. This context reveals the tensions in the state's calculus on how to deal with terrorism threats, with primacy nonetheless accorded to maintaining national security. Second, I aim to shed light on how Islam discursively figures within terrorism trials. What assumptions about Muslim practice and belief animate the courtroom's deliberations and undercut the chances of the accused obtaining an acquittal?

I proceed in three steps. First, I highlight the tension between national security imperatives and the rights of citizens by focusing on the US government's internal disagreement about whether or not to assassinate Muhanad. Second, I examine the irregularities in the run-up to the trial. I highlight how national security imperatives hindered Muhanad's legal team from adequately preparing for trial and placed undue pressure on Muslim witnesses to provide testimony that would secure a guilty verdict. And finally, I turn to theoretical insights from legal scholars Anver Emon and Aaqib Mahmood to make the case that the prosecution and judge disadvantaged Muhanad by blurring the line between the moderate Muslim and the radical Muslim. This blurring rendered innocuous actions seemingly dangerous.

* * *

September 9, 2017, 4 pm. I make my way to my aisle seat at the very front of coach. I have missed my connecting flight from Toronto to New York due to delays at customs. Air Canada has issued me a new boarding pass. I say hello to the African American woman in the seat beside me as I sit down.

"Where are you coming back from?" she asks.

"Oh, I'm actually traveling to New York on business. I live in Vancouver."

Her teenage daughter beside her asks me, "You're . . . you're . . . you're from Vancouver?"

"Yes," I respond, noticing her difficulty speaking.

"Oh, we've gone to Vancouver," the woman says. "Last summer we took a major trip to the Western seaboard. We went down to Vancouver, then Seattle, and Portland. From there we took a flight to Long Beach and rented a car to visit San Francisco."

"Wow, that's quite a trip."

"Oh yes, Kamie and I love traveling. We go all over. The trick is to look for sales. And to fly from smaller airports. Then we rent a car and visit different sites. We put so much mileage on the last car we rented, they must have been pretty surprised when we brought it back."

"I really appreciate these tips," I say, "because my wife and I have been talking about going on a few vacations. You know, I just finished my PhD and when I was writing my thesis it was hard to find time to just relax and enjoy life. Now that I'm done, my wife and I have committed ourselves to finding family things to do together."

We continue to talk throughout the flight. The woman's name is Vinette. Her daughter, Kamie, has a disability, which affects not only her speech but also her learning. She is nonetheless very inquisitive. I see that Vinette cares deeply for Kamie's happiness and growth. Their travels together are part of that care. Kamie asks about my background.

"My mother's French Canadian and my father is Algerian."

"Algeria is near Turkey?"

"Actually, it's just by Morocco."

Vinette interjects, "You know Kamie met a woman from Morocco recently. The woman told her all about the food and the culture. And after a short conversation Kamie knew all about the country." Vinette then asks, "And you're Muslim?"

I sense no hostility, and I feel no unease in speaking about my Muslim identity to Vinette. "Yes, I am."

"Let me show you something," Vinette says. She pulls out her cell phone and shows me a picture of Kamie wearing a headscarf. "I took this picture at my friend Shereen's house. Kamie doesn't understand the religious significance, she just found it beautiful and wanted to wear it. She's like that, she doesn't see differences in the world the way we do."

KILLING CITIZENS: THE LEGITIMACY OF TARGETED ASSASSINATIONS

Muhanad's trial might not have happened. As his letter to his senior al-Qaeda leader tells us, most of his comrades-in-arms had been targeted by drone strikes.[2] But Muhanad was an American. Though he had spent most of his life in Jordan, the UAE, and Canada, he was born in Texas, and this fact changed everything. Neither Ferid nor Miawand were as lucky. As Ahmad Yar recognized, his brother's life was rendered dispensable because he possessed the wrong passport. In a 2015 interview, Ahmad provided the *Globe and Mail* with an impassioned critique of the Canadian government's failure to protect his brother. Ahmad was ready to tolerate his brother paying for his crimes: it "doesn't matter if he gets 100 years [in prison]."[3] But he wanted Miawand to be tried, not killed. Unfortunately for Ahmad, Canada was not the country flying drones in North-West Pakistan. Nor did the Canadian government have much desire to petition the United States for Miawand's safety. In contrast, the US government could not take the matter of assassinating Muhanad lightly. The modern liberal democratic notion of citizenship is meant to grant citizens equal rights before the law. Muhanad's US citizenship afforded him the right to be tried before being punished for any crimes he committed—at least in principle.

Muhanad was lucky in another respect. Ironically, Al-Awlaki, the man who had led Muhanad down a path he would ultimately regret, also indirectly saved Muhanad's life. It was Al-Awlaki's death that made targeting Muhanad for assassination controversial. Al-Awlaki was killed in 2011 in the northern region of Yemen known as al-Jawf. He had become unbearable to the Obama administration. His spiritual guidance to Umar Farouk Abdulmutallab, a Nigerian man who attempted to detonate a bomb over Detroit in December 2009, and Major Nidal Hasan, who attacked military personnel at the Fort Hood military base the month before, jeopardized national security. Even more, it jeopardized the Obama administration's credibility. Obama had heavily criticized the Bush administration's War on Terror, and his campaign had embraced a new direction for Middle East policy. But his critique was only politically viable if he could also provide security for the nation. Without security, Republicans could accuse him of being soft on terrorists and irresponsible in the face of an unmistakable threat.

The Obama administration had made the radical decision to target Al-Awlaki in 2010. In September 2011, the CIA and JSOC (the military's Joint Special Operations Command) tracked down and killed Al-Awlaki.[4] Al-Awlaki was not considered a soldier operating in a clearly demarcated war zone, and the decision to carry out the assassination was therefore far from uncontroversial. The US government had long opposed targeted assassinations, deemed illegal under international law. More important, the fact that Al-Awlaki was abroad did not render null his rights of citizenship. In dealing with Al-Awlaki, the United States was legally bound to follow the same procedures that its law enforcement agencies follow with regard to domestic territory. Police procedures sanction the use of violence only when officers have reason to believe that a suspect poses an *imminent* threat to others. Al-Awlaki, who was miles away from US citizens, did not readily fall under this category and, thus, we would have expected him to be tried for his alleged crimes. But the secrecy of national security meant that Obama was exempt from publicly discussing his decision to target Al-Awlaki, even after the media learned of it. When a team of lawyers representing Al-Awlaki's father challenged the constitutional legality of the assassination order, the judge affirmed that the decision fell within the purview of "the political branch of government" and was therefore beyond judicial oversight.[5]

After Al-Awlaki was killed, the legality of targeting Americans became a heated topic. Legal experts and human rights groups looked upon Al-Awlaki's killing with great concern. It set a new and worrying precedent.[6] Was his killing a slippery slope toward making American lives dispensable? Compounding this fear was the fact that Al-Awlaki was not the only American killed in September. The drones that targeted him also killed Samir Khan, a Charlotte, North Carolina, resident who had joined Al-Awlaki in Yemen and served as the designer for *Inspire*, the magazine of AQAP (al-Qaeda in the Arabian Peninsula). Two weeks later, another drone strike mistakenly killed Al-Awlaki's American-born teenage son, Abdurrahman. All indications are that Abdurrahman was not involved in any terrorist activities. Though the United States had not consciously targeted Khan or Abdurrahman, their actions did show a tolerance for taking American lives as long as doing so protected national interests.

The Obama administration was forced to make public its justification for the legitimacy of targeting US civilians. The Attorney General, Eric Holder, presented the administration's rationale in an address at Northwestern University in March 2012. His position depended on reinterpreting the traditional notion of *imminent* harm that justified the decision to carry out an assassination. "The evaluation of whether an individual presents an 'imminent threat,'" Holder stated, "incorporates considerations of the relevant window of opportunity to act, the possible harm that missing the window would cause to civilians, and the likelihood of heading off future disastrous attacks against the United States."[7] Under this reasoning, "imminence" was determined by weighing the harms and benefits of delaying action. If the President felt that delaying action would lead to a future terrorist attack, he was justified in using lethal force. The problem with Holder's description is precisely that it undercuts the legal mechanisms in place to determine whether the accused actually does pose a threat. As legal scholar Jameel Jaffer notes, "in Holder's imagined scenario, the government is dealing with *known* terrorists who are *known* to be planning attacks continuously—but this assumes a degree of certainty the government will rarely, if ever, have."[8]

Muhanad very easily could have been placed on a "kill list." Kill lists had become the norm in the Obama administration: Bureaucrats gathered to identify whom the administration should target next.[9] The meetings had become banal and the targets ample. No sooner did JSOC dispose of a target than it set its sights on another. Killing Muhanad would have been easy. Drones had spotted him and monitored him throughout 2013. And many individuals and agencies within the government wanted him dead: Both the Pentagon and the CIA were pushing for his assassination; so too were members of the House Intelligence Committee who, in July 2013, expressed surprise that Muhanad was still alive.[10] But the increased public scrutiny after Al-Awlaki's death pushed the Obama administration toward caution. The question of whether Muhanad should be placed on the kill list became a divisive matter within government. Though Holder had justified Al-Awlaki's assassination, he was not so sure about Muhanad. Holder doubted Muhanad had a key role in al-Qaeda or that he posed a great threat to the United States—two doubts eventually substantiated by Muhanad's intercepted letters to his senior al-Qaeda commanders. In accordance with Obama's move to restrict who could be targeted, the decision was made to attempt to capture and prosecute Muhanad. And thus, his life was spared.

On the surface, the move toward capture and prosecution appeared to be a victory for the rule of law. If capture was successful, Muhanad would be tried by his peers. He would have to be proven guilty beyond a shadow of a doubt or released to enjoy the same freedoms as other

Americans. But a line marking a point of no return had already been crossed. The attempt to move the case into the realm of legal process was marred from the beginning because the state never really knew how to classify Muhanad: He occupied a space of ambiguity between foreign enemy and accused criminal. This ambiguity existed for Al-Awlaki as well. US District Judge John Bates, who had presided over the petition to have Al-Awlaki removed from a kill list three years earlier, had expressed consternation at the paradoxical set of legal rights to which a citizen accused of terrorism was subject. On the one hand, this accused citizen of terrorism living abroad had rights to his passport, privacy, and property. The US government could not strip him of these rights without recourse to judicial review. And yet, on the other hand, the government had given itself the right to take his life at its discretion. "How does that all make sense?" Bates asked the attorneys for the government.[11] One way to answer his question would involve taking note of how the citizen-terrorist blurred the usual bureaucratic separation between the military and the judiciary. Military violence is typically aimed at foreign enemies, in situations where the elimination of a suspected threat is the foremost objective. In contrast, the judiciary recognizes rights and places limits on government intrusion in citizens' lives until evidence is shown in a court of law. In short, the military and the judiciary function according to separate logics. In the case of Muhanad, these two logics could never be fully untangled, as was evident in his capture.

At the request of the US government, the Pakistani military made a daring raid on Muhanad's home in Waziristan in late 2014. Muhanad was captured, but he was not transferred to American custody immediately. Had the FBI taken custody of him, he would have been read the Miranda warning, advising him of his right to remain silent. This was not an option the US state was willing to entertain. Muhanad was too valuable an asset: He had spent seven years with al-Qaeda, he knew the organization's structure, and perhaps he also knew where some of its leadership resided. In normal circumstances, the US government had the duty to petition foreign governments who arrest its citizens to respect their rights and to ensure that due process is carried out. Instead, the United States asked the Pakistani military to question Muhanad for them. Eventually, the High-Value Detainee Interrogation Group

(HIG), composed of FBI, CIA, and US military officers, interrogated Muhanad while he remained in Pakistani custody.[12] The HIG claims to use the most scientifically proven interrogation methods while respecting the rule of law.[13] The Obama administration created the HIG in 2009 as part of a move away from the questionable interrogation tactics, like waterboarding, that were implemented during Bush's tenure. Nonetheless, by the time the FBI agent Aaron Sherbondy took custody of Muhanad as part of an extradition agreement on April 1, 2015, from the Bhutto International Airport in the Islamabad-Rawalpindi metropolitan area, Muhanad was in a pitiable state. Muhanad's family does not know the specifics of his treatment at the hands of either the HIG or the Pakistani military but affirm matter-of-factly that Muhanad experienced torture before being extradited to the United States.[14] Considering the documented use of torture by Pakistan's police and military, their claims are more than likely true.

Had Muhanad been subject to torture at the hands of US or Pakistani officials, it would have been relevant to his prosecution. A jury might come to distrust a government narrative about an accused were it to discover that this government either tolerated or actively sought to violate the rights of the accused. A jury may come to see itself in their fellow citizen and to identify a common interest in preventing the state's violation of a citizen's bodily safety. This in turn may make a jury examine state evidence with greater scrutiny. One of Muhanad's lawyers recognized the importance of his client's treatment in Pakistani custody. Sean Maher is quick-witted and pugnacious in the courtroom. During the trial, Maher pressed Sherbondy on the state of Muhanad's clothing: "You say that you observed that Mr. Al Farekh's clothes that he had on at the time you first saw him appeared soiled or dirty, words to that effect; right?"[15] He then tried to ask Sherbondy about the length of time that Muhanad had spent in Pakistani custody and the cause of his soiled clothes. It was clear that Maher wanted to shed light on Muhanad's treatment. But the prosecution objected and the presiding judge, Judge Cogan, quickly put a stop to Maher's line of questioning. Sherbondy did not work on Muhanad's case until his extradition and Judge Cogan considered his answer hearsay. The prosecution had been careful to build a case on evidence that did not depend, at least directly, on evidence gathered while Muhanad was in Pakistani custody. Thus, the defense had no means to shine a light on Muhanad's ill treatment and its implications for the trial. In short, Muhanad's possible torture in Pakistan was effectively sidelined in the trial.

* * *

September 9, 2017. I arrive at LaGuardia Airport. I am exhausted. John, the FBI agent, greets me, accompanied by two other law enforcement officers.

"Youcef," he says warmly. "How was your flight, man?"

"It was alright."

"I'm sorry about your hardships in Toronto."

"It's okay, John, I'm more concerned about the next time."

John looks at me hesitantly: "Next time?"

"Yeah, will I continue to have trouble traveling across the border?"

"Oh, well that's it, next time you'll just travel."

I know John is lying. The border officer's stamp in my passport reads, "One week parole." Under "reason," the officer wrote "Public Benefit." This is Trump's America, and the US government has no intention of reducing my travel difficulties beyond this week.

"I'll bring you to your hotel. You should rest. Tomorrow morning the lawyers for the prosecution would like to meet with you."

On the car ride to the hotel, I ask John about his black eye. "Did you get hurt on the job?"

"Oh, no, I actually got hit doing jiu-jitsu."

"No way, you know Sabir has a black belt in jiu-jitsu."

"I know. He's actually the one who inspired me. We got to talking about jiu-jitsu and I thought to myself, I should give it a try. He's arrived already. He's in a hotel close to yours. You'll both testify the same day."

The road is fairly smooth. My hotel is about a half-hour away; it is walking distance from both the prosecutor's office and the courthouse.

"You know it's interesting," John says, "you and Sabir, you guys were on the same path as Muhanad, Ferid, and Miawand, but you turned out okay."

I am bothered. What exactly does he mean, we were on the same path? Is he implying we had the same jihadist commitments? Or did he mean that we were all Muslims in the MSA and, lo and behold, some of us were not given to violence? Either way, the comment was out of turn. "John, we were never on the same path," I say firmly.

John knows he's offended me, but nonetheless adds, "Well, I know some things, Youcef. You know, through this case, I know some things about you."

I know some things about myself too, I think, but keep my thoughts to myself. The car ride to the hotel proceeds with great tension in the air.

HOW NATIONAL SECURITY SHAPES DUE PROCESS

After Muhanad's transfer to the FBI, the state had decided he would be treated as an accused criminal, with the rights afforded to other citizens. But what I want to show is that these rights only acted as a partial check on national security imperatives. In what follows, I highlight various ways in which national security concerns shaped Muhanad's trial before it even began and produced irregularities that disadvantaged Muhanad. These irregularities can be divided into three categories: mental fitness for trial, ability to prepare for trial, and undue pressures on witnesses.

Muhanad's treatment in US custody affected his mental fitness in making decisions related to his trial. While one type of ill treatment ended with Muhanad's arrest, another, legally sanctioned, form began in the two years before Muhanad faced his jury. Muhanad awaited trial at the Metropolitan Correctional Center in New York, where he spent twenty-three hours a day in a small cell.[16] Solitary confinement is a common tool for disciplining inmates in US prisons. It involves removing them from human contact. Its constitutional legality is questionable because of the Eighth Amendment, which denies cruel and unusual punishment, but courts have typically desisted from ruling against it completely.[17] Instead, they have focused on the conditions of the cells, such as cleanliness, space, or light. Thus, putting Muhanad in solitary confinement was not itself counter to the law. Nonetheless, it was unusual. Typically, solitary confinement is justified to ensure prisoner compliance and safety to others. In Muhanad's case, the office of the Attorney General argued that he should be isolated based on the nature of his alleged crime. Muhanad was considered too great a threat to be allowed freedom of mobility or communication with others—be they inmates or visitors. A memo from the Attorney General referred to Muhanad's "proclivity for violence,"[18] and expressed worries that he might find a way to communicate with other terrorists and endanger American lives or property. But was there really a reason to believe that Muhanad was dangerous? Several factors seem to indicate not. First, the JSOC had monitored his movements closely and they knew he had little contact with anyone in the year prior to his capture. Second, the RCMP and CSIS had concluded that Muhanad, Ferid, and Miawand had acted alone. In other words, Muhanad did not have prior connections to anyone in North America who might be part of a broader conspiracy against the United States. Third, Muhanad had been imprisoned in Pakistan in the months prior to his transfer to US custody, during which he was removed from any contacts he might have had. Fourth, Muhanad was not accused of a violent crime, at least not initially. He was charged with giving material support to a terrorist organization for which he faced a maximum sentence of fifteen years.[19] And fifth, there are ways to monitor a prisoner's communications with the outside world. In sum, the chances that Muhanad could cause harm to any person or property outside of his New York prison were incredibly small. In the end, Muhanad was not put in isolation because of the level of threat that he posed but because the nature of the crime itself had been identified as a national security issue. And with national security, a minimal threat necessitates complete neutralization. Muhanad was considered so fearsome that he was incarcerated beside El Chapo, the notorious leader of the Sinaloa drug cartel.

Solitary confinement created more than psychological difficulties for Muhanad. It also affected his ability to mount a proper defense. Muhanad had lived in Pakistan for seven years. He had no assets and therefore no means to hire a defense team. He could have contacted his father were he not in isolation.[20] Muhanad's father, Dr. Mahmoud Al Farekh, was a physician in the UAE and a person of means. He was sufficiently well off to send his two sons to study abroad despite the high costs of international tuition. More importantly, he cared deeply about his son and would have paid for his legal team. But Mahmood had no access to Muhanad. As a consequence, Muhanad's defense team was state-appointed. The team consisted of Sean Maher,

David Ruhnke, and Diane Ferrone; Maher and Ruhnke would ask most of the questions at trial. They were competent: They raised important objections and asked well-thought-out questions during trial. But as public defenders, they had very limited resources. For instance, they were unable to gather witnesses who might testify in Muhanad's favor. They had no means of interviewing the many people in Winnipeg who would have spoken favorably about his character and mitigated the government's portrait of a hardened radical. Although the prosecution had interviewed me more than a year before the trial, the first time I received a call from the defense was the night before my testimony. There was simply no way that they could adequately prepare to rebut the narrative that the prosecution sought to paint based on my answers and those of other witnesses. As it was, Maher had trouble accessing Muhanad at all. He complained early on about his inability to meet with his client and perform his duties as his lawyer, stating that Muhanad was "severely limited in his access to counsel."[21]

In contrast to the defense's lack of resources, the prosecution was given all the financial resources it needed to build the strongest case possible for Muhanad's guilt. For two years, the prosecution flew all across North America and the Middle East to gather testimonies they could use in court. They had the resources to interview me twice, despite my tangential knowledge of the case. They hired two radicalization experts, two forensics experts, and three internet experts (among whom was the woman from Google I saw waiting in the hallway before my testimony); they ordered DNA testing and fingerprint testing, and paid for the room and board of more than twenty witnesses for several nights in New York. Of course, there is nothing unusual in the prosecution seeking to uncover the necessary details to win its case. That is their task, and in an ideal world both the prosecution and the defense would have had sufficient capacities to present the strongest case against and for Muhanad. The trouble was that the priority given to a national security case caused the imbalance between the prosecution and defense to become unusually pronounced. The Justice Department could not afford an acquittal. Several congressmen and members of Obama's administration had wanted Muhanad dead.[22] That he was breathing reflected government ineptitude in the eyes of one Republican congressman.[23] Muhanad's acquittal would have reinforced the view that law is a mechanism ill-suited to dealing with terrorists. Paradoxically, then, applying the rule of law to Muhanad was only palatable to the state if it produced a conviction. The rule of law could only enforce national security, not override it.

Compounding the imbalance in resources was the problem of secrecy. A principle of the rule of law is that a defendant must be able to question the credibility of evidence used against him in court. For this principle to apply, the prosecution must disclose evidence, including its origins. This principle was largely followed before trial, but there were a few documents whose origins remained shrouded in mystery: the letters that Muhanad allegedly wrote in Pakistan to other al-Qaeda members.[24] They had allegedly been acquired by a CIA operative and the state therefore considered it essential that its source remain confidential. Consequently, the defense could not question the CIA operative on where or how he obtained the letters and, in so doing, cast doubt on claims that they were composed by Muhanad (whose name does not appear anywhere in the letters). But without these letters, the evidence that Muhanad subscribed to a jihadist ideology, let alone belonged to al-Qaeda, was greatly diminished.[25]

Then there was the problem of the witnesses. Those of us who knew the three men in Winnipeg had all suffered at the hands of Canadian security agencies. These agencies' suspicion seriously impacted our livelihoods, often because it precluded our ability to travel to the United States. As a result, we were constantly trying to prove our innocence by assisting the state in meeting its national security objectives by any possible means. This put undue pressure on all of us. I have often reflected on whether my own testimony was fully honest and truthful.[26] The question is not an easy one to answer. It is simplistic to think of testimonies as either honest or perjured. There is a grey area between the two extremes. The grey often comes from how much detail, context, or qualification one provides. I am confident that everything I said the day I testified would have passed a lie detector test. I presented information as best I remembered it. But if I was nervous before my testimony, it is partly because I knew it was wrong to testify under circumstances where witnesses experienced pressure to please the government. And whether I like to admit it or not, I did experience this pressure. I could not be seen as an uncooperative or disappointing witness. And I know other witnesses such as Sabir and Ahmad Yar felt the same. John had often affirmed that he would do whatever possible to help us resolve our difficulties traveling to the United States. He was careful to remain within the sphere of legality by avoiding explicit promises that would see us testify in exchange for an end to travel restrictions. He would say things like "I'll look into it. It's not my jurisdiction but I have a friend I can ask." John walked a fine line between enticement and bribery—and he knew it. He knew subpoena laws did not apply to Canadians and sought to put subtle pressure on witnesses to attend the trial by dangling the hope that it would end the state suspicion that had so greatly affected their lives.

Other witnesses had more to gain than Sabir, Ahmad, and me. The prosecution had asked two men convicted of terrorism-related charges to testify. Najibullah Zazi and Zarein Ahmedzay were both serving time in prison for plotting an attack on Times Square in 2009.[27] Neither had met Muhanad prior to the trial. But the men had gained explosives training in Waziristan. There, they had met a Black man who spoke impeccable English. They later identified the man as Ferid. Ahmedzay would give extensive testimony about his time in Waziristan, the structure of al-Qaeda, and his interactions with Ferid. His description of Ferid certainly rang true: He spoke of Ferid's seriousness and his ability to quell conflict. There was little reason to believe that the content of his testimony was false. But, again, the circumstances of his testimony should raise eyebrows. Neither Ahmedzay nor Zazi had been sentenced at the time, and their testimonies were part of plea deals. Under cross-examination, Ahmedzay informed the court that he hoped to be sentenced to six or seven years in exchange for his cooperation. If so, he would be released on time served. Of course, plea bargains are unexceptional. Criminals are sometimes given lighter sentences in exchange for their testimony in cases that have nothing to do with national security. But it was not only a lighter sentence that Zazi and Ahmedzay desired. They were also promised that their testimony would save them from transfer to the most notorious US prison: the ADX, or United States Penitentiary Administrative Maximum Facility. The prison is located in Flushing, Colorado, and is sometimes ominously called "The Alcatraz of the Rockies." At the time of his testimony, Ahmedzay was allowed out of his cell from morning to evening, he could communicate with family for up to 300 minutes per month, he had recreational opportunities outdoors including sports, he had access to television, and the state gave him $100 a month to purchase products over and above the food he received from the prison. If he was transferred to the ADX, he would be placed in the notorious H-wing that houses terrorist convicts.[28] He would be confined to his cell for twenty-two to twenty-three hours a day for what was bound to be a lengthy prison sentence. The possibility of such a grim existence would weigh heavily on anyone's shoulders.

In sum, the state's decision to try Muhanad did not mark a clean break from the period before his capture when Obama contemplated his assassination. The state's national security imperatives continued to shape how Muhanad was tried. It is difficult to determine how fair a court case could be in such circumstances. None of the measures of the state stood squarely outside of the law: solitary confinement, a well-funded prosecution, a state-appointed defense, and witness plea bargains are all possible tools of a legal system dedicated to convicting criminals while affording the innocent the possibility of acquittal. However, collectively, the measures made the case unique. They highlight how the state's imperative to keep the nation safe tainted due process.

In 2015, Muhanad was charged with material support to a terrorist organization. In other words, the state accused Muhanad of joining al-Qaeda in Waziristan. If convicted, Muhanad would have spent fifteen years in prison. However, a year later, the state came back with eight additional charges. The most serious were conspiracy to murder US nationals and conspiracy to use a weapon of mass destruction. The state had examined fingerprints and DNA on explosive devices targeting US troops in Afghanistan. It concluded that Muhanad had been part of a planned attack on Forward Operating Base Chapman, a US base in the Afghan province of Khost, in January 2009. Muhanad now faced the possibility of life in prison. His trial was set for September 12, 2017.

* * *

September 10, 2017, 8:30 am. I meet with US prosecutor, Saritha Komatireddy, and John in an office of the Department of Justice. I don't want to be here. I'm still angry about John's claim that he knows something suspect about me. We go through my testimony again. Then Saritha says, "Youcef, I want to practice some of the questions that the defense might ask you in their cross-examination. Their goal will be to discredit your testimony."

"I understand," nodding.

"Dr. Soufi," she says in a more formal voice, "you yourself once subscribed to a jihadist ideology, didn't you?"

"No, I haven't."

"Really? Well, in 2010, you took a flight from Montreal to Winnipeg. The airport security searched your bag and found literature on suicide bombing."

So that's what John meant when he said he "knew things" about me. I'm at a breaking point; my eyes roll back in exasperation. "Well, I've gone through this with the RCMP so it's a little strange that they send you only partial information about the Muslims they investigate. It's not literature on suicide bombing, it's a book called *On Suicide Bombing*. The book is based on a series of lectures delivered at UC Irvine by a professor here at the City University of New York, and one of the most distinguished anthropologists of Islam today. It was published with Columbia University Press. So really, unless there's a conspiracy between the University of California, Columbia, and CUNY, there is not much to worry about here. Of course, that's something that anyone, let alone the best security agencies in the world, can google and see."

But that's not how it works, I think to myself. If you're a national security suspect, you remain suspect indefinitely. It doesn't matter how many times you try to justify yourself. If this is my situation, what chance does Muhanad have?

(IM)PARTIAL JUSTICE: BLURRING THE MODERATE/RADICAL LINE

I now turn to the trial itself. In particular, I focus on how assumptions about Islam shaped the courtroom. In a 2019 article, Anver Emon and Aaqib Mahmood examined how a Canadian courtroom became a site of discursive production about the Islamic tradition.[29] Emon and Mahmood analyzed the trial of Asad Ansari, arrested in

2006 as part of the Toronto 18 conspiracy to detonate explosives at the Toronto Stock Exchange. The two scholars revisit the evidence presented by the prosecution, and they express misgivings about the testimony from one of the prosecution's witnesses—an undercover Muslim informant in the case. During the course of his testimony, the witness made several claims about the Islamic tradition. In particular, he made claims about the meaning of the defendant's actions, linking them to a commitment to jihad. But drawing on their expertise in Islamic history, Emon and Mahmood contend that the defendant's actions should be considered far more open to interpretation than the witness conceded. For instance, on one occasion the witness claimed that a black flag at a camp attended by the defendant was a sign of sympathy for jihad. But Emon and Mahmood note that a black flag, particularly before the emergence of ISIS, also had other meanings within Islamic history: It was therefore presumptuous to link the flying of a black flag to an indication of sympathy with jihad. In the end, Emon and Mahmood show us how easy it is for judges and juries to accept a partial or misleading interpretation of the Islamic tradition.

In the following sections, I bear Emon and Mahmood's analysis in mind as I examine the ways in which Islam was described during Muhanad's trial. I show that the prosecution's case against Muhanad depended upon proving that he subscribed to radical Islam, but also that this attempt to prove radicalization involved blurring the line between the moderate and radical Muslim. As in the case of Ansari, the conflation is partly the product of the complexity of the Islamic tradition, in which the meaning of acts and symbols necessitates knowledge of the history and diversity of Muslim thought and practice—knowledge that most American citizens do not possess. But it is also the product of the context of a post–9/11 public sphere that has fumbled in its attempts at finding the dangerous Muslims among us. In his 2006 book, *The Great Theft*, Khalid Abou El Fadl pointed out how malleable the moderate/radical divide had become.[30] He explained that he had recently been labeled a "radical" Muslim by a "well known Islam-basher" despite his impeccable track record of standing up against violence. Depending on who wields the term, "radical" has meant wildly divergent things over and above support for militant groups, including "practising," "conservative," "proud of a Muslim heritage," or "critical of US foreign policy."[31] The consequence is that "moderate" Muslims have been vulnerable to being lumped in with the "radical." The easy blurring of the moderate/radical distinction is significant to the fairness of Muhanad's trial. In his trial, acts of blurring created a situation where mere religiosity was construed as a sign of his looming radicalization. Radicalization, in turn, not only gave the prosecution grounds to claim that Muhanad was likely to join a terrorist organization but also cast Muhanad as a foreign enemy and traitor to the nation. Notably, the blurring of lines between radical and moderate Muslim was often subtle and inadvertent: It inhered in the hidden assumptions and biases of courtroom actors, including the judge, the prosecution, and expert witnesses.

* * *

September 11, 2017, 8 am. According to Google, it was a forty-minute walk from my hotel; I am walking over the bridge into Manhattan. I arrive at the site. Police are everywhere. So too are passersby, come to remember that fateful day sixteen years prior. Muhanad's trial starts tomorrow, a short walk away. But it's here that it all began. No World Trade Center attacks = no war in Afghanistan and Iraq = no Al-Awlaki = Muhanad finishes school and lives a decent and unremarkable life. I wonder about the rawness of the emotions New Yorkers feel today. The victims' families are guests of honor at an event commemorating the anniversary alongside government officials. I think about Muhanad. Why would they hold the trial the day after 9/11? It is too symbolic. It seems bound to stir passions against him.

The ceremony is closed off. I decide to make my way to the site of the Cordoba House—the disparagingly named "Ground Zero Mosque." It was a deeply contested site a short time ago. Protesters had claimed that its organizers were disrespectful for wanting to build a mosque near the World Trade Center. A mosque was considered a symbol of conquest. It did not matter that the imam of the mosque, Feisal Abdul Rauf, had been a long-standing and vocal critic of the Salafi branch of Islam to which al-Qaeda's members subscribed.[32] The antipathy toward Abdul Rauf proved how any Muslim could be lumped in with the radicals. Regardless of his track record and his denunciation of terrorism, protesters of the Cordoba House had refused to distinguish between him and the 9/11 attackers. The controversy ended when the site's property owners determined that erecting a condo building rather than a mosque would be more lucrative.

TEMPORAL BLURRING: ISLAM AND MEDIEVAL DEVIANCY IN THE COURTROOM

Judge Bryan Cogan did not have the responsibility of convicting or exonerating Muhanad. This task belonged to the twelve women and men of the jury. But Judge Cogan did have the responsibility of determining what evidence could and could not be heard in his courtroom. He was responsible for ensuring that the evidence was pertinent to the charges and did not prejudice the fairness of the trial. And one of Judge Cogan's statements gives us insights into the blurriness of the moderate/radical Muslim category within his courtroom. The statement was made in response to an objection from the defense against allowing the prosecution's expert witness on radicalization to take the stand. Judge Cogan gave the objection some consideration. Lorenzo Vidino, an Italian academic with a recent appointment at George Washington University's International Center for Counter-Terrorism, had been invited to testify on the causes of radicalization. The defense had misgivings. The prosecution wanted to use Vidino to explain why someone like Muhanad, a well-liked university student with no track record of violence or crime, might suddenly decide to join a terrorist organization, let alone plan an attack on an American base. But Ruhnke, Muhanad's lawyer, argued that this type of expertise would be inadmissible in the context of other crimes: "I mean, your Honor[,] I believe[,] clearly would not permit a witness to testify in a case of white collar fraud to say, how could some nice college graduate stockbroker get so deep into an insider trading scheme. . . . You wouldn't allow a witness to say [']all kinds of people commit crimes,['] and that's what the Government is proposing to do here [by asking Vidino to take the stand]."[33] Ruhnke pressed the point further: "Nice people commit murders and I've met a lot of them. And it just—it's just we don't go, as I started to say this morning, into a murder case saying . . . anybody can commit a murder. It's common sense."

But Judge Cogan was not so sure. He reasoned that radicalization was not something a regular juror could understand:

> I think, that while jurors can readily understand that people get involved in crimes all the time, it may be beyond the ken of the average juror to have an understanding of why someone—I don't mean this literally—leaves humanity, and reverts to an eighth-century mentality. It's more deviant, a juror or jury could think, than simply committing a crime. So the Government is trying to help answer that possible concern.[34]

Vidino was allowed to testify. But it is not Vidino's testimony that interests me here. Rather, it is the loaded language of the judge presiding over Muhanad's case. In particular, I want to focus on Cogan's statement that a jihadist "leaves humanity, and reverts to an eighth-century mentality." The assumption that jihadism represented a reversion to an eighth-century mentality is amenable to two interpretations. A charitable interpretation of the judge's statement is that he saw history through a Western lens of progress that construed the medieval ages as a period of darkness, characterized by lack of knowledge and the rule of brute strength. It goes without saying that not all the world experienced or remembers the eighth century as a period of violence or ignorance. But regardless, for Cogan, jihadists fell within this category because they subscribed to a worldview that held little regard for reason or human life. The trope of the jihadist as a holdover of medievalism was a common one in the post–9/11 world. Groups like al-Qaeda and the Taliban were accused of inhabiting a premodern temporality.[35]

The second, less charitable interpretation is more concerning for any Muslim defendant in Judge Cogan's courtroom. Under this interpretation, Judge Cogan saw the origins of Islam itself as mired in lawlessness and barbarism. The eighth century is one century off from when Muhammad lived and formed the first Muslim community. Was Judge Cogan in lockstep with common, if vulgar, claims that the problem with Islam today is precisely its medieval origins? Islam, so it is often claimed, never reformed to fit the modern world.[36] As a consequence, Muslims lack human rights and democratic values. Christianity once suffered from a medieval mentality too, but the Protestant Reformation and the move toward the secular sciences during the Enlightenment had changed the course of Christian history. Islam was still waiting for its Martin Luther.[37] Of course, this view acknowledges that Muslims might be moderate, but such moderate voices would be the product of taking faith less seriously. The more religious a Muslim, the more likely he would exemplify these medieval tendencies.

Under this second interpretation, there was already an assumption that Muhanad was at least partly deviant by virtue of his religiosity. And of Muhanad's religiosity, there was little doubt. Copious evidence showed that Muhanad took his faith seriously. But if Judge Cogan believed that Islam was a faith whose practitioners had a tendency to drift into the inhuman and the deviant, then this might have shaped his assessment of the defendant and what counted as evidence against him. Even under the charitable interpretation of Judge Cogan's comments, we still have reason to believe that his comments prejudiced Muhanad's trial. To make the eighth century stand in for deviancy is to make it difficult for Muhanad's religiosity to be seen sympathetically. Most currents of Islamic practice today see the Prophet and his early community as objects of moral emulation. If the eighth century stands in for deviancy, then how might the judge view testimony about the hours Muhanad spent listening to lectures on the Prophet Muhammad's community? Or the community of the early Caliphs? Muhanad's faith could not easily be disconnected from the premodern and the medieval, regardless of how charitable we might be in our interpretation of the judge's comments.

Sahar Aziz, a scholar of Islamophobia and the law, contends that practicing Muslim dissidents are most likely to be seen as a threat to the United States, a perception she claims is held within both liberal and conservative circles. These practicing Muslims often face the ire of the US state and society, whether in the form of discrimination, surveillance, or prosecution. In contrast, Aziz contends that Muslims accepting a "racial bribe," in which they assimilate and tone down their Islamic practice and appearance, gain acceptance within a white and historically Protestant America.[38] Aziz's argument is that the racialization of Muslims reveals that the US aspiration toward religious freedom is "more myth than reality."[39] Her analysis shows that moderate Islam is often presumed to be an absence of Islamic practice or at least a form of Islamic practice that conforms to conservative Christian and liberal secular sensibilities around the private expression of religion. Certainly, it is possible to read Judge Cogan's comments through this lens. The same can be said of the prosecution's statements, which we will soon examine. But what is missing from Aziz's analysis is that the association of Islam with radicalization is an unstable one. Neither Judge Cogan nor the prosecution straightforwardly or even intentionally associated the Islamic tradition with radicalization. Rather, as we shall continue to see, this association takes place through subtle and often unconscious slippages between what constitutes the radical and moderate Muslim.

* * *

September 11, 2017, 10 am. Enough sorrowful brooding for today, I think. Walk around, check out the sites New York is famous for. I make my way to Times Square. But when I arrive, I'm brought right back to thinking about our turbulent times. A poster hangs in the middle of the Square. It features the outline sketch of a beheaded body with blood pouring from the neck. The caption beneath the sketch: "'Can't We Talk About This': Film Director's Last Words as He was Killed for Insulting Islam."[40] The film director is not named, but I recognize the reference. The murdered director was the Dutch filmmaker Theo Van Gogh who was murdered for his film *Fitna* in 2004. The caption was another act of blurring. Again, it suggested that Islam itself was the problem, and was the reason Van Gogh was killed. It played with the old stereotype that Muslims are anti–free speech and therefore do not fit with our values. I think about how ISIS still dominates headlines and fuels the sentiments expressed in the poster. How will Muhanad ever benefit from a fair trial tomorrow if this is the climate that surrounds us?

MUHANAD'S DESCENT INTO RADICALIZATION: (IN)EXPERTISE IN THE COURTROOM

How much did Judge Cogan's views on Islam shape his courtroom? This is a difficult question to answer. But we can point out that much of the prosecution's case rested on showing that Muhanad had become radicalized during his time at the University of Manitoba. To be clear, the prosecution did not make the crude case that Muhanad had radical ideas and was therefore guilty of attacking the US base. To prove Muhanad's guilt, the prosecution had fingerprint and DNA evidence. Thus, the first two days of trial were dedicated to establishing the facts surrounding the January 2009 attack on Base Chapman and linking the forensic evidence to Muhanad. But for the remainder of the two-week trial, the jury heard about Muhanad's descent into radicalization. This testimony was important to the prosecution because beyond the forensic evidence, the evidence linking Muhanad to al-Qaeda was thin. Unlike Miawand, Muhanad never wrote letters to his family that mentioned his jihadist companions. Unlike Ferid, the prosecution could not produce a witness who had seen Muhanad in al-Qaeda training camps. There were letters, but these letters were not signed by Muhanad; rather, they were signed by an ʻAbd Allah al-Shami, which the prosecution claimed was Muhanad's pseudonym.[41] Irrefutable evidence might have shown that Muhanad had traveled with Ferid and Miawand to Afghanistan, but what proof was there that he continued on to Miran Shah with them?

Judge Cogan allowed the prosecution to show Muhanad's descent into radicalization as a means to establish Muhanad's "state of mind" in the lead-up to the commission of his crimes. The concept of "state of mind" pertains to the motives of an accused. It is a necessary part of the criminal justice system because the prosecution must show that the accused intended to commit the act for which he is charged. But in the present case, focusing on Muhanad's descent into radicalization meant determining what radical Islam is. It meant finding traces of this radicalization in his behavior and in the behavior of his close friends.

At times, the blurring of the radical/moderate line in the prosecution's narrative was subtle but sloppy. We have seen some examples in previous chapters: for instance, the prosecution's assumption that paying one's debts is a sign of seeking martyrdom. But there were other examples too. In his summation of the prosecution's case, Assistant US Attorney Douglas Pravda noted that Ferid's letter to his family expressing his desire to be reunited with them was a sign that he was seeking to engage in jihad. Pravda stated:

> Remember, Imam sent an email on March 15th, 2007, to a family member, subject line, ["]worried,["] he's responding to the message from [a] family member. Let me start with the bottom part that we pulled out from this email. [']This is probably the last email you'll receive and I ask Allah to make us a family in Jannah like He has made us a family in this life.['] Remember, Jannah means paradise . . . that's where Ferid Imam believes that he's going[,] to paradise. Because remember, one of the things that you heard from Anwar Al-Awlaki lectures, you hear[d] that a Muslim who dies for the cause of Islam is going to Jannah.[42]

Here, I suspect that Pravda was influenced by popular post–9/11 accounts that reduced the motives of al-Qaeda fighters to a desire to enter paradise.[43] This popular account not only flattened the political motives of al-Qaeda but also caricatured how Muslims understand paradise. Many Muslims pepper their speech with references to reaching paradise as their ultimate objective. Admittedly, Ferid's email was worrisome for its tone of finality: Why was he cutting ties with his family? Why would he not see them again in this life? But nonetheless his language of paradise cannot so easily be assimilated to martyrdom. Ferid always spoke in religiously inflected language. He constantly referenced God and said prayers throughout his discussions with other Muslims. To express that he wished to be reunited with his family in paradise was less a reflection of a belief that he would go to heaven and more a wish that God would accept his deeds and those of his family and reunite them someday. By making Ferid seem confident he would achieve martyrdom and enter paradise, Pravda sought to cast suspicion over Muhanad's travels to Pakistan.

But the most consequential blurring of the moderate/radical divide emerged during the prosecution's questioning of its second terrorism expert. The prosecution's expert witness was a controversial one.

Evan Kohlmann had amassed wealth over the previous decade testifying in terrorism cases, but his credentials were questionable. He had no academic pedigree and his claim to terrorism expertise came from a book he published with an obscure press.[44] After working on counterterrorism for a Washington, DC, think tank called The Investigative Project, Kohlmann ventured into the business of counterterrorism by establishing the company Flashpoint in 2010, which sought to monitor jihadist activity online. Not knowing Arabic or the Islamic tradition, Kohlmann nonetheless established himself as an authority on jihadism. Darryl Li notes how Kohlmann has deceptively positioned himself as the go-to expert for US terrorism cases—and how this deception has profited him handsomely.[45]

In the context of Muhanad's trial, Kohlmann provided some useful information about the publication of Al-Awlaki's lectures online, giving adequate summaries of some of them and explaining where on the web they could be accessed.[46] But Kohlmann failed to make a distinction of paramount importance between Al-Awlaki's earlier mainstream lectures and his later jihadist lectures. He made no mention of Al-Awlaki's momentous shift from a Salafi scholar who believed that terrorist attacks were morally wrong to a jihadist ideologue who called for war against the United States. Many Muslims in 2006 and 2007 listened to Al-Awlaki's lectures for edification on matters of faith. They applied lessons from his stories of past prophets and religious communities to their own lives. Many had no idea Al-Awlaki had turned to radical ideas. But when Assistant US Attorney Saritha Komatireddy asked Kohlmann to shed light on who Al-Awlaki was, Kohlmann described him simplistically by stating: "Anwar Al-Awlaki has gained a reputation as being a particular radical cleric and he also appeared as a spokesman on behalf of al-Qaeda in the Arabian peninsula." This description then shaped how Kohlmann characterized the lectures that Muhanad listened to. For instance, in speaking of the lecture entitled, "It's a War Against Islam," Kohlmann stated:

> The raids [by the FBI on Muslim organizations] were allegedly counterterrorism raids. Raids that were looking for evidence of terrorist financing or terrorist recruitment. During his sermon, Anwar Al-Awlaki argued that, in fact, this was just a pretext for

> a war against Islam. In other words, that these raids were not actually in the vein of targeting terrorist fundraising. They were actually trying to target Islam and Muslims.[47]

Kohlmann's description is accurate, but the possible nefariousness of the lecture depends upon seeing Al-Awlaki as already radical when he delivered the lecture. In fact, Kohlmann omits that Al-Awlaki does not encourage armed resistance in the lecture but rather encourages his audience to follow the example of African Americans who mobilized to demand the recognition of their civil rights. As Scott Shane notes, Al-Awlaki gave this lecture in the context of a Friday sermon at his Northern Virginia mosque, and at the time of its recording he still intended to live and participate in US life.[48]

The same issue plagued Kohlmann's description of Al-Awlaki's *Lives of the Prophets*, of which he stated:

> Anwar Al-Awlaki talks about the necessity of fighting in jihad fi sabilillah, jihad in the way of God. And that Muhammad, and those who surrounded him, had no problem fighting for their beliefs. And that those who wished to emulate the life of the prophet, should also be willing to engage in jihad fi sabilillah, jihad in the way of the God.[49]

There are two problems with Kohlmann's characterization here. First, the *Lives of the Prophets* series was a fairly uncontroversial retelling of the lives of prophets in the Islamic tradition. There is mention of prophets fighting wars, but as Shane also notes, the description is not very different from stories in the Bible. To claim that Al-Awlaki was preaching war in this series would be similar to accusing a Christian preacher of doing so when teaching the story of David and Goliath.[50] Moreover, Kohlmann also described the wrong set of lectures in his answer: He confused the *Lives of the Prophets* series and the *Life of Muhammad* series. The confusion is a testament to Kohlmann's insouciance when describing differences between Al-Awlaki's lectures.[51]

A consequence of Kohlmann's failure to distinguish between Al-Awlaki's non-jihadist and jihadist lectures was to make it difficult for the audience to understand other reasons why Muhanad might have listened to Al-Awlaki. If, as Kohlmann intimated, Al-Awlaki was a radical when he recorded all of his lectures, then Muhanad's interest in them inevitably became suspect. Why would Muhanad listen to so many of them? Why didn't he prefer moderate Muslim lecturers? Surely only a radical Muslim shows so much enthusiasm for a radical's lectures? But in fact we have little proof that Muhanad listened to Al-Awlaki's radical lectures. The only radical lectures we are certain he listened to were *Constants on the Path of Jihad*. But this fact was hardly incriminating, since there are many reasons we can imagine for why Muhanad would have listened to them. For one, he had already listened to several "moderate" Al-Awlaki lectures before *Constants* became accessible to him. We can imagine that he would have had little reason to suspect that *Constants* was a radical series of lectures when he first heard of it. It is plausible that he finished listening to it out of curiosity, wanting to understand how the ideas of a prominent figure among Anglophone Muslims were changing. For another, Muhanad might have listened to the lectures at the behest of his friends, Ferid and Miawand, without finding much value in them. It is a mistake to assume that listening to the lectures is equivalent to sympathizing with their radical content.

Muhanad's defense sought to cast doubt on Kohlmann's credibility during the trial. But Kohlmann should not have been allowed to testify. His lack of knowledge about the shifts in Al-Awlaki's thought and his lack of intimacy with Muslim communities should have disqualified him from providing expert testimony. His continued status as an expert reflected the state's interest in employing him in terrorism trials. The state had an expert who was happy and willing to assist in putting suspected terrorists behind bars. Once again, the concerns of national security shaped the (im)possibility of a fair trial.

* * *

September 14, 2007. That's that, I think. Whatever misgivings I have about this trial I now need to put aside. I follow an FBI agent into the courtroom, an opulent and imposing room with marble floors and walls, and high ceilings. The judge and the witness stand are in front of me, at a distance of maybe thirty meters or so. But my attention is only on one spot. There he is. Muhanad. Unlike in the movies,

Muhanad is not facing the judge. His table is positioned sideways to my right. Our gazes lock. He smirks, recognizing me. I am irked. I can read him: "Youcef, after all this time you're going to come and help put me in jail, help the people who tortured me, and then put me in isolation. You're a good friend, Youcef." My gaze becomes more piercing and my face turns to disgust. He has no right. He has no right to sit in judgment of me, of us. Of the community who stayed behind and picked up the pieces. He has no idea what we've been through because of his stupidity. I'm tired of these lines being drawn: us/them, civilization/barbarity, West/Islam, terrorism/jihad, modern/medieval, radical/moderate. I'm tired of needing to appear loyal to anyone. His expression turns serious. The intensity of his gaze matches mine. This is our only conversation. Our reunion. After ten years and five months. Our eyes are still locked as I arrive at the witness stand.

TREASON!

In this final section, I want to make the case that prosecutors can exploit the label of traitor to secure the conviction of a Muslim accused of terrorism. In liberal democratic states, accusations of treachery often undercut the accused's right to be judged by his peers. Take, for instance, the stance of some members of the Republican Party in the aftermath of the Boston Marathon Bombing of 2013.[52] These politicians claimed that the accused, Dzokhar Tsarnaev, should be treated as an "enemy combatant" with no recourse to courts. The push to have Muhanad killed before his capture was also exemplary of the impulse to strip accused traitors of their right to due process. But my claim here is that even when a Muslim accused of terrorism is afforded the right to a trial, he must do more than prove that he did not break the law: He must also prove his loyalty to the nation. In other words, Muhanad needed not only to cast doubt on the charge that he had joined al-Qaeda and conspired to kill American soldiers, but also to show that he was not ideologically aligned with the enemy. Muhanad needed to show that he was a "good Muslim," who merited his American citizenship.[53] Failure to prove his loyalty would jeopardize how the jury saw him, regardless of evidence. To sustain my claim, I will examine the most damaging court evidence against Muhanad's character: a video recorded shortly before his departure for Pakistan. The prosecution presented this video to support its claims that Muhanad had become radicalized in Canada. Judge Cogan allowed parts of this evidence to be admitted in court, claiming again that it revealed Muhanad's state of mind.[54]

Mahdi, Muhanad's friend and roommate, shot the recording in February 2007. The recording is scarcely a minute long. In it, we see Miawand and Muhanad in their apartment. Miawand is cooking food in the kitchen and Muhanad is at a computer. At one point in the recording, Muhanad shouts in excitement for the men to come. He tells them that he has located a "very good" video on the internet. The video in question is titled "Lee's Life of Lies." Mahdi's recording shows the first few seconds of the video but nothing more. It is clear neither how much of the video Muhanad watched nor why he watched it. However, we know that the video was produced by a jihadist organization calling itself the Islamic Army in Iraq. Moreover, the video shows several scenes of violence against US troops. This violence against US troops was a point of great importance for the prosecution.[55] If the prosecution could show that Muhanad was excited about watching American troops die, then they could comfortably claim that Muhanad supported jihad and they could therefore prove the intent behind the attack against American troops in Afghanistan. But the possibility I would like to raise is that the prosecution knew that this evidence did more than simply reveal Muhanad's state of mind. It also served to position him as a traitor to his nation. In its opening statement, the prosecution had claimed that Muhanad had "turned his back" on his country.[56] Muhanad's excitement at watching the killing of his own country's troops was the clearest indicator of whose side he had taken in the War on Terror. If Muhanad was a traitor, did he not perhaps already deserve to be punished, regardless of the evidence as to whether he had committed a crime?

As the defense argued, exposing the jury to the video created unfair prejudice against Muhanad. To his credit, Judge Cogan recognized this problem.[57] But he sought to strike a balance between the prosecution's right to show Muhanad's state of mind and Muhanad's right not to be subject to an unfairly prejudiced jury. Judge Cogan therefore asked the prosecution to limit the court's viewing of the video. They would only show the jury the first attack against American soldiers and then use Kohlmann to corroborate that similar scenes are shown throughout the video. But we ought to be skeptical that any prejudice could be undercut in this fashion. The problem was not only the affective attachment of many Americans to their troops; it was also the inability to imagine that Muhanad might have watched this video for reasons other than sympathy with jihadists.

In fact, it is clear to me that Muhanad's excitement was not directed at the video's scenes of violence but rather at what it purported to reveal about the War in Iraq. The video itself began from the premise that the US government and media was lying to its citizens about the justification for the war. To uncover these lies, the video's makers presented a letter found on a USB drive allegedly belonging to a fallen American soldier named Lee. The letter is addressed to Lee's family. Within it, Lee reveals his increasing disillusionment with the war: "Why are we even here? The people hate us, and they still don't want our presence, a lot of the kids throw stones at us." The letter goes on to compare the occupation of Iraq to the British occupation of pre-Independence America. It also laments the failure of the United States to learn from its mistakes in Vietnam. It is not difficult to imagine that Muhanad took an interest in this video for what it "revealed" about the war in Iraq. As a young Muslim man, Muhanad knew that the narrative about the War on Terror in popular media distorted the Middle East in which he had grown up. In an era when social media had yet to take root, he would have taken an interest in alternative sources of information on the war in Iraq. We might consider Muhanad naïve and misguided for his failure to recognize that a jihadist source did not exemplify the highest standards of journalism, but his naïveté did not make Muhanad a supporter of violence against US troops. If anything, we might conclude that Muhanad lamented that young US soldiers like Lee had gone to die in a war they no longer considered morally justified.

Muhanad's defense team understood Muhanad's motives as well. In petitioning Judge Cogan not to show the video, Ruhnke explained the wider premise of the footage.[58] But Ruhnke also knew that the jury was unlikely to look favorably upon Muhanad's viewing of enemy propaganda. It was even less likely to forgive his watching of attacks against men and women in uniform. Muhanad may not have shown excitement *because* of the attacks against American troops, but he clearly did not share the sense of disgust that many Americans would have felt about the video. Ruhnke's cross-examination was therefore exceedingly brief. He sought only to emphasize the disjuncture between viewing violence and acting upon it. Muhanad, he implied, was like countless others who watched the video without becoming terrorists:

> Question: Fair to say that the video "Lee's Life for Lies" probably [has] been downloaded by millions and millions of people since it [was] posted?
>
> Answer [Kohlmann]: Millions sounds like a lot. But I would say if the question is, have a lot of people downloaded [it], I think a lot of people have downloaded [it].

In its closing statements, the defense attempted to assimilate Muhanad among other immature college kids who watch ill-advised videos online. They also emphasized that we do not know how much of the video Muhanad watched or why he was excited about it. The points were valid, but too brief to place Muhanad outside of the category of treasonous Muslim.

In the end, understanding, subtlety, and complexity were casualties of the dichotomies created by the War on Terror. Muhanad's act could not be understood on its own terms: The possibility that a young Arab American man, perturbed by the War on Terror and seeking to better understand the War in Iraq, might watch a video that includes imagery his fellow citizens would find deeply hurtful remained unimaginable. Instead, the trope of the treacherous Muslim haunted Muhanad during his trial. Evidence was not scrutinized with sufficient rigor. The adversarial nature of the court process was blunted as a consequence.

* * *

September 29, 2017. I am walking toward my afternoon class. I reflect on the lecture I will deliver. The September air is crisp in Vancouver, and scattered clouds shield some of the sun's rays. Suddenly, my phone vibrates. As I take it from my pocket, I read "John FBI" on my caller ID. What does he want? I think.

"Hi, John."

"Hi, Youcef. I'm here with Saritha."

"Hi, Saritha, how are you?"

"I'm good, Youcef. We have news to share with you. The jury has returned with a verdict. They have found Muhanad guilty on all counts."

I pause. I suspected Muhanad would be found guilty of at least some of the charges. I never really doubted that he had gone to Pakistan to join a jihadist organization. Why else would he have left with Miawand, who openly shared his adulation for jihad? If he didn't share Miawand's commitment to jihad, why did he sever ties with his family and friends?

"Well, it's no real surprise, I guess. I expected this verdict," I finally say.

Saritha continues: "I want to thank you for your testimony. It was really powerful and important to the case."

Now I really don't know what to say. My misgivings about the trial come flooding back. I had convinced myself that I had not testified for or against Muhanad. My testimony merely sought to fill in the blanks of who he was before he left for Pakistan. But I knew I had answered unfair and loaded questions. I had testified to Ferid's lack of empathy for terrorist victims without being asked to give a fuller account of its background. I had testified that the men listened to Al-Awlaki without being asked to offer a broader context for why. And I had testified that Muhanad seemed rigid and dogmatic the last time I had seen him, though I knew I might have imagined that moment as more ominous than it had been—after all, I had spent ten years trying to figure out if there were signs that the men were about to join a jihadist organization.

If I believe Muhanad is guilty, I am nonetheless uneasy with my role in his conviction. Why didn't the defense contact me, I think to myself. I could have helped them create greater clarity about my testimony. I begin to feel like a pawn of the US state in its War on Terror.

"Yeah, well, you know. It was a hard week, for sure," I tell Saritha. My voice trails off as I finish my sentence. "Thank you for letting me know about the verdict, Saritha," I add as we finish the call.

CONCLUSION

I left New York feeling emotionally drained. But I also left committed to being a different type of witness than the one I had been on the stand. Surely, fate had placed me in this situation. Had I never met Muhanad, Ferid, and Miawand, then no one with my training in Islamic studies would be able to tell their story. No one would have witnessed Muhanad's trial and seen how the justice system had failed to meet its aspirations to fairness and impartiality. My commitment was not to free Muhanad or to declare the courtroom a show trial. I saw the hard work that Saritha and others had done to gather evidence against Muhanad. In fact, I appreciated how they helped me understand the story of the three men. Still, there were deep flaws with the judicial process. Flaws that could be attributed to the ambiguous position that Muhanad occupied between national security threat and accused citizen. This ambiguity shaped the period before the trial—the possible torture, the isolation, the lack of access to a lawyer, the imbalanced resources between the prosecution and the defense, and the pressures that witnesses like myself felt to please the state. And it shaped the trial itself by creating an unstable and blurry dichotomy between "radical"/"treasonous" Muslim and "moderate"/"loyal" Muslim. Muhanad's trial was meant to be a triumph for the rule of law. Instead, it laid bare the structural problems that beset trials of Muslim citizens accused of terrorism.

EPILOGUE

Today, Muhanad languishes in a cell in the ADX Supermax in Florence, Colorado—the Alcatraz of the Rockies. His family reports that he is doing well, all things considered. "At least he hasn't lost his marbles yet," his brother recounts. The Winnipeg Muslim community has moved on from the darkest years of the War on Terror. It has grown in numbers, wealth, and political influence. It continues to face various forms of overt and subtle Islamophobia from fellow citizens and institutions. But Canadian security agencies seem to be moving on. CSIS has been increasingly chastised for following simplistic models of radicalization and de-radicalization. In spring of 2023, the Ministry of Public Safety, which is responsible for both the RCMP and CSIS, asked me to present on Islamophobia in an effort to repair trust with Muslim communities. Instead, a new enemy appears to be on the horizon—white supremacists and populist politics driven by conspiracy theories and characterized by a propensity for violent political confrontation.

But the escalation of violence in Gaza in the aftermath of Hamas's bloody incursion into Israel on October 7, 2023, signals the ever-looming prospect of a return to darker times. In this context, I aim to delve into the core claims of this book. I underscore how these claims on state violence and anti-Muslim racism resonate amid the Israeli assault on Gaza for two important reasons. One, I wish to illuminate how my arguments shed light on deeply ingrained aspects of liberal democratic states that persist across shifts in foreign policy. Analyzing the responses of both the US and Canadian states to Hamas's violence on October 7 reveals the enduring state anxieties surrounding consensus-building in the face of foreign threats, pervasive racist assumptions about Muslims, and the persistence of national security strategies of the War on Terror, despite the withdrawal of ground troops from Afghanistan, the dismantling of ISIS in Iraq and Syria, and the scaling back of drone warfare across Muslim majority lands. Likewise, Muslim responses to the Gaza crisis are rooted in entrenched facets of North American Muslim life discernible in the context of the War on Terror. Two, the brutal and inhumane violence inflicted upon Gazan civilians will continue to reverberate in global and domestic US and Canadian politics for years to come. A renewed surge of frustration and feelings of powerlessness characterize Muslim-majority lands, while domestic Muslims are unlikely to forget the shamelessness with which their leaders tolerated, and in some cases justified, the indiscriminate killing of civilians. In this critical context, it is imperative to reflect on why and how the future of Muslim politics in North America is intricately linked to the Gaza crisis.

To begin, I have argued that a key function of liberal democratic states is the continual reimagining of the contours of the nation to render certain forms of violence acceptable. In times of war, the state seeks to unify the population against an enemy by controlling the images of who and what belongs to the nation. In so doing, it renders violent acts righteous and civilian deaths palatable. The devaluation of Muslim life during the War on Terror was a function of the US and NATO's efforts to create boundaries between the civilized and the savage. It relied on the insistence that taking Muslim life abroad was necessary for the preservation of civilization and for the ultimate good of the populations under bombardment and occupation.

The US, Canadian, and European support for Israel's destruction of Gaza followed a similar script. Hamas's violence became a pretext to dehumanize Palestinians as savages—"human animals," to quote Israeli Defense Minister, Yoav Gallant. In an act that once again redrew the collective national imaginaries of their citizens, the US President and Canadian Prime Minister insisted that their nations stand with Israel and that "Israel has a right to defend itself." In so doing, they rendered palatable the taking of life in Gaza, where children are continually killed, and millions have been brought to the brink of dehydration and starvation, for a purported political end deemed necessary at all costs—the destruction of Hamas. At home, this dehumanization made Muslims again suspect by virtue of their cultural and religious proximity to Palestinians and Arabs. On October 14, 2023, a seventy-one-year-old white man stabbed a six-year-old boy twenty-six times in Chicago, reportedly saying, "You Muslims must die."[1] In Winnipeg, a man yelling anti-Muslim slurs attacked a visibly Muslim woman on November 3, 2023, as she brought her child to school.[2] There are differences, of course: Unlike the War on Terror, Israeli violence appears tightly bound to the objective of deterrence and ethnic cleansing. By pounding Gaza indiscriminately and making it uninhabitable for the Palestinian population, Israel asserts its overwhelming capacity and resolve to punish populations that threaten its security. But the immense violence to the civilian population has also made it impossible to keep up the pretense of acting within the limits of the laws of war. This is at least partly why protests typically have been larger and have lasted longer than those organized during the War on Terror.

Second, I have argued that anti-Muslim racism depends upon the blurring of the line between "radical" and "moderate" Muslims. The radical/moderate divide was a product of the United States' post–9/11 strategy to create alliances with Muslims abroad and protect populations at home. North American Muslims themselves accepted the divide, partly because the notion of moderation (*wasatiyya*) is integral to their religious self-understanding, but also because they welcomed the protection it offered them. However, the acceptance of the radical/moderate divide was a Faustian bargain insofar as it created the conditions that permitted state agencies, political leaders, self-declared pundits, and courts to exploit and blur the line between the radical and the moderate. Did subscription to "shariʿa law"—that ill-defined and ambiguous term—make one a radical, as many Ontarians and their politicians proclaimed in 2005;[3] how about wearing a face cover (*niqab*), as Conservative Prime Minister Stephen Harper intimated; or maybe simply praying in public, as some Quebequers reported feeling in 2007?[4] Depending on where one drew the line, Muslims could become the object of repression and suspicion. The division between radical and moderate did not go away when more "Muslim-friendly" administrations came to power. Obama and Trudeau were simply more circumspect about whom they called a radical, and they attempted to avoid explicitly linking Islam to the radical's beliefs or actions. But the line between moderate and radical could still be—and often was—blurred.

The Israeli assault on Gaza in the fall of 2023 shows a similar blurring of lines. Like al-Qaeda once was, Hamas has become the paradigmatic figure of the terrorist, the savage, and the radical—whose killing is barbaric because senseless, causeless, and unprovoked in contrast to Israeli violence, which is presented in popular media as necessarily proportionate self-defense and always righteous. Some politicians have construed pro-Palestinian protests as pro-Hamas rallies and "hate rallies," to quote the Premier of Canada's most populous province, Doug Ford—even as the protesters demand an end to all violence and the preservation of all life. Trudeau, like Biden, followed a familiar playbook of trying to keep peace at home by denouncing Islamophobia, alongside anti-semitism, and asserting the right to peaceful protest, while continuing to support and offer diplomatic shelter for Israel's bombardment and killing of Gazans. However, Muslim communities have rejected any tacit acceptance of militarism abroad. The shamelessness with which Gazans were targeted and blamed for Hamas's crimes, not to mention the decades-old solidarity with Palestinians languishing under military occupation, made it difficult for many of them to stay silent or support the Liberal party. The same is true of American Muslims partly responsible for a large dip in Democratic Party support among swing states. Thus, while the situation in Gaza shows that the blurring of the radical/moderate line is still essential to modern North American states' attempts to drum up support for militarism abroad, its mystifying effects have somewhat dissipated for Muslims, who no longer fear labels that have no empirical basis and are overused (when every form of anti-war protest is tarnished as pro-terrorist, the insult loses all efficacy).

Third, I have argued that the moderate/radical divide masks the commonalities between those labeled moderates and radicals. The analysis of post–9/11 mosque-going Muslims revealed a shared and pervasive concern and love for their sisters and brothers facing the catastrophic devastation of the War on Terror. Their embodied sensibilities toward the *umma*—a community whose existence depends upon moral exhortations and practices of mutual care—made them unsympathetic to Bush's and NATO's civilizational justifications for military campaigns abroad. While a minority, including Muhanad, Ferid, and Miawand, garnered attention for their attempts to right the wrongs of the War on Terror through armed violence, many Muslims coming of age after 9/11 did so through engagement in professions relating to the law, journalism, academia, and grassroots or electoral politics. They should be credited not only with surviving the War on Terror but also contributing to discrediting its claims to necessary or righteous violence.

In the Gaza crisis, a similar Muslim instinct of solidarity is at play. On October 14, 2023, the Manitoba Islamic Association invited me to speak to Winnipeg Muslims about the situation in Gaza. The Muslim community I addressed was acutely aware that 2.2 million Gazans, half of whom were children, were on the precipice of death. The emotions and concerns of those in attendance were strong, and Canadian Muslim communities engaged in solidarity with Canadians of all backgrounds to call for an end to bloodshed abroad. As my colleague working with the Manitoba Islamic Association impassionedly told two members of Parliament: "Do not forget: We are the children of 9/11. Some of us have given our lives to studying Islamophobia and colonial violence; do not believe we will let our children experience this violence and racism again."

The notion of the umma and solidarity with Muslims abroad is by no means a straightforward predictor of Muslim political alliances—indeed, this was Samuel Huntington's mistake in imagining a monolithic Muslim civilization.[5] No clear political program arises inherently from sentiment and attachments alone. But just as Saba Mahmood once pointed out that Muslim piety is the foundation of many Muslims' political commitments in Egypt, North American Muslim sensibilities around the umma form the basis upon which different foreign policy projects are judged and responded to.[6] Care for the umma will be an important factor in American and Muslim politics for decades to come.

Fourth, I have argued that Al-Awlaki's theory of jihad was the product of a rupture with classical Islamic thought. Al-Awlaki belongs instead to a branch of modern jihadist thought that I have termed utopian jihad. Utopian jihad is distinct from the classical legal doctrines of Muslim scholars by virtue of its emphasis on God's alleged promise to bring about military victory to the faithful against all rational odds. It contrasts the pragmatism of premodern jurists who saw the need for leaders to accommodate themselves to the realities of existing political power. But Al-Awlaki's success in compelling some North American Muslims, like Muhanad, Ferid, and Miawand, depended on more than a mere translation of Arab jihadists' ideas into English. Al-Awlaki produced a theory that proffered an explanation and solution to the seeming passivity of Muslims when confronted with their brethren's suffering around the world: They had become attached to worldly life but would gain victory if they sacrificed for God's sake. Al-Awlaki provided these disaffected Muslims with a program that addressed their sense of affective injury over the loss of Muslim life.

Al-Awlaki's influence today has waned. His lectures are difficult to find online and Anglophone Muslim preachers continue to warn their flocks against listening to him. But Al-Awlaki may yet make a reappearance, or if not him, someone of his ilk. The violence in Gaza once again became a moment of deep disorientation for North American Muslims. A common refrain was that the West has lost even the pretense to humanity. How else would they allow children's bodies to be dismembered and charred, wandering hopelessly in crowded hospital courtyards, without hospital beds or even water to keep their wounds clean? How could the human rights discourse that the post–World War II era ushered in so ferociously under the aegis of "Western" leadership be jettisoned in favor of cheering on ethnic cleansing and genocide? A new generation of Muslims is coming of age, and some may again grow impatient with our national complicity in violence abroad. Time will tell.

But I nonetheless remain hopeful that we have entered a new political dawn. A fundamental difference between politically engaged Muslims today and those who, like Ferid, Miawand, and Muhanad, deeply resented post–9/11 militarism under the Bush administration, is the broad coalition to which they now belong—a coalition that cuts across religious, racial, and cultural backgrounds. Without seeking to generalize, their moral compass on Gaza does not distinguish between international law, Islamic scripture, and notions of basic human decency. All three contribute to a principled commitment to human dignity and the preservation of all life—Palestinian and Israeli. They mourned the Israelis killed on October 7 and showed due concern for those that Hamas held hostage, alongside their outrage at Israel's response and indefensible occupation. Muslim and Jewish student protesters celebrating the Passover Seder while calling for Palestinian liberation will be an enduring image of the promise of solidarity in our times. While no politics should be beyond critical scrutiny, North American Muslim communities have stood courageously and firmly in opposition to a Western world that has rendered Palestinian life disposable. For many, the War on Terror was a training ground for forging solidarity with the marginalized and wretched of this earth in ways that saw an overlap between love for the umma and justice for all. This commitment to justice has made them a sorely needed voice for a morality that refuses to sacrifice human life for the sake of political ends. It is perhaps a deep irony that the very community erstwhile under suspicion for violent political proclivities should today serve as the voice of Western moral conscience.

I wish to end by emphasizing a final insight for my reader, one I take to be of great significance to our shared future. More than two decades ago, I made the decision to be part of the Winnipeg Muslim community. By listening to its members and sharing in their form of life, I came to understand our common world differently than I once had. As this world becomes more precarious, we should all pay attention to something they have taught me, something I have sought to convey throughout this book: Solidarity is not contingent on similarity—racial, cultural, religious, linguistic, or even the similarity of common values—as the post-enlightenment concept of the nation would have us believe. Rather, solidarity can also be a choice—to cultivate a relationship of care toward the other, the stranger, the destitute, the wayfarer. It is not easy. It requires work and it requires more than state institutions enforcing agreed upon laws and rights for all. It requires transformations of the self, transformations of the heart. And it is needed now more than ever.

ACKNOWLEDGMENTS

This book benefited from the feedback and insights of several colleagues and friends: Sadaf Ahmed, Anver Emon, Elizabeth Shakman-Hurd, Arun Kundnani, Khalidah Ali, Basit Iqbal, Itrath Syed, Baljit Nagra, Sunera Thobani, Philip Sayers, Rachel Soufi, Sofiya Soufi, Jim Tully, Salman Rana, and Jennifer Selby. I am grateful to Jennifer Hammer and the editorial team at New York University Press, including its two anonymous reviewers, for their encouragement and hard work throughout. I am especially indebted to Amira Mittermaier, who helped me find my authorial voice by inspiring me to embed academic analysis within a compelling narrative. Finally, I wish to express my profound appreciation to Sadaf, Muaaz Jutt, Tasneem Vali, Ramsey Zeid, Idris Elbakri, Ruheen Aziz, Evdoxia Sotiriadou, and Nadira Mustapha for their tireless work upholding human rights in Winnipeg and beyond.

NOTES

Introduction

1 Canadian Security Intelligence Service, *CSIS Annual Report, 2020*, 12–13. See also Stephen Harper's 2011 comments in "Harper Says Islamicism Biggest Threat to Canada," *CBC*, September 6, 2011, www.cbc.ca.

2 Walter Laqueur, "The Terrorism to Come," *Hoover Institution*, August 1, 2004, www.hoover.org. For a genealogy of the concept of "radicalization," see Arun Kundnani, *The Muslims Are Coming: Islamophobia, Extremism, and the Domestic War on Terror* (London: Verso, 2014), 120.

3 *USA v. Al Farekh* (Eastern District of New York, September 12–29, 2017), 1053.

4 Edward Said, "Representing the Colonized: Anthropology's Interlocutors," *Critical Inquiry* 15, no. 2 (1989), 205–225.

5 Darryl Li notes that terrorism studies takes "for granted the globalized order of racial violence that the national security state aims to protect." Darryl Li, *The Universal Enemy* (Stanford, CA: Stanford University Press, 2019), 26. On the phrase, "bringing the state back in," see Theda Skocpol, "Bringing the State Back In: Strategies of Analysis in Current Research," in *Bringing the State Back In*, ed. Peter Evans, Dietrich Rueschemeyer, and Theda Skocpol (New York: Cambridge University Press, 1985), 3–43.

6 "Secretary Clinton Reaction to Osama bin Laden," *CSPAN*, May 2, 2011, www.c-span.org.

7 "Remarks by the President at Cairo University, 6-04-09," *The White House, Office of the Press Secretary*, June 4, 2009, https://obamawhitehouse.archives.gov.

8 Abdolmohammad Kazemipur, *The Muslim Question in Canada: A Story of Segmented Integration* (Vancouver: University of British Columbia Press, 2014), 82; Edward Curtis, *Muslims in America: A Short History* (Oxford: Oxford University Press, 2009), 72; Earle H. Waugh, *Al Rashid Mosque: Building Canadian Muslim Communities* (Edmonton: University of Alberta Press, 2018), 35–70.

9 On the history of Arab Muslims of the Midwest, see Edward Curtis IV, *Muslims of the Heartland: How Syrian Immigrants Made a Home in the American Midwest* (New York: New York University Press, 2022).

10 Haideh Moghissi, Saeed Rahnema, and Mark Goodman, *Diaspora by Design: Muslim Immigrants in Canada and Beyond* (Toronto: University of Toronto Press), 7–10, 25–27.

11 Mohamed Nimer, *The North American Muslim Resource Guide* (London: Routledge, 2002), 79.

12 See also Sadiya Durrani, "Journal of an ISNA Convention," *Manitoba Muslim*, October 2003, 13. On ISNA's place within the landscape of North American Muslim organizations, see Jocelyn Cesari, "Islamic Organizations in the United States," in *The Handbook of American Islam*, ed. Yvonne Y. Haddad and Jane I. Smith (Oxford: Oxford University Press, 2014), 64–86.

13 Zareena Grewal, *Islam Is a Foreign Country: American Muslims and the Global Crisis of Authority* (New York: New York University Press, 2013), 79–124; Jamila Karim, *American Muslim Women: Negotiating Race, Class, and Gender Within the Ummah* (New York: New York University Press, 2009), 25–50. Sherman Jackson, *Islam and the Black American: Looking Towards the Third Resurrection* (Oxford: Oxford University Press, 2005), 3–4.

14 For instance, Canadians have worked as part of the IMAN Centre of Chicago, which fuses hip-hop culture with Islam to combat anti-Black racism within and outside of the Muslim community; on IMAN, see Su'ad Abdul Khabeer, *Muslim Cool: Race, Religion, and Hip Hop in the United States* (New York: New York University Press, 2016), 36.

15 *Reviving the Islamic Spirit* (RIS), the largest annual Islamic conference in Canada in the post– 9/11 era, has often invited Malcolm X's daughter, Attallah Shabazz, to address attendees; https://risconvention.com. See also Jamila Karim, "Islam for the People: Muslim Men's Voices on Race and Ethnicity in the American Ummah," in *Voices of Islam: Voices of Change*, ed. Omid Safi and Vincent Cornell (Westport, CT: Praeger, 2007), 44.

16 Jerome Klassen, *Joining Empire: The Political Economy of the New Canadian Foreign Policy* (Toronto: University of Toronto Press, 2014), 104; Rey Koslowski, "Smart Borders, Virtual Borders or No Borders: Homeland Security Choices for the United States and Canada," *Law and Business Review of the Americas* 11, no. 3 (2005), 527–528.

17 Yasmeen Abu-Laban and Nisha Nath, "From Deportation to Apology: The Case of Maher Arar and the Canadian State," *Canadian Ethnic Studies* 39, no. 3 (2007), 71–98.

18 Examples of excellent studies include Baljit Nagra, *Securitized Citizens: Canadian Muslims' Experience of Race Relations and Identity Formation Post-9/11* (Toronto: University of Toronto Press, 2017), 93; and Seher Selod, *Forever Suspect* (New Brunswick, NJ: Rutgers University Press, 2018).

19 Although security agencies and politicians have also labeled members of the Shiʿa community radical, they have largely used the term "homegrown radical" to speak of Sunni groups that follow the Salafi branch of Islam to which al-Qaeda and ISIS subscribed.

20 Khaled Beydoun, *American Islamophobia: Understanding the Roots and Rise of Fear* (Oakland: University of California Press, 2018), 28.

21 On intra-Muslim debates over the meaning of "moderate Islam," see Rosemarie Corbett, *Making Moderate Islam: Sufism, Service, and the "Ground Zero Mosque"* (Stanford, CA: Stanford University Press, 2016), 5–11.

22 Bill Waiser, *Park Prisoners: The Untold Story of Western Canada's National Parks* (Saskatoon: Fifth House, 1995); Bohdan S. Kordan, *No Free Man: Canada, the Great War, and the Enemy Alien Experience* (Montreal: McGill University Press, 2016), 152–153.

23 Kassandra Luciuk, "Reinserting Radicalism: Canada's First National Internment Operations, the Ukrainian Left, and the Politics of Redress," in *Civilian Internment in Canada: Histories and Legacies*, ed. Rhonda L. Hinther and Jim Mochoruk (Winnipeg: University of Manitoba Press, 2020), 47–48.

24 Mona Oikawa, *Cartographies of Violence: Japanese Canadian Women, Memory, and the Subjects of the Internment* (Toronto: University of Toronto Press, 2012), viii.

25 "Banff Pavilion Highlights WWI Internment Camps," *CBC*, September 13, 2013, www.cbc.ca (accessed December 28, 2020). Dawn Walton, "Controversy Dogs Exhibit on First World War Internment," *Globe and Mail*, June 10, 2013, www.globeandmail.com. The theme of national contrition is also common in media and political discussions of the internment of Canadian Japanese internees in the Second World War; see Pamela Hickman and James Fasuko, *Japanese Canadian Internment in the Second World War* (Toronto: James Lorimer and Company, 2011).

26 Beydoun, *American Islamophobia*, 83–90.
27 Surveillance went hand in hand with camps during the First World War when 80,000 enemy aliens were given identity papers and requied to regularly report to the police authority for monitoring. Luciuk, "Reinserting Radicalism."
28 On the historical origins of the state's claims to legitimate violence, see Janice Thomson, *Mercenaries, Pirates, and Sovereigns* (Princeton, NJ: Princeton University Press, 1994), 3.
29 Zuhair Kashmeri's journalistic reporting unveiled the surveillance of Canadian Arabs and Muslims during the First Gulf War. Kashmeri claimed that the impact of the surveillance on Muslim communities would take years to mend. Zuhair Kashmeri, "When CSIS Comes Knocking: Canadian Arabs, Racism, and the Gulf War," in *Whose National Security*, ed. Gary Kinsman, Dieter K. Buse, and Mercedes Steedman (Toronto: Between the Lines, 2000), 256–266; Zuhair Kashmeri, *The Gulf Within* (Toronto: James Lorimer & Company, 1991), 12.
30 Baljit Nagra and Paula Maurutto, "Crossing Borders and Managing Racialized Identities: Experiences of Security and Surveillance Among Young Canadian Muslims," *Canadian Journal of Sociology* 41, no. 2 (2016), 165–194.
31 Mayanthi Fernando provides a probing example of how the liberal state seeks to define the nation, focusing on France's use of secularism to define the French nation in the face of increasing social fragmentation in the age of neoliberal markets. *The Republic Unsettled: Muslim French and the Contradictions of Secularism* (Durham, NC: Duke University Press, 2014), 9.
32 Talal Asad, *Formations of the Secular: Christianity, Islam, Modernity* (Stanford, CA: Stanford University Press, 2003), 3–8.
33 Benedict Anderson, *Imagined Communities*, revised edition (London: Verso, 2006), 5–6.
34 E.g., Charles Taylor, "Nationalism and Modernity," in *The State of the Nation: Ernest Gellner and the Theory of Nationalism* (Cambridge: Cambridge University Press, 1998), 191–218; Michael Ignatieff, *Blood and Belonging* (Toronto: Penguin Canada, 1994).
35 John Milloy, *A National Crime: The Canadian Government and the Residential School System 1879–1986* (Winnipeg: University of Manitoba Press, 1999), 27.
36 On the Conservative government's use of the *niqab* for political gain, see Natasha Bakht, "In Your Face: Piercing the Veil of Ignorance About *Niqab*-Wearing Women," *Social & Legal Studies* 24, no. 3 (2015), 419–441.
37 Kirby Bourne, "Alberta Muslim Group Condemns Racist Letter Received by Edmonton Mosque," *Global News*, February 6, 2019, https://globalnews.ca.
38 *Daily Nor'Wester*, August 3, 1897, 4.
39 Noah Salomon, *For Love of the Prophet: An Ethnography of Sudan's Islamic State* (Princeton, NJ: Princeton University Press, 2016), 4; see also Yael Navarro-Yashin, *Faces of the State* (Princeton, NJ: Princeton University Press, 2002), 119.
40 On the relationship between state and society, see Joe Painter, "State: Society," in *Spaces of Geographical Thought: Deconstructing Binaries* (London: Sage, 2005), 42–60.
41 Carl Schmitt, *Political Theology*, trans. George Schwab (Chicago: University of Chicago Press, 2006), 5. Giorgio Agamben, *Homo Sacer: Sovereign Power and Bare Life*, trans. Daniel Heller-Roazen (Stanford, CA: Stanford University Press, 1998), 11–12.
42 Sherene Razack, *Casting Out: The Eviction of Muslims from Western Law and Politics* (Toronto: University of Toronto Press, 2008), 11–14.
43 Craig Forcese and Kent Roach, *False Security: The Radicalization of Canadian Anti-Terrorism Law* (Toronto: Irwin Law, 2015), 23.
44 The controversial measures of the Anti-Terrorism Act were revived under Bill C-51 in 2015 and the Combating Terrorism Act of 2013 (Bill S7), which revived investigative hearings.

45 Reg Whitaker, Greg Sealy, and Andrew Parnaby, *Secret Service: Political Policing in Canada: From the Fenians to Fortress America* (Toronto: University of Toronto Press, 2012), 437.

46 Prior to 9/11, few Canadian Muslim residents had provable ties to al-Qaeda. Most of those accused of terrorist ties in the first four years after 9/11 were identified as part of the social circle of the LAX Airport millennium bomb plotter, Ahmed Ressam. Ahmed Khadr and the two Jabarah brothers (Mohammed and Abdul Rahman) are other notable exceptions. Importantly, all of these suspects had come to Canada as adults. On Ressam's circle, see Daniel Livermore, *Detained: Islamic Fundamentalist Extremism and the War on Terror in Canada* (Montreal: McGill University Press, 2018), 58–69.

47 US Department of Homeland Security, "National Strategy for Homeland Security," October 2007, 22.

48 Paul Koring, "Terror Alerts Short on Specifics," *Globe and Mail*, October 4, 2010, www.globeandmail.com. The term "homegrown terrorist/militant" itself existed before 9/11, but until the London attacks of 2005, the *Globe and Mail* used the term for Muslims in reference to other countries like Yemen and Indonesia; see for instance Oliver Moore, "Rumsfeld Finesses Coalition Partners," *Globe and Mail*, October 4, 2001, www.globeandmail.com; Dillon Paul, "Indonesians Bracing for Terror-Trial Verdict," *Globe and Mail*, September 2, 2003, www.globeandmail.com. Reid Morden's analysis of the 7/7 London attacks marks the first instance I found in which an article mentions the term homegrown terrorist/radical to refer to Muslims born in the West; see Reid Morden, "You Can't Always See Them Coming," *Globe and Mail*, July 30, 2005, www.globeandmail.com. A watershed moment in the term's use is the trial of the Toronto 18, and by 2010, the term is being used very frequently.

49 Aside from those who joined ISIS in Syria and Iraq, many others proclaimed loyalty to ISIS online; see Abdul Basit, "Foreign Fighters in Iraq and Syria—Why So Many?" *Counter Terrorist Trends and Analyses* 6, no. 9 (2014), 4–8; Greg Myre, "Americans in ISIS: Some 300 Tried to Join, 12 Have Returned to U.S.," February 5, 2018, www.npr.org.

50 On the Friday night *halaqa*, see "Regular Activities: 'Youth English Halaqa,'" *Manitoba Muslim* 1, no. 1 (1999), n.p.

51 See, e.g., "Fund Raising Dinner for Palestine," *Manitoba Muslim* 2, no. 4 (2001), n.p. "The Massacre of Sabra and Shatila: Twenty Years Later," *Manitoba Muslim* 4, no. 1 (2002), n.p.

52 On pan-Islamism, see Faiz Ahmed, *Afghanistan Rising: Islamic Statecraft between the Ottoman and British Empires* (Cambridge, MA: Harvard University Press, 2017), 13–17.

53 See the audio for the song on YouTube, at www.youtube.com/watch?v=5nsDGO_l-aQ.

54 Darryl Li, *The Universal Enemy* (Stanford, CA: Stanford University Press, 2019), 26.

55 Khalid Blankinship, "Parity of Muslim and Western Concepts of Just War," *Muslim World* 101, no. 3 (2011), 412–426.

56 Saba Mahmood's pathbreaking *Politics of Piety: The Islamic Revival and the Feminist Subject* (Princeton, NJ: Princeton University Press, 2005) and Charles Hirschkind's *The Ethical Soundscape: Cassette Sermons and Islamic Counterpublics* (New York: Columbia University Press, 2006) both show that Muslim politics is impacted by pious Muslims' self-fashioning.

57 Thus, books of theology (*kalam*) are silent on jihad and those of law reserve a modest section for its treatment. See Richard Bonney, *Jihad: From Qur'an to Bin Laden* (Basingstoke, UK: Palgrave Macmillan, 2004); Michael Bonner, *Jihad in Islamic History: Doctrines and Practice* (Princeton, NJ: Princeton University Press, 2008).

58 Karl Marx and Friedrich Engels, "Manifesto of the Communist Party," in *The Marx-Engels Reader*, ed. Robert C. Tucker, 2nd edition (New York: W.W. Norton, 1978), 497–499.

59 Ernst Bloch, *The Principle of Hope*, trans. Neville Plaice, Stephen Plaice, and Paul Knight, 3 vols. (Cambridge, MA: MIT Press, 1986), 1:142–147.
60 Herbert Marcuse, "Art and Revolution," in *Counterrevolution and Revolt* (Boston: Beacon Press, 1972), 110–111.
61 Fredric Jameson, *Archaeologies of the Future: The Desire Called Utopia and Other Science Fictions* (London: Verso, 2005), xiii.
62 See Jacques Derrida, "Force of Law: The Mystical Foundation of Authority," in *Deconstruction and the Possibility of Justice*, ed. Drucilla Cornell, Michel Rosenfeld, and David Gray Carlson (New York: Routledge, 1992), 26–27.
63 Tayeb El-Hibri, *The Abbasid Caliphate* (Cambridge: Cambridge University Press, 2021), 28–43.
64 Madawi Al-Rasheed, *A History of Saudi Arabia* (New York: Cambridge University Press, 2002), 59–62.
65 Fred M. Donner, *Muhammad and the Believers: At the Origins of Islam* (Cambridge, MA: Harvard University Press, 2010), 145–189.
66 Patricia Crone, *God's Rule: Government and Islam* (New York: Columbia University Press, 2005), 125–144.
67 Abu al-Hasan al-Mawardi, *al-Ahkam al-Sultaniyya*, ed. Ahmad Mubarak al-Baghdadi (Kuwait: Dar Ibn Qutayba, 1989), 8–9.
68 Muslim ibn al-Hajjaj, *Sahih Muslim*, ed. Muhammad ʻAbd al-Baqi (Cairo: ʻIsa al-Babi al-Halabi, 1955), 69.
69 Ernest Gellner, *Muslim Society* (Cambridge: Cambridge University Press, 1981), 54–56.
70 Although Asad wrote his essay in 1986, its influence became more pronounced by the late '90s and early 2000s. Talal Asad, *The Idea of an Anthropology of Islam* (Center for Contemporary Arab Studies, Georgetown University, Working Paper Series, 1986).
71 Kundnani, *The Muslims Are Coming*, 58–59.
72 Abu al-Hasan al-Mawardi, *al-Hawi al-Kabir*, ed.ʻAli Muhammad Muʻawwad and ʻAdil Ahmad ʻAbd al-Mawjud, 18 vols. (Beirut: Dar al-Kutub al-ʻIlmiyya, 2009), 14:351.
73 Ibn al-Humam, *Sharh Fath al-Qadir*, ed. ʻAbd al-Razzaq Ghalib al-Mahdi, 10 vols. (Beirut: Dar al-Kutub al-ʻIlmiyya, 2003), 5: 443–444.
74 Religion is sometimes seen as a form of brainwashing where it "pushes" its followers like automatons toward violence; Stephen Nemeth, "Rational Choice and Religious Terrorism: Its Bases, Applications, and Future," *The Cambridge Companion to Religion and Terrorism*, ed. James Lewis (New York: Cambridge University Press, 2017), 106.
75 For a critique of studies that eliminates religion from their analysis, see Lorne Dawson, "Trying to Make Sense of Home-Grown Terrorist Radicalization: The Case of the Toronto 18," in *Religious Radicalization and Securitization in Canada and Beyond*, ed. Lorne Dawson and Paul Bramadat (Toronto: University of Toronto Press, 2017), 82.
76 The challenge of understanding political violence demands a proper account of the relationship between political circumstances and cultural/religious sensibilities and beliefs. To emphasize the cultural/religious and neglect the political is to fall prey to a long-standing European colonial tendency to see the other as a savage inevitably prone to violence. However, to emphasize politics alone risks distorting the diversity of human societies and reducing them to "our" Western self-understandings and embodied sensibilities.
77 On the history of salafi-jihadism, see Shiraz Maher, *Salafi-Jihad: The History of an Idea* (New York: Oxford University Press, 2016).
78 See Evelyn Alsultany, *Broken: The Failed Promise of Muslim Inclusion* (New York: New York University Press, 2023).

79 In the context of the anthropology of Islam and the Middle East, see Ted Swedenburg, *Memories of Revolt: The 1936–1939 Revolt and the Palestinian National Past* (Minneapolis: University of Minnesota Press, 1995). See Johannes Fabian, *Memory Against Culture: Arguments and Reminders* (Durham, NC: Duke University Press, 2006), 132.
80 On al-Ghazali's famous quest for knowledge, see *al-Munqidh min al-Dalal*, published as *The Faith and Practice of al-Ghazali*, trans. Montgomery Watt (Oxford: Oneworld, 1994).
81 Although for reasons of style, I do not always add quotation marks around the term radical, the reader that encounters these terms should imagine their presence. Among the goals of this study would be for us to transcend this term altogether.

Chapter 1. Can the Muslim Speak?

1 Scott Atran, "Who Becomes a Terrorist Today?" *Perspectives on Terrorism* 2, no. 5 (2010), 3–10. Marc Sageman, *Understanding Terror Networks* (Philadelphia: University of Pennsylvania Press, 2004); Rik Coolsaet, *Al-Qaeda, the Myth: The Root Causes of International Terrorism and How to Tackle Them* (Ghent, BE: Academia Press, 2005); Marc Sageman, "Facing the Fourth Foreign Fighter Wave: What Drives Europeans to Syria, and to Islamic State? Insights from the Belgian Case," *Royal Institute for International Relations* (2016); S. Cottee and K. Hayward, "Terrorist (E)motives: The Existential Attractions of Terrorism," *Studies in Conflict and Terrorism* 34, no. 12 (2011), 963–986; L. L. Dawson and A. Amarasingam, "Talking to Foreign Fighters: Insights into the Motivations for Hijrah to Syria and Iraq," *Studies in Conflict and Terrorism* 40, no. 3 (2017), 191–210.
2 Jeffrey Monaghan and Adam Molnar, "Radicalisation Theories, Policing Practices, and 'the Future of Terrorism?'" *Critical Studies on Terrorism* 9, no. 3 (2016), 393–413.
3 Reid Morden, "You Can't Always See Them Coming," *Globe and Mail*, July 30, 2005, www.globeandmail.com.
4 US prosecutors commonly spoke of Muhanad, Miawand, and Ferid as "ordinary" young men; *USA v. Al Farekh*, 885.
5 Gerhard Enns, *Homeland to Hinterland: The Changing Worlds of the Red River Metis in the Nineteenth Century* (Toronto: University of Toronto Press, 1996).
6 Alan Artibise, *Winnipeg: A Social History of Urban Growth, 1874–1914* (Montreal and London: McGill University Press, 1975), 129–148; Arthur Ross, *Communal Solidarity: Immigration, Settlement, and Social Welfare in Winnipeg's Jewish Community, 1982–1930* (Winnipeg: University of Manitoba Press, 2019).
7 On Muslim families who settled in Manitoba prior to the postwar period, see Ismael Mukhtar's *Manitoba Muslims: A History of Resilience and Growth* (Altona: FriesenPress, 2021), 1–26.
8 *Prairie Mosque* (2018) by Snow Angel Films, run by two Winnipeg Muslim sisters, Nilufer Rahman and Saira Rahman, presents testimonies by Muslim immigrants to Winnipeg in the 1950s and 1960s of their early experiences in the city. See also Mukhtar, *Manitoba Muslims*, 27–39.
9 "Community Profile," *Manitoba Muslim*, November 5, 1999, n.p.
10 A few prayer spaces, though not full-fledged mosques, did pop up in the intervening years. These included the Education Foundation on Sargent Avenue as well as the Pakistan Centre in the downtown region, which had a prayer room, largely for Friday prayers.
11 To celebrate its fortieth anniversary, the mosque was renamed the Pioneer Mosque in 2016. www.cbc.ca.
12 Sarah F. Howell, "Inventing the American Mosque: Early Muslims and Their Institutions in Detroit, 1910–1980" (PhD diss., University of Michigan, 2009), 48.

13 On the gendered Muslim campus experience, see Shabana Mir, *Muslim American Women on Campus: Undergraduate Social Life and Identity* (Chapel Hill: University of North Carolina Press, 2014); see also Marcia K. Hermansen, "How to Put the Genie Back in the Bottle: Identity Islam and Muslim Youth Cultures in the United States," in *Progressive Muslims: On Pluralism, Gender and Justice*, ed. Omid Safi (Oxford: Oneworld, 2003), 303–319.

14 The *hadith* whereby Muhammad affirms that God rewards prayer in congregation more than prayer alone motivates Muslims to attend prayer spaces. On women in mosque spaces, see Marion Katz, *Women in the Mosque: A History of Legal Thought and Social Practice* (New York: Columbia University Press, 2021).

15 Anthony Leek, "Muslim Students Association Presents Fast-a-Thon," *The Manitoban*, November 17, 2004, 3. https://digitalcollections.lib.umanitoba.ca. Accessed January 21, 2022.

16 For examples, see "Islam Awareness Week," *Manitoba Muslim* 2, no. 2 (2000), n.p.

17 In April 2006, Ferid had challenged Ezzedin for the presidency of the MSA. Ezzedin won the election but then abandoned his role. Ferid stepped in to fulfill the organizational gap.

18 "Whoever believes in God and the Last Day, let him speak well or remain silent (*fa'l-yaqul al-khayr aw li-yasmut*)." *Hadith* 15 in al-Nawawi's collection. Al-Nawawi, *Kitab al-Arba'in al-Nawawiyya*, ed. Ahmad al-Bakri, 4th ed. (Cairo: Dar al-Salam, 2007), 12.

19 Haideh Moghissi, "Multiculturalism and Belonging: Muslims in Canada," in *New Horizons of Muslim Diaspora in North America and Europe*, ed. Moha Ennaji (Cham, CH: Springer, 2006), 91–102.

20 This is not to say that Ferid knew no variability in his practice: Life events continually shaped how he approached religion in his life. For instance, in the winter of 2005–2006, Ferid was diagnosed with tuberculosis. When Dawud and I visited him, we could see how the illness had made him rethink his purpose in life. His sister also remembers a time in high school when she struggled to get him to pray. For Muslim shifts in religiosity, see Samuli Schielke, *Egypt in the Future Tense: Hope, Frustration, and Ambivalence Before and After 2011* (Bloomington: Indiana University Press, 2015).

21 Ebrahim Moosa, "Ethical Landscape: Laws, Norms, and Morality," in *Islam in the Modern World*, ed. J. Kenney and E. Moosa (London: Routledge, 2014), 35–56.

22 Khaled Abou El-Fadl, *The Great Theft: Wrestling Islam from the Extremists* (New York: Harper Collins).

23 The difficulty in pinning down Salafism is that the term has been appropriated by different groups at different historical junctures. The word itself has roots in the expression *al-salaf al-salih* (the pious predecessors), which refers to the first three generations of Muslims (the prophet's companions, then their successors [*al-tabi'in*] and then *their* successors). Thus the term Salafism is tied to the idea of following the example of the early community of Muslims and rejecting later accretions to the faith. However, those who have invoked the term have meant wildly divergent things when deploying it. In the premodern period, the term was used to refer to a theological approach that shunned speculative thinking on the attributes of God in favor of deference to the text; see Henri Lauziere, *The Making of Salafism: Reform in the 20th Century* (New York: Columbia University Press, 2016). However, in the early twentieth century, the term was invoked by a circle of Muslim reformers, foremost among them the Syrian Rashid Rida. Jonathan Brown usefully calls the movement of these reformers "salafi-modernism" because of its desire to interpret early Islam in ways compatible with modernity. By the 1970s, Salafism had become most associated with preachers in Saudi Arabia who claimed to rely on a literal interpretation of hadith to determine correct practice.

24 Caner Dagli, "The Phony Islam of ISIS," *The Atlantic* (2015), www.theatlantic.com.

25 Abou El Fadl, *The Great Theft*, 95–112. See Stéphane Lacroix, "Between Revolution and Apoliticism: Nasir al-Din al-Albani and His Impact on the Shaping of Contemporary Salafism al-Albani," in *Global Salafism*, ed. Roel Meijer (New York: Oxford University Press, 2014), 58–70. Aaron Rock-Singer, *In the Shade of the Sunna: Salafi Piety in the Twentieth Century Middle East* (Oakland: University of California Press, 2022), 14.

26 See, for instance, the obituary in the *Manitoba Muslim* for a prominent Salafi scholar, "Obituary—Sheik Bin Othaimeen," *Manitoba Muslim* 2, no. 3 (2001), n.p. Salafism in Winnipeg was partly strengthened by an influx of Muslims from North Africa; see Frederic Wehrey and Anouar Boukhars, *Salafism in the Maghreb: Politics, Piety, and Militancy* (Oxford: Oxford University Press, 2019).

27 The subtle presence of Salafism is evident in a seeming contradiction in the interview of a founding member of the Manitoba Islamic Association in the documentary *Prairie Mosque*: The founding member lamented the increase of dogmatic and strict religious positions among the Winnipeg community in the decades after the Hazelwood Mosque was built, but in the same interview, he also praised King Faysal of Saudi Arabia for providing funds for the mosque in 1975. The founding member seemed unaware that the Saudi Kingdom played a strong part in strengthening the attitudes he lamented in the Winnipeg Muslim community.

28 For examples of the arguments made against celebrating non-Muslim holidays, see the lecture of Abdullah Hakim Quick, *Holiday Myths* (Toronto: Sound Vision, 1997).

29 Muslim b. al-Hajaj, *Sahih Muslim* (Riyadh: Dar al-Tayyiba, 2006), 1230.

30 Khaled Abou El Fadl, *Speaking in God's Name: Islamic Law, Authority, and Women* (London: Oneworld, 2001), 468. I should caution the reader against thinking that Salafism is the only branch of Islam that cares about sexual morality or shows concern with retaining a Muslim identity. My point is only that these twin concerns are strongly emphasized within Salafi discourse.

31 On Alshareef's al-Maghrib Institute, see Zareena Grewal, *Islam Is a Foreign Country: American Muslims and the Global Crisis of Authority* (New York: New York University Press, 2013), 330–332.

32 Sadek Hamid, "Abdur-Raheem Green, the Life of a British Convert to Salafism," in *Global Salafism*, ed. Roel Meijer (New York: Oxford University Press, 2015), 445–446; Sadek Hamid, *Sufis, Salafis and Islamists: The Contested Ground of British Islamic Activism* (London: IB Tauris, 2016). See also Green's website: www.islamsgreen.org.

33 On March 1, 2007, Ferid sent an email rhetorically asking if the men singing the *Burda* in a video were truly religious scholars.

34 On Salafism's reputation for dogmatism and rebuking the ungodly, see Abou El Fadl, *The Great Theft: Wrestling Islam from the Extremist* (New York: Harper, 2005), 250.

35 Greg McArthur, Patrick White, Joe Friesen, and Christie Blatchford, "The Lost Boys of Winnipeg," *Globe and Mail*, October 1, 2010, A14.

36 *USA v. Al Farekh*, 598–560.

37 *USA v. Al Farekh*, 669.

38 *Queen v. Yar*, Provincial Court of Manitoba, April 26, 2006, 2–104.

39 Lewis R. Rambo, *Understanding Religious Conversion* (New Haven, CT: Yale University Press, 1994).

40 Nada Moumtaz, "Refiguring Islam," in *A Companion to the Anthropology of the Middle East* (Hoboken, NJ: John Wiley & Sons, 2015), 125–150.

41 Schielke, *Egypt in the Future Tense*, 135–136.

42 See the episode "The Convert," season 1, episode 7 of the TV show *Little Mosque on the Prairie*, produced by CBC, which features a white convert who tells others how to practice Islam; both conversion and a return to the faith involves *iltizam* (a commitment to ritual practice); see Schielke, *Egypt in the Future Tense*, 130–131.

43 Recent studies on South Asia have brought to light the importance of ongoing contestation in the Islamic tradition: Shir Ali Tareen, *Defending Muhammad in Modernity* (Notre Dame, IN: Notre Dame University Press, 2020); Naveeda Khan, *Muslim Becoming: Aspiration and Skepticism in Modern Pakistan* (Durham, NC: Duke University Press, 2012), 7; Irfan Ahmed, *Religion as Critique: Islamic Critical Thinking from Mecca to the Marketplace* (Chapel Hill: University of North Carolina Press, 2017); Youcef Soufi, *The Rise of Critical Islam: 10th–13th Century Debate* (New York: Oxford University Press, 2023).

44 See Anver Emon, *Islamic Natural Law Theories* (New York: Oxford University Press, 2010); Felicitas Opwis, *Maslaha and the Purpose of the Law: Islamic Discourse on Legal Change from the 4th/10th to 8th/14th Century* (Leiden, NL: Brill, 2010).

45 Given many converts' desire to diligently apply religious rules without a full awareness of historical legal debates, it is unsurprising that radicalization experts have noted newfound religiosity as a common variable among radicals. On conversion, see Amy Melissa Guimond, *Converting to Islam: Understanding the Experiences of White American Females* (Cham, CH: Springer, 2017); Patrick D. Bowen, *A History of Conversion to Islam in the United States, Volume 1 White American Muslims before 1975* (Leiden, NL: Brill, 2015); Karin Van Nieuwkerk, ed., *Women Embracing Islam: Gender and Conversion in the West* (Austin: University of Texas Press, 2006); Karin Van Nieuwkerk, "'Conversion' to Islam and the Construction of a Pious Self," in *The Oxford Handbook of Religious Conversion*, ed. L. Rambo and C. Farhadian (Oxford: Oxford University Press, 2014).

46 Luisa Gandolfo, *Palestinians in Jordan* (London: IB Taurus, 2012), 42.

47 Medina Tenour Whiteman shows the privilege and power of white Muslims, able to navigate white society by avoiding the racialization of the Muslim majority. But they are also highly prized in Muslim communities as indicators of Islam's universalism and its ability to attract peoples from economically and politically dominant societies; Whiteman, *The Invisible Muslim: Journeys through Whiteness and Islam* (London: Oxford University Press, 2020).

48 On the effects of neoliberalism and economic growth on faith in the UAE, see Joud Alkorani, "Dubai Detours: Being Muslim After the Islamic Revival and Arab Spring" (PhD diss., University of Toronto, 2021).

49 The few widely available English language books for Muslims were published by Salafi presses like Dar-us-Salam Publications. An example of the type of Islamic literature that Muhanad gravitated toward was 'Aaidh al-Qarni's *Don't Be Sad* (Riyadh: International Islamic Publishing House, 2005), a text that uses Qur'anic verses, prophetic reports, and stories from Muslim history to help individuals cope with their life trials.

50 Dale Eickelman, "Mass Higher Education and the Religious Imagination in Contemporary Arab Societies." *American Ethnologist* 19, no. 4 (1992), 643–655.

51 The question of finding an iteration of Islam compatible with a Western environment was popular after 9/11: Tariq Ramadan, *Western Muslims and the Future of Islam* (New York: Oxford University Press, 2005); Sherman Jackson, *Islam and the Black American: Looking Toward the Third Resurrection* (New York: Oxford University Press, 2005); Justine Howe, *Suburban Islam* (New York: Oxford University Press, 2018).

52 *USA v. Al Farekh*, 590.

53 Talal Asad, *Formations of the Secular: Christianity, Islam, Modernity* (Stanford, CA: Stanford University Press, 2003), 10–11.

54 Arun Kundnani, *The Muslims Are Coming: Islamophobia, Extremism, and the Domestic War on Terror* (London: Verso, 2014), 65–69.

55 "Community Programs and Services: Publications," *Manitoba Muslim* 2, no. 2 (2001), n.p.

56 Paul Bramadat, "The Public, the Political, and the Possible," in *Religious Radicalization and Securitization in Canada and Beyond*, ed. L. Dawson and P. Bramadat (Toronto: University of Toronto Press, 2014), 20.

57 Patrick White and Colin Freeze, "Family Fears U.S. Has Killed Winnipeg's 'Lost Boys' of Jihad," April 23, 2015, www.globeandmail.com.
58 Colin Freeze, "Former CIA Director Knew of Canada's 'Lost Boys'," November 19, 2010, www.globeandmail.com.
59 Abu 'Abd Allah al-Bukhari, *Sahih al-Bukhari* (Damascus: Dar ibn Kathir, 2002), 860.
60 For the verse's exegesis, see Muhammad b. Jarir al-Tabari, *Jami' al-Bayan* (Beirut: Dar Ibn Hazm, 2013), 3, 60.
61 Kristen Stilt, *Islamic Law in Action: Authority, Discretion, and Everyday Experiences in Mamluk Egypt* (Oxford: Oxford University Press, 2012), 73–75.
62 Muslim jurists sometimes speak of "communal obligations"—acts that God expects some to undertake, such as ensuring that the bodies of the deceased are washed and proper funeral prayers are observed. When these obligations are not fulfilled, the entire Muslim community is held accountable for failing to fulfill God's law.
63 Victor Hugo, *Les Misérables* (Paris: J. Hetzel et A. Lacroix, 1867), 60.
64 McArthur et al., "The Lost Boys," A14.
65 Nicole Nguyen, *Suspect Communities: Anti-Muslim Racism and the Domestic War on Terrorism* (Minneapolis: University of Minnesota Press, 2019), 6–8.
66 See James Tully, *Strange Multiplicity: Constitutionalism in an Age of Diversity* (Cambridge: Cambridge University Press, 1995), 35.
67 Talal Asad speaks of a "democratic ethos" as a sensibility that takes the fact of our togetherness as foundational and therefore makes us attentive to the needs, views, and struggles of fellow citizens; "Thinking about Secularism," in *Multitudes* 59, no. 2 (2015), 69–82. See also Hussein Agrama, "Reflections on Secularism, Democracy, and Politics in Egypt," *Amercian Ethnologist* 39, no. 1 (2012), 26–31.
68 Alasdair MacIntyre, *After Virtue: A Study in Moral Theory*, 3rd ed. (Notre Dame, IN: Notre Dame University Press, 2007), 244.

Chapter 2. Lives That Mattered and Lives That Didn't

1 On the eve of 9/11, Canadian Muslims struggled with the negative depiction of their faith: see Bob Harvey, "Air Farce Apologizes for Muslim Skit: Routine Depicted Muslims as Terrorists, Complainants Say," *Ottawa Citizen*, January 29, 2000, A8.
2 The concept of *haram* is part of a complex typology of Islamic law; see Bernard Weiss, *The Search for God's Law: Islamic Jurisprudence in the Writings of Sayf al-Din al-Amidi*, revised edition (Salt Lake City: University of Utah Press, 2010), 94. For a primary source, see Abu Ishaq al-Shirazi, *Sharh al-Luma'*, ed. Majid Turki (Tunis: Dar al-Gharb al-Islami, 1988).
3 *USA v. Al Farekh*, 537–538.
4 Kathy Gilsinan, "Where Were You on 9/11? Stories from the New York Area," *The Atlantic*, September 9, 2016, www.theatlantic.com.
5 Jane Gadd, "Day of Infamy Canadian Reaction: Muslims Fear Backlash; Jewish Group Issues Alert," *Globe and Mail*, September 12, 2001, www.globeandmail.com.
6 Susan Baer and David Greene, "'Face of Terror Not True Faith of Islam,' Bush Declares," *Baltimore Sun*, September 18, 2001, www.baltimoresun.com.
7 Debates (Hansard), 37th Parliament, 1st Session, no. 79 (September 17, 2001) (Ottawa, House of Commons of Canada), 5115, www.ourcommons.ca.
8 Debates (Hansard), no. 79, 5117.
9 Debates (Hansard), no. 79, 5124.
10 Robert J. C. Young, *Postcolonialism: An Historical Introduction* (Oxford: Blackwell, 2001), 22, 30.

11 For a nineteenth-century history of "the West," see Christopher Lloyd GoGwilt, *The Invention of the West: Joseph Conrad and the Double-Mapping of Europe and Empire* (Stanford, CA: Stanford University Press, 1995).
12 James Mill, J.S.'s father, sought to provide a precise typology of stages of civilization; see Jennifer Pitts, *A Turn to Empire: The Rise of Imperial Liberalism in Britain and France* (Princeton, NJ: Princeton University Press, 2009), 129–133. See also Michael Levin, *J.S. Mill on Civilization and Barbarism* (New York and London: Routledge, 2004).
13 John Stuart Mill, "Civilization," in *Essays on Politics and Society (Complete Collected Works, Vol. 18)* (Toronto: University of Toronto Press, 1977), 119.
14 Alexander Morris, *The Treaties of Canada with the Indians of Manitoba and the North-West Territories Including the Negotiations on Which They Are Based, and Other Information Relating Thereto* (Toronto: Willing & Williamson, 1880), 292.
15 Debates (Hansard), no. 79, 5118.
16 Debates (Hansard), no. 79, 5116. Day, for his part, explicitly spoke of "other radical Middle Eastern groups," and, in so doing, positioned the region as a whole as a potential battleground (p. 5118).
17 Samuel Huntington, "The Clash of Civilizations?" *Foreign Affairs* 72, no. 3 (1993), 22.
18 Samuel P. Huntington, *The Clash of Civilizations and the Remaking of World Order* (New York: Simon & Schuster, 1996), 183.
19 Tanja Collet, "Civilization and Civilized in Post–9/11 US Presidential Speeches," *Discourse & Society* 20, no. 4 (2009), 458.
20 "Text: President Bush Addresses the Nation," *Washington Post*, September 20, 2001, www.washingtonpost.com.
21 Deepa Kumar, *Islamophobia and the Politics of Empire: 20 Years after 9/11* (New York: Verso, 2021), 129.
22 Junaid Rana, *Terrifying Muslims: Race and Labor in the South Asian Diaspora* (Durham, NC: Duke University Press, 2011), 5.
23 Lila Abu-Lughod, *Do Muslim Women Need Saving?* (Cambridge, MA: Harvard University Press, 2013); Sherene Razack, *Casting Out: The Eviction of Muslims from Western Law and Politics* (Toronto: University of Toronto Press, 2008), 83–84.
24 "National Prayer Service," September 14, 2001, www.c-span.org.
25 Dana Milbank and Emily Wax, "Bush Visits Mosque to Forestall Hate Crimes," *Washington Post*, September 18, 2001, www.washingtonpost.com.
26 "Text: President Bush Addresses the Nation."
27 Debates (Hansard), no. 79, 5116.
28 Debates (Hansard), no. 79, 5122–5123.
29 Bob Harvey, "Churches Urge End to Bombing: Seek Non-Military Solutions to Crisis," *Ottawa Citizen*, October 2001, A8.
30 Judith Butler, *Frames of War: When Is Life Grievable?* (London: Verso Books, 2016), 38.
31 Mike Davis, *Late Victorian Holocausts: El Nino Famines and the Making of the Third World* (London: Verso Books, 2002).
32 See Makau Mutua, "Savages, Victims, and Saviors: The Metaphor of Human Rights," *Harvard International Law Journal* 42, no. 1 (2001), 201–245.
33 James Farrell, "The Story behind the Friendly Fire Tragedy: Misguided Bomb," *Calgary Herald*, October 5, 2002, OS06.
34 Debates (Hansard), 37th Parliament, 1st Session, No. 171 (April 18, 2002) (House of Commons of Canada), 10537.
35 Allison Dunfield, "Canadian to Co-Chair U.S. Friendly-Fire Inquiry," *Globe and Mail*, April 23, 2002. www.globeandmail.com.

36 Barry Bearak, "Uncertain Toll in Fog of War: Civilian Deaths from American Raids in Afghanistan," *New York Times*, February 10, 2002, 1.
37 Carlotta Gall and Eric Schmitt, "Shocked Afghans Criticize U.S. Strike; Toll Is Some 40 Dead and 100 Wounded," *New York Times*, July 3, 2002, A3.
38 Carlotta Gall, "Hunt for Taliban Leaves Village with Horror," *New York Times*, July 8, 2002, A1.
39 Dexter Filkins, "War Blunders Kill Hundreds: Flaws in U.S. Air Campaign Have Left Upward of 400 Afghan Civilians Dead," *Times Colonist*, July 21, 2002, A1.
40 See Charles Abrogast, "U.S. Attack Hits Wedding; Stray Bomb Leaves Scores of Afghans Dead, Injured," *Toronto Star*, July 2, 2002, A01.
41 For instance, Mohamed Elmasry told the Standing Committee on Justice and Human Rights, House of Commons of Canada, 2001: "We are familiar with terror, because for most of us coming from developing countries terrorist acts are a way of life," 6. Bruce Culp, "Keeping Their Faith: Muslims across the Country Live in Fear of Retribution for Recent Terrorist Attacks in the United States," *The Standard*, September 22, 2001, A1.
42 Sheema Khan argued that popular assumptions that the "West Knows Best" covered up Muslim histories of seeking human rights and their dismantling of oppressive strictures like misogyny. Sheema Khan, "Dismantling Oppressive Strictures Takes Guts," *Toronto Star*, August 12, 2002, A17.
43 "MSA 10th Annual Conference," *Manitoba Muslim* 1, no. 2 (2000), n.p.
44 For Green's discussion of the conference, see his blog, Abdurraheem Green, "Welcome to Heathrow!" Islam's Green, www.islamsgreen.org.
45 Green also gives a similar speech on the Islam channel: *Chechnya The Forgotten Land*, https://www.youtube.com/watch?v=cngUqrljq10.
46 On Chechnya's history of resistance to Russian imperialism, see Rebecca Ruth Gould, *Writers and Rebels: The Literature of Insurgency in the Caucasus* (New Haven, CT: Yale University Press, 2016).
47 Green, *Chechnya The Forgotten Land*.
48 The Qur'an deploys the concept of umma frequently but in different ways: for instance, to refer to the Muslim community (3:110), past religious communities (10:47), all humankind (10:19), the community of animals (6:38), and to the conduct of pious individuals like Abraham (16:120).
49 Nikki Keddie, "Pan-Islamism as Proto-Nationalism," *Journal of Modern History* 41, no. 1 (1969), 17–28.
50 Tahseen Shams, *Here, There, and Elsewhere: The Making of Immigrant Identities in a Globalized World* (Stanford, CA: Stanford University Press, 2020), 6.
51 Cemil Aydin, *The Idea of the Muslim World: A Global Intellectual History* (New York: Columbia University Press, 2017).
52 Benedict Anderson, *Imagined Communities*, revised edition (London: Verso, 2006), 5–6.
53 See "Words of Revelation," *Manitoba Muslim* 1, no. 2 (2000), n.p., for an example of the type of Qur'anic verses that were used to promote mutual care among Muslims.
54 Zareena Grewal, *Islam Is a Foreign Country: American Muslims and the Global Crisis of Authority* (New York: New York University Press, 2013), 83.
55 Shams, *Here, There, and Elsewhere*.
56 The Manitoba Islamic Association wrote in its e-newsletter: "Appeal for donations for the victims of the disaster in South Asia: The death toll from the devastating tsunamis in Asia has reached 44,000, and could dramatically increase in the coming days. The Manitoba Islamic Association is requesting all members of the community and all friends to act immediately to assist the victims of this horrifying disaster. Please remember, in your prayers, the victims of this catastrophe and their families. Please donate generously today." *Manitoba Muslim*, E-Newsletter, December 28,

2004. On January 7, the Ellice Avenue mosque preceded its fundraising efforts for Tsunami relief with a lecture entitled "Core Values of the Muslim Community." Email correspondence, December 28, 2004.

57 Al-Nawawi, *al-Arba'in*, 11.

58 Al-Nawawi, *al-Arba'in*, 26: "Do not envy each other, do not outbid each other (in marketplaces), do not turn away from each other, and do not outsell each other. Rather, be servants of God as brothers. The Muslim is the brother of another Muslim, he does not wrong him or humiliate him or look down upon him. Righteousness is here (and the prophet pointed to his heart). It is enough evil for a man to look down upon his Muslim brother. The entirety of the Muslim is sacred to another Muslim: his life, his property, and his dignity."

59 Muslim b. al-Hajaj, *Sahih Muslim* (Riyadh: Dar al-Tayyiba, 2006), 1201: Al-Nu'man b. Bashir reported: "The Messenger of God, peace and blessings be upon him, said, 'The parable of the believers in their affection, mercy, and compassion for each other is that of a body. When any limb aches, the whole body reacts with restlessness and fever.'"

60 Saba Mahmood, *Politics of Piety: The Islamic Revival and the Feminist Subject* (Princeton, NJ: Princeton University Press, 2005), 22–27. For a critique of the focus on self-cultivation, see Samuli Schielke, "Being Good in Ramadan: Ambivalence, Fragmentation, and the Moral Self in the Lives of Young Egyptians," *Journal of the Royal Anthropological Institute* 15, no. 1 (2009), 24–40.

61 Talal Asad, "Remarks on the Anthropology of the Body," in *Religion and the Body*, ed. Sarah Coakley (Cambridge: Cambridge University Press, 2000), 48.

62 For instance, on March 20, 2004, a group of Muslims shared the announcement of the No War Coalition of Manitoba association, regarding an upcoming rally at city hall. The announcement read: "End the Occupation of Iraq! End the War at Home and Abroad. No to 'Pre-emptive War.' Space for Peace! Palestine and Afghanistan—End the Occupations!" March 11, 2004. Personal email correspondence.

63 The association "No one is Illegal" organized a rally in support of a Muslim community member facing deportation. November 6, 2004. Personal email correspondence.

64 Haideh Moghissi, "Multiculturalism and Belonging," in *New Horizons of Muslim Diaspora in North America and Europe*, ed. Moha Ennaji (Cham, CH: Springer, 2006), 96–99; Rubina Ramji, "A Variable but Convergent Islam: Muslim Women," in *Growing Up Canadian: Muslims, Hindus, Buddhists*, ed. Peter Beyer and Rubina Ramji (Montreal: McGill-Queen's University Press, 2013), 112–144. Rogers Brubaker, "Categories of Analysis and Categories of Practice: A Note on the Study of Muslims in European Countries of Immigration," *Ethnic and Racial Studies* 36, no. 1 (2013), 1–8.

65 This sentiment of "finding Islam" is documented in Zarqa Nawaz, *Me and the Mosque* (National Film Board of Canada), 2005, www.nfb.ca.

66 Paul Wiecek, "A Death Sentence for Iraq's Children," *Winnipeg Free Press*, April 2, 1998, A1.

67 For instance, the Qur'an claims that God has ennobled "all Children of Adam" (17:70); the MIA also published articles speaking of the need to help all humankind; see "The Meaning of Ramadan," *Manitoba Muslim* 2, no. 1 (2000), n.p.

68 See Asad's essay "Redeeming the 'Human' in Human Rights," in *Formations of the Secular* (Stanford, CA: Stanford University Press, 2003), 127–158.

69 See Anne Phillips, *The Politics of the Human* (Cambridge: Cambridge University Press, 2015), 1–20.

70 Hannah Arendt, *The Origins of Totalitarianism* (New York: Brace Jovanovich, 1966), 299–300.

71 Following the "Friendly Fire" incident, several Canadians demanded that their country revisit its commitment to the War in Afghanistan.

72 This anti-war sentiment was particularly strong in Quebec; see Lysianne Gagnon, "The Doves of Quebec," *Globe and Mail*, February 23, 2003, A11.
73 Tim Harper, "Canadians Back Chretien on War, Poll Finds; 71% Approve of Decision to Stay Out," *Toronto Star*, March 22, 2003, A01.
74 Wiecek, "A Death Sentence."
75 Personal email correspondence, October 26, 2006.
76 See the movie *Rambo III* (Tri-Star Pictures, 1988), portraying Afghan Mujahideen as freedom fighters ennobled by their religious convictions.
77 See Nilufer Rahman, "Finding Our Niche in These Troubling Times," *Manitoba Muslim* 5, 2 (2003), n.p.
78 On affect and emotion, see Charles Hirschkind, *The Ethical Soundscape: Cassette Sermons and Islamic Counterpublics* (New York: Columbia University Press, 2006), 82.
79 Omid Safi, "The Times They Are A-Changing," *Progressive Muslims: On Justice, Gender and Pluralism* (Oxford: Oneworld, 2003), 1–32.
80 Su'ad Abdul Khabeer, *Muslim Cool: Race, Religion, and Hip Hop in the United States* (New York: New York University Press, 2016), 3–8.
81 Talal Asad, *On Suicide Bombing* (New York: Columbia University Press, 2007), 2.

Chapter 3. The Emergence of the Homegrown Jihadist

1 See bin Laden's speeches in Gilles Kepel, ed., *al-Qaeda in Its Own Words*, trans. Pascale Ghazale (Cambridge, MA: Belknap Press of Harvard University Press, 3008), 11–80.
2 Al-Awlaki was hired as the Imam of the Dar al-Hijra Mosque in Falls Church, Virginia; Scott Shane, *Objective Troy: A Terrorist, A President, and the Rise of the Drone* (New York: Tim Duggan Books, 2015), 83.
3 Andrea Elliot, "Why Yasir Qadhi Wants to Talk about Jihad," *New York Times*, March 17, 2011, www.nytimes.com.
4 Knut Vikhor, *Between God and Sultan: A History of Islamic Law* (Oxford: Oxford University Press, 2005), 8.
5 Al-Shirazi, *Sharh al-Luma'*, ed. Majid Turki (Lebanon: Dar al-Gharb al-Islami, 1988), 1012–1013; Ibn al-Qassar, *Muqaddima fi Usul al-Fiqh*, ed. Mustafa Makhdum (Riyadh: Dar al-Ma'lama li'l-Nashr wa'l-Tawzi', 1999), 140; al-'Ukbari, *Risalat al-'Ukbari*, ed. Badr al-Subay'i (Amman: Arwiqa, 2017), 77; Ibn al-Farra', *al-'Udda fi Usul al-Fiqh*, Muhammad 'Ata (Beirut: Dar al-Kutub al-'Ilmiyya, 2002), 2:444.
6 Abu al-Husayn al-Basri, *al-Mu'tamad fi Usul al-Fiqh*, ed. Khalil al-Mays, 2 vols. (Beirut: Dar al-Kutub al-'Ilmiyya, 1983), 2:384; Abu Bakr al-Jassas, *Usul al-Jassas al-Musamma al-Fusul fi al-Usul*, ed. Muhammad Tamir, 2 vols. (Beirut: Manshurat Muhammad 'Ali Baydun, 2000), 2:423; Abu al-Ma'ali al-Juwayni, *al-Talkhis fi Usul al-Fiqh*, ed. 'Abd Allah al-Nibali and Shabir al-'Amri, 3 vols. (Beirut: Dar al-Basha'ir al-Islamiyya), 3:35; Abu Hamid al-Ghazali, *al-Mustasfa fi 'Ilm al-Usul*, ed. Hamza b. Zuhayr Hafiz, 4 vols. (Medina: n.p., 1993), 4:71.
7 Al-Shirazi, *Sharh al-Luma'*, 1038.
8 Since 9/11, a plethora of secondary literature has examined jihad. Examples include Richard Bonney, *Jihad: From Qur'an to Bin Laden* (Basingstoke, UK: Palgrave Macmillan, 2004); Michael Bonner, *Jihad in Islamic History: Doctrines and Practice* (Princeton, NJ: Princeton University Press, 2008), 97–117; F. E. Peters, *Muhammad and the Origins of Islam* (Albany: State University of New York Press, 1994); David Cook, *Understanding Jihad* (Berkeley: University of California Press, 2005), 19–22, 56–63; Patricia Crone, *Medieval Islamic Political Thought* (Edinburgh, Edinburgh University Press, 2005), 297–300, 362–373; and Asma Afsaruddin, *Striving in the*

Path of God: Jihad and Martyrdom in Islamic Thought (New York: Oxford University Press, 2013), 1–3.

9 The term is *jihad al-nafs*, meaining one's struggle with the lower self. Cook, *Understanding Jihad*, 32–48. Another modern use of the term is the meaning "struggle for a good cause." This is the way that Amina Wadud uses the term in *Inside the Gender Jihad: Women's Reform in Islam* (Oxford: Oneworld, 2006).

10 Khalid Blankinship, "Parity of Muslim and Western Concepts of Just War," *Muslim World* 101, no. 3 (2011), 412–426.

11 S. Frederick Starr, *Lost Enlightenment: Central Asia's Golden Age from the Arab Conquest to Tamerlane* (Princeton, NJ: Princeton University Press, 2013), 101. George Makdisi, *The Rise of Colleges: Institutions of Learning in Islam and the West* (Edinburgh: Edinburgh University Press, 1981), 35.

12 Burhan al-Din al-Marghinani, *al-Hidaya: Sharh Bidayat al-Mubtadi*, ed. Muhammad ʿAdnan Darwish (Beirut: Dar al-Arqam b. Abi al-Arqam, 1997), 2: 424; Al-Sarakhsi identifies the purpose of jihad with "breaking the strength of the polytheists (*kasr shawkat al-mushrikin*) and to strengthen [the Islamic] religion (*iʿzaz al-din*)." Al-Sarakhsi, *Kitab al-Mabsut* (Beirut: Dar al-Maʿrifa, 1989), 10, 3.

13 Al-Shaybani, *Kitab al-Siyar al-Saghir: The Shorter Book on Muslim International Law*, ed. and trans. Mahmood Ahmad Ghazi (Islamabad: Islamic Research Institute, 1998), 10.

14 Abu Zayd Al-Dabbusi, *Taqwim al-Adilla fi Usul al-Fiqh*, ed. Khalil al-Mays (Beirut: Dar al-Kutub al-ʿIlmiyya, 2001), 45; Badr al-Din al-ʿAyni, *al-Binaya: Sharh al-Hidaya*, ed. Ayman Salih Shaʿban (Beirut: Dar al-Kutub al-ʿIlmiyya, 2000), 7:96.

15 Qur'an 47:5.

16 Qur'an 8:61.

17 Abu Ishaq al-Shirazi, *al-Muhadhdhab fi Fiqh al-Imam al-Shafiʿi*, ed. Muhammad Zuhayli (Damascus: Dar al-Qalam, 1992), 5:228–229.

18 Al-Marghinani, *al-Hidaya*, 2: 462. See Khaled Abou El Fadl, *Rebellion and Violence in Islamic Law* (Cambridge: Cambridge University Press, 2001), 37.

19 Realism's description of the international arena as an anarchic realm is mirrored in the jurists' concept of *dar al-harb* (a realm of war) which jurists invoked to speak of non-Muslim governed states; Giovanna Calasso and Giuliano Lancioni, eds., *Dar Al-Islam/Dar al-Harb: Territories, People, Identities* (Leiden, NL: Brill, 2017).

20 Al-Shirazi, *al-Muhadhdhab*, 5:228–229.

21 ʿAla al-Din al-Samarqandi, *Tuhfat al-Fuqaha'* (Beirut: Dar al-Kutub al-ʿIlmiyya, 1984), 3:295.

22 Al-Jassas, *Sharh Mukhtasar al-Tahawi*, ed. ʿIsmat Allah ʿInayat Allah Muhammad and Zaynab Muhammad Fallata (Beirut: Dar al-Basha'ir al-Islamiyya, 2010), 7:10.

23 Al-Sarakhsi, *al-Mabsut*, 10:86.

24 See for instance, al-Shirazi, *al-Muhadhdhab*, 5: 347–348.

25 Abu al-Hasan al-Mawardi, *al-Hawi al-Kabir fi Fiqh Madhhab al-Imam al-Shafiʿi*, ed. ʿAli Muhammad Muʿawwad and ʿAdil Ahmad ʿAbd al-Mawjud (Beirut: Dar al-Kutub al-ʿIlmiyya, 1994), 14: 296–297.

26 Youcef L. Soufi, "From Conquest to Co-existence: Burhan al-Din al-Marghinani's Reinterpretation of Jihad Doctrine," *Journal of Islamic Studies* 32, no. 2 (2021), 203–236.

27 Abu al-Qasim al-Zamakhshari, *al-Kashshaf ʿan Haqaʿiq Ghawamid al-Tanzil wa-ʿUyun al-Aqawil fi Wujuh al-Tanzil*, ed. Muhammad ʿAbd al-Salam Shahin (Beirut: Dar al-Kitab al-ʿArabi, 1986), 2:233.

28 Abdullahi Ahmed An-Naʿim, "Islamic Law, International Relations, and Human Rights: Challenge and Response," *Cornell International Law Journal* 20, no. 2 (1987), 317–335 at 334–335; Tariq Ramadan, *To Be a European Muslim: A Study of*

Islamic Sources in the European Context (Leicester: Islamic Foundation, 1999), 124; Yusuf al-Qaradawi, *Fiqh al-Jihad: Dirasa Muqarana fi Ahkamihi wa-Falsafatihi fi Daw' al-Qur'an wa-Sunna* (Cairo: Maktaba Wahba, 2009).

29 Michael Walzer, *Just and Unjust Wars: A Moral Argument with Historical Illustrations*, 4th edition (New York: Basic Books, 2006).

30 Charles Hirschkind, *The Ethical Soundscape: Cassette Sermons and Islamic Counterpublics* (New York: Columbia University Press, 2006), 2.

31 Al-Awlaki sold his lectures first through two companies, Al-Fahm and Al-Basheer; Shane, *Objective Troy*, 100.

32 Al-Awlaki, *Lives of the Prophets*, Al-Basheer, 2001, 21 compact discs, CD 1.

33 Al-Awlaki drew on Ibn Kathir's *al-Bidaya wa'l-Nihaya*, a larger history of the Islamic prophets.

34 Ibn Kathir, *The Lives of the Prophets*, trans. Muhammad Mustapha Geme'ah (Riyadh: Dar-us-Salam, 2003).

35 The need to quote past scholarly authorities results from the Islamic teaching that scholars are inheritors of the prophets (*warithat al-anbiya'*). Hamid Dabashi, *Authority in Islam: From the Rise of Muhammad to the Establishment of the Umayyads* (New Brunswick, NJ: Transmission Publishers, 1989), 71; Patricia Crone, *God's Rule: Government and Islam* (New York: Columbia University Press, 2004), 219.

36 Su'ad Abdul Khabeer, "Black Arabic: African American Muslims and the Arabic Language," in *Black Routes to Islam*, ed. Manning Marable and Hishaam D. Aidi (New York: Palgrave Macmillan, 2009), 167–190. Zareena Grewal, *Islam Is a Foreign Country: American Muslims and the Global Crisis of Authority* (New York: New York University Press, 2013), 131–132.

37 Al-Awlaki, *The Life of Muhammad*, Awakening, 53 compact discs, divided over three periods.

38 Shane has convincingly refuted claims that Al-Awlaki was a closet jihadist, *Objective Troy*, 100–101.

39 Shane, *Objective Troy*, 82.

40 Ray Suarez, "My Post-9/11 Interview with Anwar Al-Awlaki," *PBS*, November 11, 2009, www.pbs.org.

41 For instance, in the UK, Al-Awlaki would record a lecture series on Ibn Nuhhas's book of jihad, *Mashari' al-Ashwaq ila Masari al-'Ushaq*, ed. Idris 'Ali and Muhammad al-Istanbuli (Beirut: Dar al-Basha'ir al-Islamiyya, 1990).

42 Before the three men's disappearance in March 2007, there were reports of Canadian Somali youth joining al-Shabab. However, Canadian Somalis' personal ties to Somalia distinguished their case from that of Ferid, Miawand, and Muhanad, who joined a deterritorialized international fighting force. "Somali Militant Group Recruiting Canadian Youth," January 26, 2011, www.cbc.ca.

43 Qutb famously described modern Egyptian society as one of "ignorance" about divine guidance. The implication was that societies who do not apply God's law should be fought. Sayyid Qutb, *Ma'alim fi al-Tariq* (Beirut: Dar al-Shuruq, 1979), 8.

44 Qutb wrote a chapter on jihad in *Milestones* (see *Ma'alim*, 55–82) that argued against modern claim that Muhammad undertook jihad purely out of self-defense. He claimed that jihad is a struggle for human freedom from servitude to other human beings. Although Qutb never spells out his conclusions explicitly, the implication is that societies who do not apply God's law should be fought.

45 Thomas Hegghammer, *The Caravan: Abdullah Azzam and the Rise of Global Jihad* (Cambridge: Cambridge University Press, 2020), 463.

46 'Abd Allah 'Azzam, *al-Difa' 'an Aradi al-Muslimin Ahamm Furud al-A'yan* (N.p.: Mu'assasat al-Murabitin, 2016), 32–33.

47 Quintan Wiktorowicz popularized the division between salafis into three categories: quietists, politicos, and jihadis. Quintan Wiktorowicz, "Anatomy of the Salafi Movement," *Studies in Conflict & Terrorism* 29, no. 3 (2006), 207–239.

48 Lara Deeb, *An Enchanted Modern: Gender and Public Piety in Shi'i Lebanon* (Princeton, NJ: Princeton University Press, 2006), 3–6; Shanthie Mariet D'Souza and Routray Bibhu Prasad, "Jihad in Jammu and Kashmir: Actors, Agendas and Expanding Benchmarks," *Small Wars & Insurgencies* 27, no. 4 (2016), 557–577; Cabeiri deBergh Robinson, *Body of Victim, Body of Warrior: Refugee Families and the Making of Kashmiri Jihadists* (Berkeley: University of California Press, 2013), 11.

49 'Azzam attracted Salafis around him as a result of his professorial appointment in Saudi Arabia and the Saudi support for the anti-Soviet jihad; Hegghammer, *The Caravan*, 46; Gilles Kepel, *Jihad: The Trail of Political Islam*, trans. Anthony Roberts (Cambridge, MA: Belknap Press of Harvard University Press, 2002), 139, 146. But 'Azzam never adopted the Salafi methodology of the likes of Nasir al-Din al-Albani or Bin Baz.

50 Stephane Lacroix, *Awakening Islam: The Politics of Religious Dissent in Contemporary Saudi Arabia*, trans. George Halach (Cambridge, MA: Harvard University Press, 2011), 55; Joas Wagemakers, *A Quietist Jihadi:The Ideology and Influence of Abu Muhammad al-Maqdisi* (New York: Cambridge University Press, 2012), 35.

51 'Azzam, *al-Difa'*, 76–78.

52 Bronislav Ostřanský, *The Jihadist Preachers of the End Times: ISIS Apocalyptic Propaganda* (Edinburgh: Edinburgh University Press, 2019), 3.

53 While I use the term "utopian jihad" to refer to al-Qaeda's ideology, Muslim history is witness to many other groups that have considered military mobilization as the best means to correct an unjust state of affairs. Some of these groups, like the kharajites, who rebelled against the Caliph 'Ali for failing to apply God's law, are remembered as extremists. Others, however, like the 'Abbasids, who came to power by means of religious fervor, are remembered more positively. The list of these groups is lengthy and includes, in more recent times, the Saudis. Classical jurists' discourse of jihad sought to temper Islamic revolutionary impulses through their theorizations.

54 Roel Meijer, "Yusuf al-'Uyairi and the Making of a Revolutionary Salafi Praxis," *Die Welt des Islams* 47, no. 3 (2007), 431.

55 Yusuf al-'Ayayri, *al-Thawabit 'ala Darb al-Jihad*, n.d., available online at https://ketabonline.com.

56 W. J. Berridge, *Hasan al-Turabi: Islamist Poliltics and Democracy in Sudan* (Cambridge: Cambridge University Press, 2017), 207–208.

57 Ray Suarez, "My Post-9/11 Interview."

58 Charles Hirschkind (*The Ethical Soundscape*, 8) employs Arendt's concept of politics to explain the relationship between piety and politics. Hirschkind sees politics as "the activities of ordinary citizens who, through the exercise of their agency in contexts of public interaction, shape the conditions of their collective existence."

59 Saba Mahmood, *Politics of Piety: The Islamic Revival and the Feminist Subject* (Princeton, NJ: Princeton University Press, 2005), 34, 35.

60 Hussein Agrama, *Questioning Secularism: Islam, Sovereignty, and the Rule of Law in Modern Egypt* (Chicago: University of Chicago Press, 2012), 2–3; Mayanthi Fernando, *The Republic Unsettled: Muslim French and the Contradictions of Secularism* (Durham, NC: Duke University Press, 2014), 10; Saba Mahmood, *Religious Difference in a Secular Age: A Minority Report* (Princeton, NJ: Princeton University Press), 3–4.

61 Shane, *Objective Troy*, 82.

62 Anwar Al-Awlaki, *Constants on the Path of Jihad*, 6 mp3 files, 2005, lecture 1.

63 Al-Awlaki, *Constants*, lecture 1. On the topic of the saved sect, see al-Ghazali, *On the Boundaries of Theological Tolerance in Islam*, trans. Sherman Jackson (Oxford: Oxford University Press, 2002), 125–127.
64 On the Salafi notion of the saved sect, see Roel Meijer, "Introduction," in *Global Salafism*, ed. R. Meijer (Oxford: Oxford University Press, 2013), 5.
65 Muhammad b. Jarir al-Tabari, *Jamiʿ al-Bayan* (Beirut: Dar Ibn Hazm, 2013), 3:64–70.
66 Al-Awlaki, *Constants*, lecture 1.
67 Al-Awlaki, *Constants*, lecture 2.
68 Al-Awlaki, *Constants*, lecture 2
69 The refrain of needing to show non-Muslims the beauty of Islam was often uttered in the aftermath of 9/11. E.g., *Frontline*'s interview with Feisal Abdul Raouf in March 2002, www.pbs.org.
70 Al-Awlaki, *Constants*, lecture 4.
71 The story of Abraham's sacrifice as a paradigm of faith has attracted long-standing discussions across the Abrahamic faiths. Soren Kierkegaard, *Fear and Trembling* in *Fear and Trembling and The Sickness unto Death*, trans. Walter Lowrie (Princeton, NJ: Princeton University Press, 2013), 1–234; Derrida, "Abraham: The Other," in *Judeities: Questions for Jacques Derrida*, ed. Bettina Bergo, Joseph D. Cohen, and Raphael Zagury-Orly (New York: Fordham University Press, 2007), 1–35.
72 Al-Awlaki, *Constants*, lecture 4; The Qur'an states (20:71): "You [i.e. the magicians] believed him before I gave you permission. Indeed, he is your leader who has taught you magic. So I will surely cut off your hands and your feet on opposite sides, and I will crucify you on the trunks of palm trees, and you will surely know which of us is more severe in [giving] punishment and more enduring."
73 Al-Awlaki, *Constants*, lecture 6.
74 Al-Awlaki, *Constants*, lecture 5.
75 Al-Awlaki, *Constants*, lecture 1.
76 Al-Awlaki, *Constants*, lecture 2.
77 Ferid Imam, "Anwar Al-Awlaki!!!." March 16, 2006. Personal email correspondence,
78 Al-Awlaki would leave shortly thereafter, Shane, *Objective Troy*, 118.
79 Judith Miller, "A Nation Challenged; Raids Seek Evidence of Money-Laundering," *New York Times*, March 21, 2002, www.nytimes.com.
80 Anwar Al-Awlaki, *It's a War Against Islam*, 2002, mp3 file.
81 Cindy Holder provides a trenchant critique of the power relations at stake in the Danish Cartoons episode. "Debating the Danish Cartoons: Civil Rights or Civil Power?" *UNB Law Journal* 55 (2006), 179–185.
82 See Saba Mahmood, "Religious Reason and Secular Affect: An Incommensurable Divide," in *Is Critique Secular?: Blasphemy, Injury, and Free Speech* (New York: Fordham University Press, 2013), 58–94 at 68–73.
83 Sabir forwarded the email written by a Vancouver-based imam, entitled, "Let's Move On," February 11, 2006.
84 *USA v. Al Farekh*, 1282.
85 Anwar Al-Awlaki, *'Umar ibn al-Khataab: His Life and Times*, al-Basheer, 18 compact discs.
86 Janice Gross Stein and Eugene Lang, *Canada's Unexpected War* (Toronto: Penguin Canada, 2008), 136, 183–187.
87 Mohamed Haji Ingiriis, "From Al-Itihaad to Al-Shabaab: How the Ethiopian Intervention and the 'War on Terror' Exacerbated the Conflict in Somalia," *Third World Quarterly* 39, no. 11 (2018), 2034, 2044.
88 Ferid Imam, "Quote. . . ." July 27, 2006. Personal email correspondence.

89 Shiraz Maher, *Salafi-Jihad: The History of an Idea* (New York: Oxford University Press, 2016), 47. Al-Qaeda justified attacks against civilians by claiming that American democracy made US citizens culpable for its government's actions. Al-Qaeda, "A Statement from Qa'ida al-Jihad Regarding the Mandates of the Heroes and the Legality of the Operations in New York and Washington," April 2002. https://scholarship.tricolib.brynmawr.edu.
90 *USA v. Al Farekh*, 605–608.
91 Elliot, "Why Yasir Qadhi." On Sunni quietism, see Crone, *God's Rule*, 124, 228–233. The Muslim preacher, Hamza Yusuf, has encouraged political quietism in the last decade. His theory of politics emerged as part of a response to the devastation of civil war in places like Syria and Libya in the aftermath of the Arab Spring in 2011. "Hamza Yusuf Issues Apology for 'Hurting Feelings' with Syria Comments," *Middle East Eye*, September 13, 2019, www.middleeasteye.net.
92 William Connolly, *Why I Am Not a Secularist* (Minneapolis: University of Minnesota Press, 1999), 3.
93 Suzanne Van Geuns, "Seductive Methods: Sexual Success in the Computational Imagination" (PhD diss., University of Toronto, 2022).
94 Matthew Avery Sutton, "The Capitol Riot Revealed the Darkest Nightmares of White Evangelical America," *New Republic*, January 14, 2021, https://newrepublic.com; Peter Manseau, "Some Capitol Rioters Believed They Answered God's Call, Not Just Trump's," *Washington Post*, February 11, 2021, www.washingtonpost.com.
95 Edward Curtis IV shows how US political leaders have used the example of fallen US Muslim soldiers to counter Islamophobia; Edward Curtis IV, *Muslim American Politics and the Future of US Democracy* (New York: New York University Press, 2019), 121–142.

Chapter 4. Under Suspicion

1 Reg Whitaker, Greg Sealy, and Andrew Parnaby, *Secret Service: Political Policing in Canada: From the Fenians to Fortress America* (Toronto: University of Toronto Press, 2012), 350–357. John Starnes, *Closely Guarded: A Life in Canadian Security and Intelligence* (Toronto: University of Toronto, 1998), 164–165.
2 Whitaker et al., *Secret Service*, 367.
3 Whitaker et al., *Secret Service*, 365.
4 Mary Jo Leddy, *Our Friendly Local Terrorist* (Toronto: Between the Lines, 2010). Leddy was witness to CSIS's request that Goven become an informant for them.
5 Targeting of Muslims and particularly Arabs had intensified after the First Gulf War; see Zuhair Kashmeri, *The Gulf Within* (Toronto: James Lorimer & Company, 1991).
6 Andrew Mitrovica, *Covert Entry: Spies, Lies, and Crimes Inside Canada's Secret Service* (Toronto: Random House Canada, 2002), 17–18.
7 An example was that a senior officer used CSIS funds to rent an apartment for his university age daughter; Mitrovica, *Covert Entry*, 9.
8 Whitaker et al., *Secret Service*, 435.
9 Whitaker et al., *Secret Service*, 450–451.
10 Whitaker et al., *Secret Service*, 486; Paul Koring, "Sudan Is Your Guantanamo," *Globe and Mail*, July 23, 2009; Joanna Smith, "Strange Case of Tortured Canadian," *Toronto Star*, July 24, 2009.
11 Ashley Burke and Kristen Everson, "A Muslim Former Intelligence Officer Says Systemic Racism at CSIS Is a Threat to National Security," CBC, June 29, 2021, www.cbc.ca.

12 Security Intelligence Review Committee, *SIRC Annual Report 2007–2008: An Operational Review of the Canadian Security Intelligence Service* (2008), 21–22.
13 Khaled Beydoun, *American Islamophobia: Understanding the Roots and Rise of Fear* (Oakland: University of California Press, 2018), 28.
14 See Su'ad Abdul Khabeer, Arshad Ali, Evelyn Sultani, Sohail Dolatzai, Lara Deeb, Carol Fadda, Zareena Grewal, Juliane Hammer, Nadine Naber, and Junaid Rana, "Islamophobia Is Racism," www.islamophobiaisracism.wordpress.com.
15 Erik Love, *Islamophobia and Racism in America* (New York: New York University Press, 2017), 4.
16 Evelyn Alsultany, *Arabs and Muslims in the Media: Race and Representation after 9/11* (New York: New York University Press, 2012), 2.
17 Jasmin Zine, *Under Siege: Islamophobia and the 9/11 Generation* (Montreal: McGill-Queen's University Press, 2022).
18 Stephanie Carvin, "The Canadian Security Intelligence Service and the Toronto 18 Case," *Manitoba Law Journal* 44, no. 1 (2021), 106.
19 Baljit Nagra, *Securitized Citizens: Canadian Muslims' Experience of Race Relations and Identity Formation Post-9/11* (Toronto: University of Toronto Press, 2017), 93–123.
20 Radicalization studies is premised on the presumption that radical ideas circulate between a group of individuals. For the major theories of radicalization, see *Radicalization*, ed. Peter Neumann (Abingdon: Routledge, 2016).
21 Arun Kundnani, *The Muslims Are Coming: Islamophobia, Extremism, and the Domestic War on Terror* (London: Verso, 2014), 94.
22 "[Over the last year,] CSIS continued to grow and increase its capabilities in 2006–07. Even with additional resources and capacity, there is no guarantee that intelligence will always be available to forestall those who would do us harm. Like all open and democratic societies, Canada is vulnerable to terrorism." Canadian Security Intelligence Service, *Public Report 2006–2007* (2007).
23 On critiques of radicalization, see Peter Neuman, "The Trouble with Radicalization," *International Affairs* 89, no. 4 (2013), 873–893.
24 Forcese explains what constitutes a legitimate national security threat according to courts: "The Court concluded that a person constitutes a 'danger to the security of Canada' where he or she poses a direct or indirect threat to the security of Canada that is 'serious'—that is, grounded in an objectively reasonable suspicion based on evidence." Craig Forcese, *National Security Law: Canadian Practice in International Perspective* (Toronto: Irwin Law, 2007), 5.
25 On the experience of Somali immigrants just south of the Canadian border, see Cawo M. Abdi, *Elusive Jannah: The Somali Diaspora and a Borderless Muslim Identity* (Minneapolis: University of Minnesota Press, 2015), 169–230; Rima Berns McGown, *Muslims in the Diaspora: The Somali Communities of London and Toronto* (Toronto: University of Toronto Press, 2022), 94.
26 A similar threat was issued to Abousfian Abdelrazak before his detention and torture in Sudan; Whitaker et al., *Secret Service*, 487.
27 The international border has often been a fertile site of research on discrimination against Muslims; Baljit Nagra and Paula Maurutto, "Crossing Borders and Managing Racialized Identities: Experiences of Security and Surveillance Among Young Canadian Muslims," *Canadian Journal of Sociology* 41, no. 2 (2016), 165–194; Anna Pratt and Sara K. Thompson, "Chivalry, 'Race' and Discretion at the Canadian Border," *British Journal of Criminology* 48, no. 5 (2008), 620–640; Anna Pratt, "Between a Hunch and a Hard Place: Making Suspicion Reasonable at the Canadian Border," *Social & Legal Studies* 19, no. 4 (2010), 461–480. Sherene Razack, "Abandonment and the Dance of Race and Bureaucracy in Spaces of Exception," *States of*

Race: Critical Race Feminism for the 21st Century, ed. Sherene Razack, Sunera Thobani, and Malinda S. Smith (Toronto: Between the Lines, 2010); Anna Pratt, *Securing Borders* (Vancouver: University of British Columbia Press, 2005).

28 "Legal Wrangling Risks Chill Effect," in *Open Secrets: Wikileaks, War, and American Diplomacy*, ed. Alexander Star (New York: New York Times, 2011), n.p.

29 Allan Woods, "The Two Faces of Jim Judd," *Toronto Star*, December, 2010, www.thestar.com.

Ironically, the 2006–2007 CSIS report states: "In her 2006 Certificate to the Minister of Public Safety, the Inspector General stated that the Service 'has not acted beyond the framework of its statutory authority, has not contravened any Ministerial Directions, and has not exercised its powers unreasonably or unnecessarily.'" CSIS, *Public Report 2006–2007*, 7.

30 David Lyon, "Airport Screening, Surveillance, and Social Sorting: Canadian Responses to 9/11 in Context," *Canadian Journal of Criminology and Criminal Justice* 48, no. 3 (2006), 397–411.

31 The sharing of information between Canada and the United States was the product of the Smart Border Declaration established after 9/11; Jessica Shultz, *The Role of Integrated Border Enforcement Teams in Maintaining a Safe and Open Canada-United States Border* (MA thesis, Windsor University, 2009); Rey Koslowski, "Smart Borders, Virtual Borders or No Borders: Homeland Security Choices for the United States and Canada," *Law and Business Review of the Americas* 11, no. 3/4 (2005), 527.

32 On Canadians' inability to travel across borders, see Youcef L. Soufi, "Guilt-by-Association: The Shaky Foundations of Canada-US Intelligence Sharing and Its Consequences for Muslim Canadians' Mobility," in *Systemic Islamophobia in Canada: A Research Agenda*, ed. Anver Emon (Toronto: University of Toronto Press, 2023), 263–278.

33 On Canada's no-fly list, see Colin J. Bennett, "Unsafe at any Altitude: The Comparative Politics of No-Fly Lists in the United States and Canada," *Politics at the Airport*, ed. Mark B. Salter (Minneapolis: University of Minnesota Press, 2008); Uzma Jamil, "Can Muslims Fly? The No Fly List as a Tool of the 'War on Terror,'" *Islamophobia Studies Journal* 4, no. 1 (2017), 72–86; Baljit Nagra and Paula Maurutto, "No-Fly Lists, National Security and Race: The Experiences of Muslim Canadians," *British Journal of Criminology* 60, no. 3 (2020), 600–619.

34 See Daniel Livermore, *Detained: Islamic Fundamentalist Extremism and the War on Terror in Canada* (Montreal: McGill University Press, 2018).

Chapter 5. "I Want Out"

1 Arun Kundnani, "Radicalization: The Journey of a Concept," *Race and Class* 54, no. 2 (2012), 21.

2 On deviance, see Wagemakers, *A Quietist Jihadi: The Ideology and Influence of Abu Muhammad al-Maqdisi* (New York: Cambridge University Press, 2012), 147–190.

3 Gilles Kepel, *Jihad: The Trail of Political Islam*, trans. Anthony Roberts (Cambridge, MA: Belknap Press of Harvard University Press, 2002), 313–322.

4 Name changed to protect family privacy.

5 Ferid Imam, "Email to Family, March 15, 2007," filed as government exhibit 822 in *USA v. Al Farekh*.

6 Paul Powers, *Intent in Islamic Law: Motive and Meaning in Medieval Sunni Fiqh* (Leiden, NL: Brill, 2005), 25–60.

7 The term in Arabic to designate the duty to keep familial relationships is *silat al-rahm* (joining relations of the womb).

8 Yar, "Letter to Family March 2007," filed as government exhibit 1201 in *USA v. Al Farekh*.
9 Yar, "Letter to Family March 2007."
10 *USA v. Al Farekh*, 610.
11 Miawand Yar, "Letter to Family March 2007."
12 *Her Majesty v. Miawand Yar*.
13 *USA v. Al Farekh*, 609–610.
14 *USA v. Al Farekh*, 586.
15 *USA v. Al Farekh*, 586.
16 *USA v. Al Farekh*, 614.
17 *USA v. Al Farekh*, 617.
18 Farish A. Noor, *Islam on the Move: The Tablighi Jama'at in Southeast Asia* (Amsterdam: Amsterdam University Press, 2012).
19 *USA v. Al Farekh*, 636–637.
20 *USA v. Al Farekh*, 646.
21 Muslim b. al-Hajaj, *Sahih Muslim* (Riyadh: Dar al-Tayyiba, 2006), 1186.
22 On the theory behind CVE programs, see Daniel Kohler, *Understanding Deradicalization: Methods, Tools, and Programs for Countering Violent Extremism* (Abingdon: Routledge, 2017), 65–94.
23 Patrick White and Colin Freeze, "Family Fears U.S. Has Killed Winnipeg's 'Lost Boys' of Jihad," *Globe and Mail*, April 23, 2015, www.globeandmail.com.
24 Imam, "Email to Family, March 15, 2007."
25 *USA v. Al Farekh*, 608.
26 *USA v. Al Farekh*, 1417–1428.
27 *USA v. Al Farekh*, 682.
28 Anver M. Emon, "*Huquq Allah* and *Huquq Al-'Ibad*: A Legal Heuristic for a Natural Rights Regime," *Islamic Law and Society* 13, no. 3 (2006), 325–391.
29 Baber Johansen, *Contingency in a Sacred Law: Legal and Ethical Norms in the Muslim Fiqh* (Boston: Brill, 1999), 211–215.
30 Burhan al-Din al-Marghinani, *al-Hidaya: Sharh Bidayat al-Mubtadi*, ed. Muhammad 'Adnan Darwish (Beirut: Dar al-Arqam b. Abi al-Arqam, 1997), 1:426; Abu Ishaq al-Shirazi, *al-Muhadhdhab fi Fiqh al-Imam al-Shafi'i*, ed. Muhammad Zuhayli (Damascus: Dar al-Qalam, 1992), 5:254–255.
31 See Anver Emon and Aaqib Mahmood, "'Canada v Asad Ansari': Avatars, Inexpertise, and Racial Bias in Canadian Anti-Terrorism Litigation," *Manitoba Law Journal* 44, no. 1 (2021), 255–293.
32 Abdulkader Sinno, "Explaining the Taliban's Ability to Mobilize the Pashtuns," ed. Robert Crews and Amin Tarzi (Cambridge, MA: Harvard University Press, 2008), 59–79. On the Taliban's military makeup and tactics in 2007, see Antonio Giustozzi, *The Taliban at War: 2001–2018* (New York: Oxford University Press, 2019), 43–76.
33 M. J. Gohari, *The Taliban: Ascent to Power* (Oxford: Oxford University Press, 2000), 26–43.
34 *USA v. Al Farekh*, 1016.
35 Kepel, *Jihad*, 147–148.
36 Barak Mendelsohn, *The al-Qaeda Franchise: The Expansion of al-Qaeda and Its Consequences* (Oxford: Oxford University Press, 2016), 61.
37 *USA v. Al Farekh*, 927.
38 Thomas Hegghammer, "Weeping in Modern Jihadi Groups," *Journal of Islamic Studies* 31, 3 (2020), 358–387.
39 *USA v. Al Farekh*, 1017.
40 *USA v. Al Farekh*, 591–592. Email is dated May 28, 2007.

41 On al-Nawawi's pietistic writings, see Fachrizal Halim, *Legal Authority in Premodern Islam: Yahya b. Sharaf al-Nawawi in the Shafi'i School of Law* (Abingdon: Routledge, 2015), 20–24.
42 Miawand Yar, "Letter to Family, June 26, 2009," filed as government exhibit 1202 in *USA v. Al Farekh*.
43 Muhammad 'Abd al-Salam Faraj, *The Neglected Duty*, trans. Roxanne L. Euben and Muhammad Qasim Zaman (Princeton, NJ: Princeton University Press, 2009), 321–343.
44 Yar, "Letter to Family," June 26, 2009, 3.
45 On the concept of *hijra* (migration from non-Muslim lands), see Khaled Abou El Fadl, "Islamic Law and Muslim Minorities: The Juristic Discourse on Muslim Minorities from the Second/Eighth to the Eleventh/Seventeenth Centuries," *Islamic Law and Society* 1, no. 2 (1994), 141–187.
46 *USA v. Al Farekh*, 1020.
47 All names of members of Miawand's family are changed to preserve their privacy.
48 On dream interpretation in the Islamic tradition, see Amira Mittermaier, *Dreams that Matter: Egyptian Landscapes of the Imagination* (Berkeley: University of California Press, 2011), 54–83.
49 *USA v. Al Farekh*, 591–592.
50 *USA v. Al Farekh*, 664.
51 Patrick White and Colin Freeze, "Family Fears U.S. Has Killed Winnipeg's 'Lost Boys' of Jihad," April 23, 2015, www.globeandmail.com.
52 *USA v. Al Farekh*, 666.
53 "US Strikes in Pakistan," *The Long War*, https://public.tableau.com.
54 "Pakistan Army Pushes Taliban Back," *Reuters*, April 30, 2009, www.reuters.com.
55 Colin Freeze, "Case of Alleged Canadian Terrorist Highlights the World of Targeted Killings," *Globe and Mail*, April 16, 2012, www.globeandmail.com.
56 *USA v. Al Farekh*, 927
57 *USA v. Al Farekh*, 929
58 *USA v. Al Farekh*, 927.
59 Muhanad Al Farekh, "Letter to a Senior Commander," n.d., filed as government exhibit 729, 2.
60 Nathan French, *And God Knows the Martyrs: Martyrdom and Violence in Jihadi-Salafism* (New York: Oxford University Press, 2020), 3.
61 Alan Feuer, "Texas Man Convicted of Helping Attack U.S. Army Base in Afghanistan," *New York Times*, September 29, 2017, www.nytimes.com.
62 *USA v. Al Farekh*, 929.
63 *USA v. Al Farekh*, 927.
64 Fawaz Gerges, *A History of ISIS* (Princeton, NJ: Princeton University Press, 2021), 127.
65 Al Farekh, "Letter to a Senior Commander," 4.
66 *USA v. Al Farekh*, 6.
67 *USA v. Al Farekh*, 3.
68 David Kloos, *Becoming Better Muslims: Religious Authority and Ethical Improvement in Aceh, Indonesia* (Princeton, NJ: Princeton University Press, 2018), 123.
69 Talal Asad, "Autobiographical Reflections on Anthropology and Religion," *Religion and Society* 11, no. 1 (2020), 1–7 at 2. Clark McCauley and Sophia Moskalenko, "Mechanisms of Political Radicalization: Pathways Toward Terrorism," *Terrorism and Political Violence* 20, no. 3 (2008), 415–433. Peter R. Neumann, "The Trouble with Radicalization," *International Affairs* no. 89, 4 (2013), 873–893; Zeyno Baran, "Fighting the War of Ideas," *Foreign Affairs* 84, no. 6 (2013), 68–78.
70 The closest parallel is with the case of the Sudanese-Canadian Abousfian Abdelrazik; Whitaker et al., *Secret Service*, 486.

Chapter 6. Prosecuting Terrorism

1 Wadie E. Said, *Crimes of Terror: The Legal and Political Implications of Federal Terrorism Prosecutions* (New York: Oxford University Press, 2018), 1.
2 Muhanad Al Farekh, "Letter to a Senior Commander," 6.
3 Patrick White and Colin Freeze, "Family Fears U.S. Has Killed Winnipeg's 'Lost Boys' of Jihad," April 23, 2015, www.globeandmail.com.
4 Scott Shane, *Objective Troy: A Terrorist, A President, and the Rise of the Drone* (New York: Tim Duggan Books, 2015), 269.
5 Shane, *Objective Troy*, 229–232.
6 "With Death of Anwar Al-Awlaki, Has U.S. Launched New Era of Killing U.S. Citizens Without Charge?" *Democracy Now!*, September 30, 2011, www.democracynow.org.
7 Eric Holder, "Remarks of Eric Holder, Attorney General of the United States Northwestern University School of Law, Chicago, IL. March 5, 2012," in *The Drone Memos: Targeted Killing, Secrecy, and the Law*, ed. Jameel Jaffer (New York: New Press Books, 2016), 191–198.
8 Jameel Jaffer, "Introduction," in *The Drone Memos: Targeted Killing, Secrecy, and the Law*, (New York: New Press Books, 2016), 42–43.
9 A Committee within the National Security Council took on the role of nominating targets.
10 Mark Mazzetti and Eric Schmitt, "Terrorism Case Renews Debate Over Drone Hits," *New York Times*, April 12, 2015, www.nytimes.com.
11 Jameel Jaffer, "Introduction," 45.
12 Adam Goldman and Tim Craig, "American Citizen Linked to al-Qaeda Is Captured, Flown secretly to U.S." The Washington Post, April 2, 2016, www.washingtonpost.com.
13 See www.fbi.gov.
14 *USA v. Al Farekh*, 1336–1337.
15 *USA v Al Farekh*, 1336.
16 Vera-Lynn Kubinec and Katie Nicholson, "'Barbaric' Conditions Imposed on Former Winnipeg Student Accused of Terrorism: Lawyer," *CBC News*, August 26, 2015, www.cbc.ca.
17 David Polizzi and Bruce Arrigo, "Cruel but Not Unusual: Solitary Confinement, the 8th Amendment, and Agamben's State of Exception," *New Criminal Law Review* 21, no. 4 (2018), 615–639.
18 "Based upon information provided to me regarding al-Farekh's proclivity for violence, I find that there is substantial risk that his communications or contacts with persons could result in death or serious bodily injury." Kubinec and Nicholson, "'Barbaric' Conditions."
19 "Indictment," *USA v. Al Farekh* (Eastern District Court of New York, May 15, 2016), 1–5; "Superceding Indictment," *USA v. Al Farekh* (Eastern District Court of New York, January 6, 2016), 1–8.
20 Kubinec and Nicholson, "'Barbaric' Conditions."
21 Kubinec and Nicholson, "'Barbaric' Conditions."
22 Jameel Jaffer, "Introduction," 19–20.
23 Alan Feuer, "Texas Man Convicted of Helping Attack U.S. Army Base in Afghanistan," *New York Times*, September 29, 2017, www.nytimes.com.
24 *USA v. Al Farekh*, 895–897.
25 The only other piece of evidence was a deposition given by a Jordanian prisoner named Sufwan Murad. *USA v. Al Farekh*, 867.
26 *USA v. Al Farekh*, 503.
27 *USA v. Al Farekh*, 32.

28 *USA v. Al Farekh*, 1086.
29 Emon and Mahmood, "'Canada v. Asad Ansari,'" 255–293.
30 Abou El Fadl, *The Great Theft: Wrestling Islam from the Extremist* (New York: Harper, 2005), 1–8.
31 Mahmood Mamdani, *Good Muslims, Bad Muslims* (New York: Three Leaves Press, 2004), 17–23.
32 On the controversy of the ground zero mosque, see Rosemarie Corbett, *Making Moderate Islam: Sufism, Service, and the "Ground Zero Mosque"* (Stanford, CA: Stanford University Press, 2016), 1–16.
33 *USA v. Al Farekh*, 885.
34 *USA v. Al Farekh*, 886.
35 E.g., Thomas Barfield, "Is Afghanistan 'Medieval'?" June 2, 2010, https://foreignpolicy.com. For a critique of this discourse, see Christian Lange, "The Taliban Aren't Taking Afghanistan Back to the Middle Ages—They're Subverting Islam's Sound Medieval Legal Principles," October 4, 2021, https://theconversation.com.
36 See, for instance, Ayaan Hirsi Ali, *Heretic: Why Islam Needs a Reformation Now* (Toronto: HarperCollins Canada, 2015).
37 For many years after 9/11, the French academic, Tariq Ramadan, was called Islam's Martin Luther: Nicholas Tampio, "Constructing the Space of Testimony: Tariq Ramadan's Copernican Revolution," *Political Theory* 39, no. 5 (2011), 600–629.
38 Sahar Aziz, *The Racial Muslim: When Racism Quashes Religious Freedom* (Oakland: University of California Press, 2022), 173.
39 Aziz, *The Racial Muslim*, 25.
40 The ad was for a propaganda video featuring pseudo-experts on Islam known for making statements about Muslims' proclivities toward violence. See www.amazon.com.
41 I have relied upon these letters in my own narrative of Muhanad's life in Pakistan. But the standard of proof in condemning a person to prison ought to be higher than those applied to the interpretations of a historian.
42 *USA v. Al Farekh*, 1417.
43 Marianne Bray, "Why Young Muslims Line Up to Die," *CNN*, August 18, 2003, www.cnn.com.
44 Trevor Aaronson, "A Terrorism Expert's Secret Relationship with the FBI," *The Intercept*, July 27, 2015, https://theintercept.com.
45 Darryl Li, *The Universal Enemy*, 34–35.
46 *USA v. Al Farekh*, 1286–1291
47 *USA v. Al Farekh*, 1282.
48 Shane, *Objective Troy*, 118
49 *USA v. Al Farekh*, 1297–98.
50 Shane, *Objective Troy*, 101.
51 *USA v. Al Farekh*, 1292. There were also lectures whose status within the corpus of Al-Awlaki's teachings were more ambiguously related to jihad. Thus, the prosecution made much of Muhanad's email to his father recommending him to purchase the "Hereafter" series from Al-Awlaki: Kohlmann described the Hereafter series in the following manner: "According to 'The Hereafter' [series,] one of the ways that one can avoid the punishment of the hellfire, one of the ways that one can be rewarded on the day of judgment, is if you are martyred. If you become a shaheed, in the cause of Islam. In other words, if you are killed in the cause of Islam, you will be saved from the hellfire and you will be transported to paradise." It is true that the Hereafter series was produced after Al-Awlaki's jihadist turn. As such, some references to martyrdom are shaped by Al-Awlaki's positive view of jihadist groups fighting the United States in 2004. But the lecture is also 22 hours long, and most of it deals with

eschatology, i.e., the science of the ends of time. As such, many "moderate" Muslims would have gravitated toward the lecture to learn about life in the "Hereafter," rather than contemporary politics.

52 Philip Bump, "Lindsey Graham, Dzhokhar Tsarnaev, and the Fight Over What to Do with Terrorist Suspects," *Washington Post*, May 15, 2015, www.washingtonpost.com.

53 There have been many instances where liberal democratic governments have sought to strip accused terrorists of citizenship: Shamima Begum's case in the UK is well-known: Ashitha Nagesh, "Nationality and Borders Bill: Can You Lose Your Citizenship?" BBC, April 26,· 2022, www.bbc.com.

54 *USA v. Al Farekh*, 1312–1313.

55 *USA v. Al Farekh*, 1415.

56 *USA v. Al Farekh*, 24.

57 *USA v. Al Farekh*, 1315.

58 The defense recognized the intent of the video. In speaking to Judge Cogan, the defense stated: "I suppose Mr. Kohlmann will describe, 'Lee's Life for Lies.' But the premise of it is that there is a member of the United States military who is stationed in Iraq who becomes disillusioned with the mission and writes a lengthy letter home to his parents explaining what has caused him to become disillusioned . . . It's a little confusing when you first see it [what's] going on. There are scenes in the longer video, United States soldiers basically physically mistreating civilians in their homes. There's a lot more to it than was presented."

Epilogue

1 Marlene Lenthang, Kailani Koenig, Samira Puskar, and Corky Siemaszko, "Suspect in Death of 6-Year-Old Palestinian American Boy Was Obsessed with Israel-Hamas War, Prosecutors Say," *NBC*, October 16, 2023, www.nbcnews.com.

2 "Winnipeg Woman Harassed with Anti-Muslim Slurs During School Drop-Off Fears for Her Safety," *CBC*, November 3, 2023. www.cbc.ca/news.

3 Sherene Razack, *Casting Out: The Eviction of Muslims from Western Law and Politics* (Toronto: University of Toronto Press, 2008), 145.

4 "Des Accommodements Raisonnables à la Cabane à Sucre!" *TVA*, March 19, 2007, www.tvanouvelles.ca.

5 Edward Said, "The Clash of Ignorance," *The Nation*, October 4, 2001, www.thenation.com.

6 Saba Mahmood, *Politics of Piety: The Islamic Revival and the Feminist Subject* (Princeton, NJ: Princeton University Press, 2005), 194.

INDEX

'Abbasids, 22, 102, 103, 237, 249
Abdul Rauf, Feisal, 207, 250n69
Abou El Fadl, Khaled, 45, 206
Abu Bakr (the First Caliph), 119
Abu-Lughod, Lila, 77
adhan (call to prayer), 41
ADX Supermax Penitentiary, 203–204, 223
affective injury, 71, 92, 93, 95, 116, 118, 128, 228
Afghanistan, 21, 48, 53, 74–75, 78, 81–82, 84, 88–89, 92–93, 97–98, 106, 112–113, 116, 123, 127, 129, 131, 132, 155, 161–162, 168, 171–172, 186, 204, 207, 212, 218, 224
African American, 8, 191, 215
Agrama, Hussein, 117, 133
ahl al-baghy (Muslim rebels), 23
ahl al-hadith (the people of hadith), 23
Ahmedzay, Zarein, 203
al-akhira (otherworldly matters), 34
Al-Albani, Nasir al-Din, 45
Algeria, 79, 192
'Ali (Fourth Caliph), 23
Almohads, 22–23
Alshareef, Muhammad, 46, 240n31
Anderson, Benedict, 86
Anglo-American law, 147
Anglophone Muslims, 14, 26, 30, 92, 109, 110, 114, 116, 136, 216
Ansari, Asad, 205–206
anti-semitism, 226
Anti-Terrorism Act, 17, 147
anti-war, 90, 226
Aquinas, Thomas, 101
'Arafa, 33, 97
Arar, Maher, 8
Arendt, Hannah, 90
Asad, Talal, 25–26, 56, 96, 133, 186, 237n70, 242n67
Al-Assad, Bashar, 8, 182–183
Augustine (saint), 101
Austro-Hungarian Empire, 11
auto-ethnography, 29, 89
Al-Awlaki, Anwar: assassination of, 99, 193–196; influence of, 24–26, 136, 147–148, 164, 168–169, 171, 179–181, 185; intellectual lineage of, 21, 107–123; life in US, 99, 127, 246n2, 248n31; moderate lectures of, 107–110, 257n51; Muhanad's prosecution and, 213–216, 227–228; 9/11 and, 98; utopian theory and, 123–135, 180–181, 227–228
Al-'Ayayri, Yusuf, 113–116, 131, 135, 168
Aydin, Cemil, 86
Aziz, Sahar, 210–211
Aziza, 154–155
'Azzam, 'Abd Allah, 112–116, 130–131, 171

Banff National Park, 10–11
Bangladesh, 18
benefit (*maslaha*), 125–126
Benjamin, Walter, 16
Beydoun, Khaled, 9, 141
the Bible/biblical, 56, 108, 124
Bin Baz, 'Abd al-Aziz, 45
Bin Laden, Osama, 6, 72, 74–75, 112–113, 172, 180
Black American, 156; African American, 8, 191, 215
Black Lives Matter, 28
Black Muslim, 8, 92
Black struggle for equality, 94
Bloch, Ernst, 21

Boko Haram, 112
book of military conduct (*kitab al-siyar*), 101
Bosnia, 18–19, 78, 88, 92, 112
Brooklyn, New York, 189
Bush, George W., 6, 11, 16, 18, 56, 75–77, 80–81, 128–129, 136, 178, 179, 193, 197, 226, 228
Butler, Judith, 79, 82

Caliphs: Abu Bakr, 119; ʿAli, 23; Umar, 129
call to prayer (*adhan*), 41
Canadian, French, 2, 7, 30, 37, 72, 96, 133, 137, 192
Canadian Muslims, US relations with, 6–10
Canadian police. *See* Royal Canadian Mounted Police
Canadian Secret Intelligence Services (CSIS), 12, 17, 27, 59, 67, 138–153, 161–162, 188, 200, 223; Agent Nick with, 143–144, 145, 153–154, 157–160; 9/11 and, 141; targeting practices of, 144–148
Canadian universities: University of British Columbia, 2; University of Manitoba, 5, 31, 37–39, 47, 51–52, 84, 106, 126–128, 137–138, 143, 147–148; University of Toronto, 66, 158
Central Intelligence Agency (CIA), 6, 162, 179, 193, 195, 197, 202
Chebib, Farouk and Laila, 37
Chechnya, 19, 88, 91, 112, 244n46; Chechen people, 85, 86, 107
Chrétien, Jean, 18, 73, 77, 90
Christians, Evangelical, 133, 137
CIA. *See* Central Intelligence Agency
City of the Prophet, 45
civilization, 9, 12, 72–80, 83, 94, 96, 217, 224, 226–227
Civil Wars (the *Fitna*), 23
Clark, Joe, 73
Clinton, Bill, 88
Clinton, Hillary, 6
Cogan (Judge), 197, 208–212, 218–219, 258n58
Cold War, 10, 12
Conservative Party, 17, 73, 188
Cordoba House (Ground Zero Mosque), 207
counterterrorism, 214
Counterviolent Extremism (CVE), 168, 254n22
COVID-19, 67
CSIS. *See* Canadian Secret Intelligence Services
CVE. *See* Counterviolent Extremism

al-dalal (misguidance), 36, 61, 238n80
Darfur, 85, 91–92
Day, Stockwell, 73, 75
deradicalization, 65
Detective Paul (of RCMP), 1–4, 28
drones, 178–181, 185–186, 192–195, 224
al-dunya (the worldly life), 34, 118, 134

Eastern European, 11, 15
Egypt, 28, 91, 108, 112, 133, 183, 227, 248n43
Eickelman, Dale, 54
Emon, Anver, 191, 205–206
empire(s), 115; American, 6; Austro-Hungarian, 11; Muslim, 22–24, 99–105
enforcement of public morality (*hisba*), 63
Enlightenment, 73, 90, 210, 229
ethno-nationalism, 14
Evangelical Christians, 133, 137
exception, state of, 16–17

faith, qualitative changes of, 110, 186
Faraj, ʿAbd al-Salam, 175
fard (obligation): *fard kifaya* and, 102; *fardʿayn* and, 114
Al-Farekh, Mahmood, 166, 200
Al-Farekh, Muhanad. *See* Muhanad
Al-Farekh, Reem, 55
Federal Bureau of Investigation (FBI), 70, 189, 198, 199, 203–204, 220–221
Ferid (Imam): affective injury, 69–71, 93–96; Danish cartoons, 128; early life, 41–46; email to family, 163; the Hajj and, 33–34; radicalization, 126–129; weapons training, 203
Fernando, Mayanthi, 117, 133, 235n31
fighters of jihad (mujahideen), 19, 20, 32, 84, 98, 125
Fitna (film), 211
the *Fitna* (Civil Wars), 23
fitra (natural disposition), 118
Forward Operating Base Chapman, 204, 212
France, 6, 122, 125, 235n31
Franco-Manitoban, 7, 30
French Canadian, 2, 7, 30, 37, 72, 96, 133, 137, 192
friendly fire, 81–82
fundraising, for *umma*, 87

Gazan genocide, 223–229
Gellner, Ernest, 24
geopolitical, 9, 128
Al-Ghazali, Abu Hamid, 31, 61, 91, 238n80
Green, Abdurraheem, 45, 84–88, 92, 107
Ground Zero Mosque (Cordoba House), 207
Guantanamo Bay, 16
guilt by association, 13, 14, 146–147

habitus (self-cultivation), 52, 88
hadith (oral tradition of Prophet Muhammad), 23, 25, 44–45, 87–88, 109, 173–174, 239n14, 239n23
hajj (pilgrimage), 8, 25, 33–34, 57, 97, 107, 110–111, 118, 127, 129, 130, 156–159
halaqa (learning circle), 19
Hanafi School, 102–105, 124
haram (prohibited in Islamic law), 70, 98, 242n2
Harper, Stephen, 16, 188, 225, 233n1
headscarf (*hijab*), 2, 125, 141, 176, 192
Hegghammer, Thomas, 172
Hezbollah, 29, 112
hijab (headscarf), 2, 125, 141, 176, 192
Hirschkind, Charles, 108
hisba (enforcement of public morality), 63
House of Commons, 2, 72, 80
Hudaybiyya Peace Treaty, 25, 105
Hugo, Victor, 63–64
Huntington, Samuel, 75–76, 227
Husayn (grandson of Muhammad), 23
husn al-zunn (thinking well of others), 58
Hussein, Saddam, 89, 91
hypocrite (*munafiq*), 111, 121

Ibn Humam, 25
Ibn Kathir, 108
Ibn Qayyim al-Jawzīyyah, 173
ICU. *See* Islamic Courts Union
India, 18, 79, 88, 167
Indian Act, 14
Indigenous Peoples, 14, 37, 74, 94
Indonesia, 87, 236n48
injury, affective, 71, 92, 93, 95, 116, 118, 128, 228
interlocutors. *See* Mahdi
Internet, 18, 201, 218
Intifada, 19
Iran, 28, 51, 63
Iranian Revolution, 76
Iraq, 7, 21, 23, 28, 78, 85, 88–93, 98, 102, 112, 116, 123, 128–132, 134, 138, 144, 172, 182–183, 207, 218–220, 224, 236n49, 238n1, 245n62, 258n58
ISIS, 2, 4, 5, 7, 18, 28, 98, 111–113, 129, 136, 159, 182, 206, 211, 224, 227
Islam: as a lens, 25–26; tradition and, 9, 24–25, 31, 32, 36, 44, 49, 54, 60–62, 66, 68, 100–101, 132, 148, 164, 167–168, 173, 205–206, 211, 215, 240n43, 255n48
Islamic Courts Union (ICU), 129
Islamic law (*shari'a*), 25, 29, 53, 100–101, 111, 126, 158, 170, 225; *haram* (prohibited in), 70, 98, 242n2
Islamic Society of North America (ISNA), 7–8
Islamophobia (anti-Muslim racism), 8–10 28, 76, 134, 141–142, 210, 223, 225, 228
Isma'il I (Shah), 24
ISNA. *See* Islamic Society of North America
Israel, occupation of Palestine, 19, 51, 88–89, 92, 223–228

Jaan and Melanie, 109, 137
Al-Jassas, Abu Bakr, 104
Al-Jazeera, 129
jihad: meaning, 20; in mosques, 106–107, 132; Muhanad disillusionment with, 179–186; mujahideen and, 19, 20, 32, 84, 98, 125; 9/11 and discourse about, 19, 88, 95, 107, 139; pragmatic, 100–107, 125, 135, 185, 227; Salafi, 24, 56, 112–113, 237n77; Soviet, 19, 32, 48, 84–85, 88, 92, 106, 112–113, 125, 172, 249n49; utopian, 18–27, 99, 111–116, 126
John (FBI agent), 70, 189, 198, 199, 203–204, 220–221
Joint Special Operations Command (JSOC), 193, 195
Jordan, 51–52, 112, 174, 183, 192, 241
JSOC. *See* Joint Special Operations Command
Judd, Jim, 151–152

Karzai, Hamid, 81, 83
Keddie, Nikki, 86
Kenney, Jason, 11, 15
kitab al-siyar (book of military conduct), 101
Kohlmann, Evan, 214–216, 219–220, 257n51, 258n58
Komatireddy, Saritha, 35, 204–205, 214, 221–222
Kumar, Deepa, 76
Kundnani, Arun, 25, 56, 146
Kurds, 91

learning circle (*halaqa*), 19
LGBTQ, 94
Li, Darryl, 19, 214
Liberal Party, 17, 73, 139
Libya, 18, 39, 183, 251n91
Love, Erik, 142

MacIntyre, Alasdair, 31, 35, 51, 68
Mahdi (interlocutor), 35, 60, 137–138, 143, 147–153, 160, 218

Mahdi Movement, 24
Mahmood, Saba, 117, 133, 227
Malaysia, 87
Malcolm X, 8, 234n15
Manitoba Islamic Association (MIA), 38, 45, 54, 122, 146, 227
Al-Maqdisi, Abu Muhammad, 174
Marcuse, Herbert, 21
Al-Marghinani, Burhan al-Din, 105
Marx, Karl, 21
maslaha (benefit), 125–126
Mateen, Omar, 4
Mauss, Marcel, 52
Al-Mawardi, Abu al-Hasan, 23, 25
McDonough, Alexa, 78–79
Menzies (Judge), 49
MIA. *See* Manitoba Islamic Association
Miawand (Yar), 46–50; letters, 130, 138, 169, 173–178; support for Taliban, 97–98, 110–111
military combat (*qital*), 101, 115
military conduct, book of (*kitab al-siyar*), 101
Mill, John Stuart, 74, 243n12
Miran Shah, 172, 175, 182, 190, 196, 212
misguidance (*al-dalal*), 36, 61, 238n80
Moosa, Ebrahim, 44
Morocco, 192
Morris, Alexander, 74
Mosque, 12, 15, 19–20, 30–31, 34–35, 38–40, 43–45, 58–60, 71–7
MSA. *See* Muslim Student Association
muadhdhan (prayer caller), 43
Muhammad (Prophet): grandson Husayn of, 23; oral tradition (*hadith*) of, 23, 25, 44–45, 87–88, 109, 173–174, 239n14, 239n23
Muhanad, Al Farekh: arrest of, 3–4; Al-Awlaki and prosecution of, 213–216, 227–228; disillusionment with jihad, 179–186; early life, 50–53; emails, 55, 166, 173; roommates, 60, 148, 218; solitary confinement of, 4, 199–200, 204, 217, 222
mujahideen (fighters of jihad), 19, 20, 32, 84, 98, 125
multiculturalism, 11, 14, 19, 142
multiethnic, 14, 106
munafiq (hypocrite), 111, 121
Muslim-majority countries, 7, 21, 58, 89, 91, 101, 112, 129, 224
Muslim(s), 31, 52, 68, 98, 227; Anglophone, 14, 26, 30, 92, 109, 110, 114, 116, 136, 216; Black, 8, 92; empire, 22–24, 99–105; immigration in Winnipeg, 37–38; 9/11 and surveillance of, 15, 17, 150; racism against, 8–10 28, 76, 134, 141–142, 210, 223, 225, 228; rebels, 23; *umma* (community), 19, 20, 83–94, 119, 176, 180, 183, 226–227, 229, 244n48; US relations with Canadian, 6–10; world, 8, 19, 54, 76, 78, 82–83, 92
Muslim Student Association (MSA), 39, 41–42, 52, 54, 60, 84, 89, 110, 144, 162, 198

nation, the, 2, 10–17, 65, 72, 74, 75, 82, 130, 218, 224, 229
national security, 5–6, 18, 36, 57, 59, 64, 138–140, 143–148, 152–153, 190–191, 194–195, 203–204, 207, 216–217, 222–223
nation-building, 129
nation-state, 15, 95
natural disposition (*fitra*), 118
Al-Nawawi, Abu Sharaf, 87, 173, 255n41
NDP. *See* New Democratic Party
neo-gothic, 4
neoliberal, 76, 235n31, 241n48
New Democratic Party (NDP), 78, 139
New York, 189, 191, 199, 200, 201, 205, 211, 222
Nick (CSIS agent), 143–144, 145, 153–154, 157–160
9/11: aftermath, 8, 12–13, 54, 73–74, 84, 225–226; alternative political trajectories, 6; Al-Awlaki and, 98; blurring of radical/moderate divide and, 10, 56, 77, 227; CSIS and, 141; differences with today, 228; impact on perceptions of Islam, 55, 63, 69; Islamophobia before, 9, 16, 18, 72, 76, 110, 159; jihad discourse and, 19, 88, 95, 107, 139; Muhanad's trial and, 207; Muslim surveillance and, 15, 17, 150; political imaginary after, 20, 75, 78, 100, 206, 213; victims and hijackers, 70, 171, 208

Obama, Barack, 6–7, 16, 24, 28, 56, 99, 158, 178, 193–195, 197, 201, 204, 225
obligation. *See fard*
Orientalism, 9
otherworldly matters (*al-akhira*), 34

Pakistan, 3–4, 21, 40, 48, 92–93, 131, 155, 157, 162, 165–168, 170–171, 173, 175–178, 181, 182, 193, 196–197, 198, 200, 202, 213, 218, 221, 238n10, 257n41
Palestine, 53, 85; Israel occupation of, 19, 51, 88–89, 92, 223–228
pan-Islamic, 19, 86, 236n52

Parliament, 1–4, 74, 158, 227
Pashtun, Pashto, 48, 171
Patriot Act, 16
Paul (detective of RCMP), 1–4, 28
people of hadith (*ahl al-hadith*), 23
Peshawar, 48, 166–167, 171, 177
pilgrimage (hajj), 8, 25, 33–34, 57, 97, 107, 110–111, 118, 127, 129, 130, 156–159
postcolonial, 14
Pravda, Douglas, 212–213
prayer caller (*muadhdhan*), 43
premodern, 25, 29, 63, 75, 99, 100–107, 113, 115, 135, 209–210, 227, 239n23
prohibited in Islamic law (*haram*), 70, 98, 242n2
Provincial government, 15, 30
public morality, enforcement of (*hisba*), 63

Al-Qaeda, 6, 12, 18, 98, 100, 107, 111–114, 126, 128–129
Qatar, 28, 76
qital (military combat), 101, 115
Quebec, 14, 139, 246n72
Quraysh, 22, 104, 121
Qur'an, 22, 25, 44, 45, 56, 58, 61, 63, 101–102, 105, 108–109, 113, 115, 118–119, 122, 124, 127, 130–131, 134, 174
Qutb, Sayyid, 112–113, 175, 248nn43–44

racism, 94; anti-Muslim, 8–10 28, 76, 134, 141–142, 210, 223, 225, 228; anti-semitism, 226
radicalization: causes, 34–35, 67–68; as state discourse, 5–10; as state of becoming, 30. *See also specific topics*
Ramadan, 38, 40, 44, 46, 47, 115
Rana, Junaid, 77
RCMP. *See* Royal Canadian Mounted Police
Republican Party, 193, 201, 217
Residential Schools, 74
revelation (*al-shar'*), 100
Rohingya genocide, 91
Royal Canadian Mounted Police (RCMP), 138–140, 144, 147, 152, 156–160; Detective Paul of, 1–4, 28
Ruhnke, David, 201, 208, 219, 220
Rumsfeld, Donald, 81, 99, 125

Sabir (student), 33, 35, 40, 48–49, 57–58, 60, 97, 106, 127, 137, 157, 159, 198, 203, 250n83
Safavid empire, 24
Said, Wadie, 190
Salafi-jihad. *See* jihad
Salafism, 41, 44–46, 53, 56, 67–68, 112–113, 115, 173, 207, 214, 234n19, 239n23, 240n30, 240n34, 241n49, 249n47, 249n49, 250n64
Saudi Arabia, 23, 28, 34, 44–45, 51, 63, 76, 112–113, 114, 116, 135, 155, 174, 183
Schmitt, Carl, 16
self-cultivation (*habitus*), 52, 88
Shafi'i school, 103–104
Shane, Scott, 24, 215
shari'a. See Islamic law
al-shar' (revelation), 100
Al-Shirazi, Abu Ishaq, 103, 242
Shi'a, 23–24, 29, 51, 109, 112, 234n19
Smart Border Declaration, 8, 159, 253n31
socioeconomic, 38, 41, 48, 51, 151
sociopolitical, 22
Soviet Jihad, 19, 32, 48, 84–85, 88, 92, 106, 112–113, 125, 172, 249n49
Sunni, 8, 23–24, 29, 100, 109, 234n19, 251n91

Tablighi Jama'at, 167
Taliban, 6–7, 12, 75, 77, 81, 83, 97–98, 111, 122, 171–172, 174, 180, 182, 209, 254n32
thinking well of others (*husn al-zunn*), 58
Thomas Aquinas (saint), 101
Toronto, 18, 98, 136, 170, 206, 236n48; University, 66, 158
Trinidad, 106
Trudeau, Justin, 16, 225–226
Trump, Donald, 4, 28, 44, 198
Turkey, 28, 76, 91, 140, 154, 156–157, 183–184, 192
Twin Towers, 11, 72

Ukrainians, 11, 15, 37
Umar (Second Caliph), 129
umma (Muslim community), 19, 20, 83–94, 119, 176, 180, 183, 226–227, 229, 244n48
ungrievability, 11, 15, 37, 79–83
United Arab Emirates, 21, 52, 151, 156, 192, 200, 241n48
United States (US): Al-Awlaki life in, 99, 127, 246n2, 248n31; border restrictions, 17, 150–160; relations with Canadian Muslims, 6–10
University of British Columbia, 2
University of Manitoba, 5, 31, 37–39, 47, 51–52, 84, 106, 126–128, 137–138, 143, 147–148
University of Toronto, 66, 158
US. *See* United States

Vidino, Lorenzo, 5, 208–209

Walzer, Michael, 96
War on Terror, 6, 8, 13–18, 20, 26–27, 36, 56, 65, 68–71, 80, 82–83, 90–99, 117–118, 120–121, 123–136, 139–141, 148, 151–152, 159–160, 168, 174, 193, 218–221, 223–227
West Indies, 37
West/Western world, 5–9, 12, 19–21, 24, 26, 31, 51, 55, 63, 65, 72–77
white population/individuals, 5, 14, 15, 30, 31, 38, 52, 84, 90, 156, 210, 223, 225
Winnipeg, Muslim immigration in, 37–38
Wittgenstein, Ludwig, 66
worldly life (*al-dunya*), 34, 118, 134

Yar, Ahmed, 48, 165–169, 171, 173, 177, 179, 192–193
Yasin, Khalid, 53
Yemen, 28, 92, 99, 110, 131–132, 172, 193–194, 236n48

Al-Zarqawi, Abu Mus'ab, 98, 129
Zazi, Najibullah, 203
Zihaf-Bibeau, Michael, 2
Zine, Jasmin, 142

ABOUT THE AUTHOR

Youcef Soufi is a Researcher with the University of Manitoba's Centre for Human Rights Research. He is the former head of the Connaught Global Challenge Project's international working group on Islamophobia and the former Chair of the Canadian Association for the Study of Islam and Muslims (CASIM). He is an authority in the history of premodern Islamic legal thought and the author of *The Rise of Critical Islam: 10th–13th Century Legal Debate*.

www.ingramcontent.com/pod-product-compliance
Lightning Source LLC
Chambersburg PA
CBHW031535260326
41914CB00032B/1814/J
* 9 7 8 1 4 7 9 8 3 2 2 6 2 *